ADA NIELD CHEW (1870–   ) North Staffordshire, the eldest   und in a family of thirteen. She left school at the age of eleven, when the family moved to Worcestershire, to help her mother with domestic duties. In about 1887 the family moved again, first to Malvern Wells and then to Crewe in Cheshire. Between 1887 and 1896, Ada Nield worked in a shop, and later as a tailoress in a Crewe factory, from where she wrote her famous series of letters in 1894 and began her long career in active politics. In the same year she joined the Nantwich Board of Guardians and the Crewe Independent Labour Party (ILP). She married George Chew, who she met in the ILP, in 1897. Her only child, Doris, was born in 1898.

In the first decade of this century, Ada Nield Chew worked in the Women's Trade Union League with Mary Macarthur, but in 1908 she gave up regular union work to devote herself more fully to the campaign for women's suffrage. She was a pacifist and a member of the Women's International League for Peace and Freedom in the First World War. Though she continued to work for many causes, in the later years of her life she retired from active politics. She died in Burnley at the age of seventy-five. Despite her meagre formal education, Ada Nield Chew wrote many letters, articles, sketches and stories, which were published in the magazines and newspapers (including the *Freewoman* and the *Clarion*) of the time.

DORIS NIELD CHEW was born in 1898. She took a degree in History at Manchester University and, until her retirement, taught history in secondary schools: she was Senior History Mistress at Burnley High School from 1926–58. She has been always been involved in local issues, and was a JP in Burnley from 1947–71. In 1971 she received the MBE.

The Life and Writings
of
ADA NIELD CHEW

Remembered and collected by Doris Nield Chew
with a foreword by Anna Davin

Virago

Published by VIRAGO PRESS Limited 1982
Ely House, 37 Dover Street, London W1X 4HS

'The Life' Copyright (C) Doris Nield Chew 1982

'The Writings' Copyright (C) Doris Nield Chew 1945

Foreword Copyright (C) Anna Davin 1982

Printed in Great Britain by The Anchor Press
and bound by Wm. Brendon, both of Tiptree, Essex

British Library Cataloguing in Publication Data
Nield Chew, Ada
    Ada Nield Chew: the life and writings of a
    working woman.
    1. Women—Great Britain—Social conditions
    2. Labor and laboring classes—Great Britain—
    History
    I. Title   II. Nield Chew, Doris
    305.4'0941 (expanded)   HQ1597

    ISBN 0-86068-294-3

Typeset by Colset Pte Ltd, Singapore.

Contents

CONTENTS

Sketches and Stories

Letters to the Accrington Observer

Articles

Acknowledgements

My sincere thanks to all those who have encouraged and helped me in the preparation of this book, especially to Professor Saville and Dr Bellamy, Editors of Hull University *Dictionary of Labour Biography*, who first suggested that my mother's writings should be collected and reproduced; to Gloria Parkinson for her interest and suggestions; to Janet Clunie, for typing the original; to David Read of Stockport and above all, to Anna Davin, without whose persistent encouragement and detailed and practical help the manuscript could never have been published.

List of Illustrations

Cover: Ada Nield Chew *c.* 1912

Between pages 200 and 201

Nantwich Board of Guardians, *c.* 1894
Ada Nield Chew standing with Clarion Van, 1896
Ada Nield Chew with their daughter Doris, *c.* 1903
Ada and George Nield Chew, *c.* 1911
Ada Nield Chew speaking at the Crewe by-election, 1912
Ada Nield Chew at Suffragist meeting, 1912
Ada and George Nield Chew in 1918
Ada Nield Chew, 1920
Ada Nield Chew, 1937
Ada Nield Chew, 1937
Ada Nield Chew, 1938

All illustrations reproduced by permission of Doris Nield Chew.

Foreword

Ada Nield Chew (1870-1945) was a working-class woman of great intelligence and talent who for some twenty years after 1894 devoted her formidable energies to socialist and suffrage campaigning. Along with co-workers like Selina Cooper, Sarah Reddish, Sarah Dickenson, and many others, she had been almost forgotten by historians until recently, when Jill Liddington and Jill Norris searched out and brought together the scattered evidence of another world of suffrage activity, far removed from the middle-class one of London and the Pankhursts: that of working women in the mill towns and other industrial areas of the north-east of England. (See their *One Hand Tied Behind Us*, Virago, 1978.)

Ada Nield Chew's political beliefs were shaped by her own experience, as was the case for many other working-class suffrage campaigners. As the eldest girl in a large family of mostly brothers, she was familiar from an early age with hard work and responsibility. The weight of domestic work in cramped and inconvenient houses, where the wind sweeping through left clouds of coal dust from nearby pits and slag-heaps 'covering the beds, the table, the clothes, the cupboard shelves, the food', remained always in the forefront of her consciousness, and was vividly conveyed in the sketches of working-class life which she later wrote; domestic work and childcare were always on her political agenda. She knew the frustration of the intellectual with limited access to education and to books, and with endless other demands on her time. She knew too the deadening exhaustion of factory life. All these undoubtedly contributed to her political formation.

Her initiation into public political activity took place, as far as we know, in the clothing factory where she was a tailoress in the early 1890s, in Crewe, then a thriving railway town on the Cheshire – Staffordshire border, where she lived with her family. Certainly it was only after her letters to the local paper on the exploitative conditions under which she and others worked, published in 1894 under the signature 'A Crewe Factory Girl', had provoked stormy events in the factory and brought her into contact with the Crewe branch of the Independent Labour Party (ILP),[1] that she became active in a formal sense. She was already a skilled writer though how we do not know – these were apparently her first published efforts, and she probably did not even keep a diary, since in later years she did not have that habit. She was well informed and must have followed and thought about newspaper coverage of contemporary questions: in her first letter she justifies taking up her pen by saying, 'although one cannot open a newspaper without seeing what all sorts and conditions of men are constantly agitating for and slowly but surely obtaining – as in the miners' eight-hour Bill – only very vague mention is ever made of the underpaid, overworked ''Factory Girl''.' The letters are most skilfully constructed, though we cannot know whether she initially intended a series, or whether it was the editor's encouragement that allowed her to extend and continue her original contribution. They operate cumulatively, giving more and more detail about conditions and practices in the factory and her criticisms, pausing now and then to recapitulate, arguing more and more strongly for the need to organise and force change on the employers, and also for change in the larger social structure. She comments on the lower wages paid to women, and on their lesser political power through not having the vote.

> Will you allow me to urge upon your readers, upon those of my own sex who though not yet having the privilege of voting themselves, yet have influence with those who have, to use that privilege intelligently, in the right direction? And to those of the opposite sex who do enjoy this privilege, to send only those men to Parliament, of whatever political creed, who stand pledged to do all in their power, with the utmost possible

speed, to relieve the burden of the oppressed and suffering workers of this country, not least amongst whom are the factory girls of Crewe.

(*Crewe Chronicle*, 19 May 1894)

So although she joined the socialists only after the publication of her letters, the revelation of her identity and the loss of her job, she had already directed her attention to the political issues which were to remain central for her: labour representation, women's suffrage, and the conditions of work, especially among women.

Unfortunately, the main sources of our information on Ada Nield Chew tell us very little about how she reached this point. Her writings, where they draw on that phase of her life, describe domestic conditions and work, not her own education or political development. And her daughter, Doris Nield Chew, the author of this book, who has done historians and feminists a great service in restoring to view so much of her mother's life, remembers little (to her great chagrin) from what her mother probably told her concerning those years. We know that Ada Nield's formal education was minimal, and ceased when she was eleven: this would be normal enough for the children (especially the girls) of a small farmer in the mid-nineteenth century. We know that at some point before her Crewe days she taught in a small church school, perhaps in Lincolnshire, but where it was, or how she (who was never religious) came to be teaching there, we do not know. Presumably she had by that time improved upon her initial schooling to some extent, though the requirements for an assistant in such a school might not have been very high. Probably, through teaching there she advanced her own studies. Doris Chew thinks that William Nield, Ada's father, with whom she had a close relationship, most likely encouraged her in her passion for reading; and perhaps he helped her supplement the family's small stock of books. It is even possible that he or his father passed on to her political ideas picked up decades before in the years of Owenite or Chartist ferment: some 1880s and 1890s socialists were later to attribute part of their militancy to such family traditions; but this is mere speculation. With more certainty we may conclude that, like a good many working-class intellectuals of the period, male and female, she was largely self-educated, learning more from informal than from formal education, and from experience as well as from books.

From this period onwards the evidence is less sparse. Her political activities as paid travelling speaker and organiser first for the ILP between 1894 and 1898 (when her daughter Doris was born), then for the Women's Trade Union League from 1900 to 1908, and later for the National Union of Women's Suffrage Societies (of which more below), were reported regularly in their respective publications (*Labour Leader* and *Clarion*, *Women's Trade Union Review*, and *Common Cause*), and her daughter in this period of her mother's life has been able to draw on their reports and references.

The Women's Trade Union League (originally the Women's Protective and Provident League) was founded in London in 1874 with the aim of stimulating and supporting organisation by women workers in their various trades. In the 1890s it was extending its activities more broadly in the provinces, working closely with branches of the Women's Co-operative Guild and other women's organisations. The appointment of regular organisers in the industrial north meant a more vigorous attention by the WTUL to the actual conditions of women's working lives: there was less emphasis after this on the moral and spiritual imperatives of unionisation, and more on the practical difficulties facing working women and women at home. Textile workers Annie Marland, Helen Silcock and Sarah Reddish worked for the League from 1892, 1897 and 1899 respectively, and were joined by Ada Nield Chew in 1900. All were workers themselves (the importance of paying organisers was of course that it allowed women who needed a wage to take on the work), and had already been active in trade unions, the Women's Co-operative Guild, and socialist groups.

As organisers they toured the industrial towns and villages in northern England and Scotland several times a year. They would work in a district for several weeks, contacting local trade, socialist and feminist societies, and the secretaries of women's unions if these existed. They addressed public meetings; preached sermons in chapels or occasionally churches (especially in London); sometimes fund-raising events were organised by wealthy supporters of the League. They visited local workshops and factories where women were employed, to speak to them as they arrived for and left their work, often holding impromptu meetings at the factory gates. Sometimes very few women could be drawn to a meeting, and this was usually attributed either to employers' hostility and victimisation (recalling Ada Nield's experiences at Crewe), or to ignorance among the women of the benefit of union organisation. During the 1890s and early 1900s the League workers often accused the men in the same trades, or in the women's families, of neglecting the political education of their women-folk. (The League's attitude to men varied: in the early 1890s it was suggested that the best organised unions and branches for women had male officials; by the end of the 1890s they were advocating women's self-organisation and greater share of responsibility.) But often the meetings would be large – 'well-attended' is the usual phrase – especially if there had been a strike or industrial dispute in the area which had promoted organisation. The difficulty then was to sustain organisation among the low-paid women. Wage rises were seldom achieved, and regular payments of union dues were hard to maintain. When the organisers moved on they would leave a secretary or other union officer in charge, perhaps under the friendly observation of a more firmly established unionist in another trade, and hope the union would survive the inevitable fluctuation in membership that resulted from women's conditions of employment – casual, low-paid and intermittent. Sometimes local secretaries sent in regular reports. League officers would keep in touch and make briefer consolidating visits during subsequent tours.

This life, it will be clear, was a demanding one, involving much travel and little comfort, as well as the less tangible strains of continually 'giving out' as speaker and charismatic outsider. The early death of one ILP campaigner, Enid Stacy, was thought by Sylvia Pankhurst to have resulted partly from 'the exhausting routine of open-air speaking, constant travelling, hurried meals and uncomfortable beds'. (Quoted in Liddington & Norris, *One Hand Tied Behind Us*.) But Ada Nield Chew's tougher upbringing may have helped her withstand such rigours; and there would have been compensations in the hospitality and comradeship encountered in place after place. There is respect and affection for the women depicted later on in the stories and sketches which poured from her pen after she had finally begun to cut down on her travelling, and which must have drawn on the knowledge of other working women's lives which she gained at this period. For us the range of this knowledge is exciting, and the detailed and realistic presentation of daily life provides us with first hand and intimate information in an area where most often what little we know comes from outsiders' accounts. The breathless account of Mrs. Turpin's day, for instance, in the first 'All in the Day's Work' sketch (see below), combines a meticulous list of the day's jobs with her 'stream of consciousness' – the anxieties and preoccupations accompanying and punctuating the work along with affectionate distraction of a bored baby. A late start means a rushed breakfast to get husband and children off in time, then she has a quick cup of tea herself, and sees to the baby:

Half past nine. The baby is washed and dressed, and willing to sit on the hearthrug and amuse himself with such marvellous curiosities as an empty bobbin, a newspaper, and a clothes peg. Thank goodness it's June, and likely to be dry outside, for the coals are getting low, and it takes such a lot of fire to dry all the clothes inside. A quarter to ten. As much of the weekly wash as the little backyard will hold is pegged out, and the rest is hanging on the clothes-horse in front of the fire.

Ten o'clock. The dirty pots are all in the little scullery, but there's no time to wash up now, nor is there any time to go upstairs. Miss Seaton, who came hindering yesterday, asked if she knew that milk contained all the necessary elements to sustain life; and hoped she gave her children a good milk pudding every day. Of course she said 'Yes, 'm,' it was easiest to get rid of her that way, especially when you wanted to be getting on with your work; but she [Mrs. Turpin] would like to know where the quart of milk per day (and a quart wouldn't make a pudding big enough to feed her five, leaving out herself and the baby) was to come from. Two shillings a week for milk puddings, when all she had to do upon, all told, was 28 shillings per week!

(Englishwoman, July 1912)

In the dialogues we also 'hear' working women in political discussion, again a rare opportunity. Their words, though presented as fiction, have the ring of truth and must have been based on (or distilled from) real arguments which the writer heard or took part in as she travelled around.

From her political activities and her writings, then, a basic account of Ada Nield Chew's life from 1894 until the First World War can be constructed with relative ease (certainly more easily than for many of her friends and fellow-workers, or for any ordinary working woman), although until Jill Liddington and Jill Norris' research, no historians had even begun such reconstruction. Doris Nield Chew, however, is able here to provide us with more than that. We not only have the record of her public life built up through Doris Nield Chew's research (her mother kept copies of nothing she published), but also the intimate insights and details supplied by memory, and the understanding produced by a long and close relationship between mother and daughter. This does not mean any revelations of her inmost feelings: Ada Nield Chew was a reticent and private person, both because of a strong sense of dignity, with which exposure of feeling was mostly incompatible, and paradoxically because of her lack of any sense of self-importance. The work she did, the working women whom she met through it and with whom she identified, the causes for which she fought, all these were more important to her than parading, or even perhaps examining, her own feelings.

Occasionally, though, one senses a confluence of public and private persona, of politics and emotion, as when she addresses questions relating to motherhood. She stood out against the flood of propaganda about motherhood in those pre-war years, according to which it should be every woman's highest ambition and destiny to rear healthy children for the service of the Empire, and argued with especial vehemence that not all women made good mothers, and childcare should be undertaken by those who did, that it was wrong to try to restrict the employment of married women, and that it was essential for all women to have economic independence, and not to be dependent either on husband or (through the proposed 'endowment of motherhood' – an early version of family allowances supported by many feminists and socialists) on the State. 'You cannot breed a free people from slave mothers, and husband-kept or State-kept women can never know the meaning of liberty.' In one passage the tone of her writing – usually measured though always vigorously logical – shifts into a more passionate key, when she derides the 'truly ghastly fear' of male politicians that the employment of mothers must 'weaken the maternal tie':

> This fear will merely afford a smile to any woman who has ever yearned to hold, or has ever held, that ever-new, ever-marvellous gift of ages in her arms – her own newly-born babe. Any woman who has lived through years watching the daily growth of her child, who has followed it with her yearning mother-care, surrounding it always, whether a yard or a thousand miles divide her from its physical contact, with her protecting love – she knows, freewoman or bond, that no mere presumptuous man-made or woman-made law on earth can lessen by one jot that blessed bond between her and her child.
>
> ('Mother Interest and Child-Training,' *The Freewoman*,
> 22 August 1912)

Ada Nield Chew stood out from other women of her time and

class even while identifying with them and speaking for them, and in spite of all the shared experience. She was exceptional, though by no means alone, in reaching socialist and feminist conclusions about her life and its social and economic context. In these years socialist ideas were reaching a wide audience, especially in the industrial North; they were making many converts, and, as Liddington and Norris have shown, their influence was strong among women too. Establishing numbers, however, is fraught with difficulty, and as usual women are especially difficult to count. (Liddington and Norris cite the case of a Blackburn textile worker, Billy Derbyshire, an ILP member, and his wife Ethel, who did not join herself because they could not afford two subscriptions, but who after their marriage in 1903 took part in branch activities as though she had been a member.) As a suffragist, too, Ada Nield was part of an expanding movement, though head-counting is no easier than for the socialists. One possible measure of support among working-class women lies in the thousands of signatures collected in the cotton towns of Lancashire in 1901-02 by the North of England Society for Women's Suffrage[2] for their suffrage petition: nearly 30,000 women workers had signed by the spring of 1901, out of a total of Lancashire women cotton workers amounting to 274,000 according to the census.

Feminism was of course a larger matter than the vote, and many feminists like Ada Nield Chew, while active in the suffrage struggle, saw it as a part only of a broader strategy. Most commonly, this was expressed in terms of winning for women a larger share of political power so that they could influence the administration of society, eliminate the many injustices to women, and serve their special needs, for instance by improving health provision, particularly in maternity. Ada Nield Chew's fierce independence made her wary of State support, as we have seen, but she certainly believed in the importance of involving women, especially working-class women, at every level of political power. She also saw suffrage propaganda as more effective than attempts at industrial organisation in combatting 'the practical impossibility of organising an unskilled, badly-paid, intending-to-become-a-parasite-on-marriage worker'.

> The fact is that unless you can get a woman to see the utter degradation of her industrial and political position as dependant and belonging of man, there is as little hope of industrial organisation for her as for political power. If there is, lying dormant, one spark of latent desire for freedom, for growth, you have some ground to work on, some hope of results. And one of the best means, I rather think, of appealing to this dormant quality is to rouse a sense of resentment against obvious inequality, as in the voteless condition of women compared with man. It may be this, merely, at first. But first steps must be taken, and if this is an effective way, and leads to growth and power, it is the right way.
>
> ('Let the women be alive,' *The Freewoman* 18 April 1912)

It was in this strategic context then that she placed her suffrage work. The links between women's political rights and their industrial and social position as workers and as potential or actual wives were, in Ada Nield Chew's view, all important; campaigning on one front only would be no use. These were controversial areas for the suffrage movement. The Women's Social and Political Union[3] under the Pankhursts after 1906 concentrated more and more on political aspects, and increasingly adopted tactics which would not expect or allow the participation of many working women. They also abandoned internal democracy on the grounds that militant tactics, like a military campaign, necessitated secrecy and unquestioning obedience to the hierarchy. In spite of Mrs. Pankhurst's earlier involvement with the ILP they grew steadily more antagonistic to the Labour movement. The National Union of Women's Suffrage Societies,[4] on the other hand, being an umbrella for many different kinds of group and having a democratic constitution, harboured a range of opinions, and its policies shifted over time in response both to changes in the political situation and to changes in the internal balance of power. By and large its policy towards labour questions was for a long time handicapped by the strength of Liberal support within it, though this coexisted with groups with strongly working-class sympathies. After the election of a new executive in 1907 the National Union began to move to the left; finally all hope of anything but betrayed promises from the Liberals was abandoned, and in 1912 a change of line allowed support for Labour candidates in by-elections. Ada Nield Chew took work with them as organiser for Rossendale in 1911, and started a series of articles for their publication, *The Common Cause*.

Her views were nevertheless still controversial: if the links between politics and labour were beginning to gain wider acceptance, her third strand of analysis, women's social position in the family, was not generally accepted as inextricably linked and needing transformation as urgently as women's political and economic situation. The editors prefaced one of her articles for *The Common Cause*, 'The Problem of the Married Woman' (6 March 1914, see pp. 230–4) with a disclaimer, perhaps to distance themselves from what she was saying, perhaps to invite debate. Announcing a series of articles on women's interests, they warned that 'IN NO CASE does the NUWSS take responsibility for the views set forward in signed articles. Our object is to provide a platform for free discussion'. Criticisms in subsequent articles confirm the divisions of opinion on the questions she raised. It was by no means generally agreed that married women should be economically independent of their husbands; nor that collective childcare funded by the State was the way to help woman 'free herself from that which shackles her'.

A more congenial place for the expression of Ada Nield Chew's advanced ideas was the *Freewoman*, a short-lived radical 'weekly feminist review', which appeared between November 1911 and October 1912, edited by two ex-WSPU activists, Dora Marsden and Mary Gawthorpe. Contributors included Rebecca West, H. G. Wells, Edward Carpenter, Rose Witcup, Guy Aldred and others, who by their ideas and in their lives were then challenging society. It was critical of the limited assumptions of most suffragists, but in its short life, with discussions of women's role, motherhood, reproduction and sexuality, it testified to the breadth of contemporary feminist debate. Ada Nield Chew welcomed the *Freewoman* as 'meat and drink to the sincere student . . . one feels your process of growth as you write; and one feels oneself growing as one reads'. It was 'a really free platform, whereon are expressed real, living thoughts, where there is no need to keep back half one's mind . . . [because] on saying what one really thinks one is but beating the air, since its unpopularity or its clashing with some other interest will safely ensure its never seeing the light'. Most organisations would not accept unconventional views for fear of antagonising either their membership or their influential supporters: 'each and all are governed and *paid for* by women who belong to a small and privileged class; and she who pays the piper may surely call the tune'.

> Most of these women are quite sincere in their desire to use the vote, when obtained, to abolish sweating and misery, inequalities and injustices among their poorer 'sisters'; but they have only the vaguest ideas as to how their having a vote is to enable them to do this. Most of them would be horrified at the idea of using their vote, or of helping in any other way, to bring about the evolutionary revolution which will result in every woman, as well as every man, having to work (really work – at something useful to the community) for the bread they eat. Proposals for, and work directed towards this end, come under the heading of 'Economics' or 'Socialism' – or something – with which they, as Suffragists, have no concern! The woman who frankly acknowledges that 'equality' means equality in bread-earning (apart altogether from marriage), in responsibility-sharing, who recognises that the woman who lives on 'rent', or 'interest', or 'shares', or unearned income of any kind is a parasite, just as a man who lives without working: who recognises that a woman who lives on a man's earnings, even though 'respectably' married, is as much a prostitute as her outcast sister of the streets – such a woman is repudiated as 'going too far', and as being a

hindrance to progress (in getting a vote).
('Let the women be alive!' *Freewoman*, 18 April 1912)

Her three contributions to the *Freewoman* are included in this collection. It is frustrating that the flow of her writing almost ceased not long afterwards, following the outbreak of war.

Over the twenty years in which Ada Nield Chew gave her energies to the political struggle, her work earned her the economic independence which mattered so much to her. Through her salary as a paid organiser she could contribute to household expenses and provide paid help for the domestic work which she always saw as her own responsibility. But with the outbreak of war the suffrage movement fractured and subsided, and the whole character of political activity changed. Had her mother been a man, Doris Nield Chew once remarked, she would have been a conscientious objector. As it was, she supported the pacifist movement but could afford little time for it, since now she had to find other ways of earning her living. She retained her radical views, but did not return to the fray when the war ended. The most likely reason is the one her daughter gives; that the need to earn for present and future needs became her priority and took all her time. But it is tempting to look for additional reasons for the withdrawal of one whose activity had previously been so intense. She may well have lost heart, as many socialists and internationalists did, at the crumbling of hopes and movements after August 1914, and the thought of the long haul involved in rebuilding organisations and influence; but she had always known there was 'a long row to hoe'. Possibly she felt discouraged and isolated in holding views which others were slow to come round to, but she had always before succeeded in remaining one of the people, even while holding ideas which were not yet general: indeed one of her talents was to find ways of expressing her ideas which would reach a wide audience without being patronising and without alienating their sympathy, but on the contrary relating everything to shared experience and attitudes. We can see this in her sketches; but her popularity as a speaker suggests that she used the same talent on platform or soapbox. Perhaps she was simply growing tired, or even bored. She would have been justified if in addition she had felt that it was the turn of others to carry on.

Ada Nield Chew's life and writings have been brought together here by her daughter Doris, as a tribute to her mother, and it is a tribute which by any criterion is justified. It gains force from the affection and sense of loss (still felt forty years after her mother's death) which perhaps were even stronger motives in its writing than her admiration for her mother's character and work. Her mother emerges as a sturdy and very spirited working woman, an impression confirmed by the writings, where we discover more of her vigorous articulateness and adventurous mind. The reader, once acquainted with Ada Nield Chew's life and writings, is likely to share not only her daughter's admiration, but also her sense of loss. Beyond that reaction, will perhaps be excitement.

Ada Nield Chew is of particular interest to us not only because we know so little still of the lives and thoughts of working women in the past, that a glimpse of them at any place and time is welcome, especially one as vivid as we get from her stories and sketches; not only because we can explore with her another relatively unknown territory – the attitudes and development of militant women of the working class. The questions she raised and struggled with are relevant still, and we can learn from their earlier discussion how tenacious the grip of an oppressive system still is, even though some forms may change. We are still concerned to understand the operation of sexual divisions in our society, and how work, home and political institutions reinforce women's oppression. We have come back to questions of motherhood, childcare and domestic labour, and are still divided about the answers. (Does payment from the State to the mother for domestic responsibilities constitute recognition of their essential character as work necessary to the State, or does it simply confirm her in a domestic role?) Problems of political strategy have not yet been solved – the relation between the feminist movement and the left, for instance, or between male and female workers – nor those of language, how to 'reach' people and to stimulate political discussion. (Ada Nield Chew's semi-fictional sketches, with their forthright women and their suffrage morals, may be compared in their intent with the work of women's theatre groups today.)

The best tribute to Ada Nield Chew, and to the women of the working class of whom she was one and for whom she spoke, will be for us whose turn it now is to carry on, to remember her quest for 'the truth, however unpalatable', to emulate her energy and the immediate force and clarity of her words, her will to convince people of the need for change, and to draw on her understanding of the complex nature of our own oppression and its roots in the social and economic structure.

Anna Davin

There are many people to whom I owe gratitude for helpful discussions and information when this foreword was being written, too many to name: but I'm particularly grateful to Sally Alexander, Les Garner and Jill Liddington for their contributions.

NOTES

[1] The ILP was founded at Bradford in 1893 with the ultimate object of securing the collective ownership of the means of production. Its immediate aims were to achieve an eight-hour working day and the removal of overtime, piecework and child labour; it also supported the extension of the suffrage, the heavy taxation of unearned income, and public help for the aged, infirm, widows and orphans; at this time there was neither a State pension nor social security.

[2] This society was formed in 1897 at the time of the reorganisation which also gave rise to the National Union of Women's Suffrage Societies; it was strongly influenced and helped by Esther Roper and

Eva Gore Booth, who in spite of class difference were able to work closely and effectively with local working-class activists. The Society was important as a forum and support for Liddington and Norris' 'radical suffragists' – the network of labour-oriented and mostly working-class suffragists of whom Ada Nield Chew was one.

[3] The WSPU was formed by Emmeline Pankhurst in Manchester, 1903; and moved to London with Emmeline and her daughter Christabel in 1906. From the summer of that year under their direction and with various secessions it became increasingly militant and élitist, with resulting divisions between the WSPU 'suffragettes' and other suffragists.

[4] The NUWSS, or National Union, founded in London in 1897, linked suffrage groups all over the country who believed in more conventional democratic organisation and strategy. For a time it united 'radical suffragists' such as Ada Nield Chew with middle-class suffragists. For further discussion see Jill Liddington and Jill Norris, *One Hand Tied Behind Us*, and Ray Strachey, *The Cause*.

THE LIFE
by Doris Nield Chew

Introduction

During the second half of the last century Great Britain prided itself on being the 'workshop of the world', the country where the basic industries had first been mechanised and the earliest railways built to transport their products; and until the recent invention of the silicon chip, the theory of economic growth had always assumed the employment of more and more workers, women as well as men. As the old domestic industries, in particular spinning and weaving and the making of clothes, were taken out of the home, so working women followed them into the factories. The middle-class woman, on the other hand, found her former skills unwanted and herself unnecessary, except for the production of children and, increasingly, the supervision of servants in her own home.

Historians have followed the exodus of men from field to factory, from the work of peasant to that of 'hand'; they have described the workers' struggle to achieve industrial organisation in trade unions and for political equality in universal male suffrage. But even now it is difficult to find a similar detailed account of the conditions under which women worked in a remarkably varied number of trades, and of their efforts to improve those conditions and to obtain better pay for their work – usually against the short-sighted opposition of their male colleagues as well as their employers.

My mother, as Ada Nield, a young woman of twenty-four, took the lead in one particular struggle – for better conditions and pay for sweated women workers in a Crewe clothing factory. Her chief weapon was her pen, which has meant that we have a complete account of the fight against her employers in a series of letters to the *Crewe Chronicle*, the local newspaper. For the first time these letters are reproduced in

3

their entirety, and illustrate vividly one facet of a national struggle.

Women's efforts to secure the vote are better known, largely because of the spectacular fight of the militant suffragettes led by the Pankhursts: so much so that people nowadays talk only of suffragettes, and are largely unaware that there is a distinction between them and the great mass of non-militant or constitutional suffragists. These in growing numbers had been working for the vote since the 1860s, and without their solid support the fight for political emancipation would have been as abortive as that of the Chartists earlier in the century.

The lead in both sections of the women's movement was taken in the first instance by middle-class women. Three names spring immediately to mind: Gertrude Tuckwell in the Women's Trade Union League, Mrs. Fawcett in the National Union of Women's Suffrage Societies (a federation of smaller societies, as the name implies), and the Pankhursts in the Women's Social and Political Union. Most of their immediate followers were also middle-class; these were the women who had not only education and a social conscience, but also time and often money to spare.

There was one remarkable difference, however, between the middle-class women who were involved in the two branches of the suffrage movement. When the vote had been won, the militants faded into the background, or, like Mrs. Pankhurst and Christabel, went abroad or turned to unrelated causes, like Christabel's propagation of the Second Coming of the Lord (though it is true that later she tried, unsuccessfully, to get elected to Parliament). The leaders of the National Union, however, either embarked on or continued in careers in social or political work. In national politics, for instance, there was Ellen Wilkinson, Education Minister in the Labour Government after 1945; Margaret Ashton won fame in the field of local government in Manchester; Maude Royden continued her work as a minister of religion; Mrs. Swanwick was prominent in the peace movement and in higher education; Kathleen Courtney was later made a Dame. These were women of wide interests, who wanted the vote so that their sex should win a stronger voice in a wide variety of social, political and economic causes. The pages of the *Common Cause*, from 1909 the weekly paper of the suffragist National Union, bear witness to this breadth of interest. In them one can see many facets of women's lives both in Britain and abroad, as well as the latest events in the struggle for the vote.

When the National Union decided in May 1912 to support Labour Party candidates in by-elections, since this Party, unlike the Conservatives or the Liberals, was prepared to support the cause of women's suffrage, it became increasingly important to include working women in the ranks of their speakers and organisers, and among these was my mother, now Ada Nield Chew. She was already well known for her work as a speaker for the Independent Labour Party and as an organiser for the Women's Trade Union League, (see Foreword p. xii) and she had contributed both letters and descriptive sketches of the lives of working women to the pages of the *Common Cause* and other periodicals. This she continued to do, and in addition to telling the story of her life as fully as I can, I have collected together a number of her writings.

The majority of unskilled workers, whether men or women, had repetitive and often unpleasant or even dangerous jobs in the 1900s (the woman pottery worker is a case in point), but women were even worse paid than were men, and married women had another burden to bear — housework and the care of the family, a task in which most men took no part. (I remember being told that in the days of my infancy my father, like most men, considered it beneath his dignity to wheel my pram.) It is true, of course, that most married working women still carry this double responsibility, but the methods of housework sixty to seventy years ago would appal the woman of today. Houses were heated by coal fires, and grates had to be blacked. There were no vacuum cleaners, no gas or electric ovens, washers, driers or refrigerators (much less deep-freezes). Washing was pounded in a dollytub, squeezed through a mangle, dried beside the fire if it was raining or in winter, and ironed with a flat-iron heated on the hob and tested by a drop of spittle. Floors were swept and scrubbed. There were neither electric blankets nor even rubber hot water bottles. I used to see my mother putting hot coals into the copper warming pan which she had inherited from her mother and passing it through the sheets.

Moreover, women's particular needs were ill catered for. I can remember the day before the disposable sanitary towel was generally used; and methods of birth control were crude. The women who coped with all this heavy labour, as well as struggling with the personal problems of their sex, were the women my mother worked for and wrote about. In her sketches, the modern reader can find a more intimate and detailed account of the daily life of the ordinary working woman than appears in more orthodox histories.

I suppose we all take our parents very much for granted, and are mainly concerned with their relationship with us, their all-important children; and it is only in later life – too often, alas, when it is too late – that we wish we had learned earlier to appreciate and understand them as independent human beings. Some of us are more self-absorbed than others, and looking back I realise with shame how many gaps there are in my knowledge of my mother's life, and how easy it would have been to ask the questions whose answers I would dearly like to know. This is true of my father's life too, of course, but I doubt whether questioning would have got me far with him. What was done was done, and he did not dwell on the past. Nevertheless, there is much I would like to know about his early years.

The gaps in my information came to light when it was no longer possible to fill them – when both my parents were dead along with the majority of their contemporaries. Those who have suffered bereavement will know how one treasures every memory as well as every physical reminder of the dead. In my efforts to bring my mother back I hunted through every drawer and cupboard for letters, papers, and especially for the autobiography which I knew she had written. Only a few letters remained – she had destroyed many, even those she had written to me when we were separated and which I had kept; while of the autobiography there was no sign.

I felt doubly bereaved when I discovered what an inferno there must have been (in those days we had coal fires); and worst of all, I felt the blame was largely mine. She had written the autobiography under a pseudonym as an entry in a publisher's competition (won by a ballet dancer), and had not been offered publication. I knew she had felt rejected in more ways than one. It was no doubt an unreasonable reaction, but my mother was a proud woman and only too ready to destroy what had apparently been judged as valueless. If I had known she meant to do this, I would have tried to dissuade her, but why did I not know? Why was I so self-absorbed, so indifferent, that I did not realise what her reaction was likely to be?

Early in the 1950s I had a fortunate encounter with Dr. W. S. Chaloner, then of Manchester University and author of *The Economic History of Crewe, 1780-1923*. Recognising my name, he told me of the letters written by my mother, under the pseudonym of 'Crewe Factory Girl', to the *Crewe Chronicle* from June to September 1894. He also told me that he had asked her for an interview and had been refused. On reflection, I realised why she had done this. The autobiography had been destroyed, and that part of her life was not to be resurrected. She had not even told me that Dr. Chaloner had written to her, much less kept his letter. I had heard of the Crewe letters but had never yet read them, so after this I sought them out, and they are reproduced in this book.

Her writings from 1894 onwards, where I have succeeded in culling them from the newspapers of the day, convey much of her experience and her ideas during those years. They overlap with times when my own memory can begin to serve as a source. But for the early years of my mother's life my memories of what she told me, scrappy and inadequate as they are, remain necessarily the main source.

7

Early Years: 1870-94

Ada Nield came from a family of Cheshire yeomen, whose only distinction lies in the fact that they can be traced back to the fourteenth century. (When my distant cousin, Dr. Patrick Nield, sent me the result of his researches into the family history, I commented unkindly that my mother appeared to me to be the only one worth writing about.) In his lifetime William, her father, worked at a variety of jobs, but his heart was in farming. Her grandfather, also William, had been a miner, but with compensation money received after a pit explosion where he worked he bought a farm known as the White Hall, not far from Butt Lane, Talke o' the Hill, in North Staffordshire. There, Ada was born on 28 January 1870. Later, when the elder William retired from farming, he handed the White Hall over to his son, who farmed it till Ada was about eleven. She always spoke of it with affection, and at one time it could be seen from the railway. Now a housing estate sprawls over the site.

My grandfather, like his daughter, was among the eldest of a large family, so although she had a number of aunts and uncles, of whom generally I knew little, the children of her youngest uncle were not much older than myself. Most of the others were known to me only by repute, but the earliest conscious memory of my life is of being taken to visit two elderly relatives in Kidsgrove, who were aged ninety and ninety-two. It gives me a thrill to realise that I have actually met two people born during the Napoleonic Wars!

William the younger and his wife Jane (née Hammond, which is all I know of her origins) had thirteen children in sixteen years. My mother was the second child and eldest daughter. Nine of the thirteen were boys; and two boys and two girls died in infancy. The three eldest were named Harry, Ada and May, but after that my grandmother indulged her fancy by culling from her favourite reading, a periodical called the *Family Herald*, names like Justinian Moore, Hilbert Edwin, Hugo Francis, William Victor and so on.

I don't know from where Ada received her meagre formal education, though I have an idea it was some kind of Dame school, but it came to an end when she was eleven, with the family's removal to Worcestershire, where her father took the Common Farm, near Malvern. The nearest she got to school after that was when she took her little brothers to the Dame school in the village of Hanley Swan.

Certainly after she left school, and to a considerable extent before, indeed as soon as she was old enough to use her hands constructively, Ada became engaged in what are usually known as domestic duties. The only other daughter, May, was born an epileptic, and became more afflicted as she grew older. Although May lived into her fifties I never knew her, and I must have been in my teens before I was even aware that she existed, for my mother's memories were too painful for her even to wish to speak of her sister. Later her brothers committed her to Chester County Asylum, where she eventually died.

Ada was therefore the only dependable daughter in a household where for many years there was a new baby every year, and her services became an indispensable adjunct to those of her mother. Boys were not expected to help with cooking, baking, cleaning, washing and the care of younger children, so Ada had to shoulder all these burdens from an early age. When she was eight she was sent over the fields in the dark to fetch the midwife, and was proud when she overheard her mother telling a neighbour that 'Ada was a good girl'. She never went out to play without a baby in her arms, never knew the joyous irresponsibility of more fortunate children.

She was not the prototype of a motherly woman; I do not think she would ever have chosen the care of young children for her lifework, but in spite of a natural feeling of resentment at

9

the burdens placed on her so early, she loved her 'little brothers', and all her life continued to feel a sense of obligation towards them. This they never fully appreciated. Looking back, I can see that their feelings towards her were ambivalent. She was the elder sister, and as such her place in the family was one of responsibility, but she had a mind and an independent will of her own even when she was living at home. In their eyes she completely abrogated her responsibility when, much to their disapproval, she married and left them, now almost all of them young men, to cope with the household. They never criticised their brother-in-law, whom they always spoke of as 'the Guvnor'; instead, they both pitied and admired him for being able to live with such a 'thrawn' [perverse, ill-tempered] creature as their sister. They wondered what sort of life their unborn niece or nephew would have with such a mother, then later criticised her for spoiling her only child. Ada had had enough, particularly of little boys. She told her mother when she married that she intended to have only one child, and hoped it would be a daughter. In spite of Mrs. Nield's openly expressed scepticism, she succeeded in both ambitions, the former by intention, the latter by luck.

There are no photographs of my mother as a child or girl, but I can visualise her, vital and eager when not weighed down by family cares, with grey-blue eyes and a mass of beautiful curly auburn hair. To the day of her death she believed her hair to be an ugly colour, because her brothers told her so and called her 'Carrots'. Her father alone admired it, but we all prefer to believe our contemporaries, even when it is to our disadvantage. Her husband told her he had always wanted to marry a girl with red hair, and she merely wondered at his taste; and when I said that at the age of five I had first realised the meaning of the word beauty through looking at her hair, she dismissed it as idle fancy. She was completely without personal vanity: her hairdresser still remembers how she crammed her hat on a head of beautifully waved hair; and she went round the world on a sixpenny tin of Pond's cold cream.

Occasionally, freed from the burden of her brothers, she

would run to the top of a neighbouring hill and hold out her arms to the wind, imagining that she could feel the earth turning on its axis. And at Malvern she gained her first taste of personal freedom at the age of seventeen when she ran a milk round on her own, driving a trap with a pony called Polly, of which she was very fond.

About this time, however, her father found it impossible to continue to work the Common Farm. As its name suggests it was poor land, and he lacked capital. For a short time after leaving the Common Farm the family moved to Malvern Wells, and it was from there that they came back to the Cheshire – Staffordshire border, this time to Crewe, which had grown from a small village to a town entirely as a result of its position on the Grand Junction Railway. I do not think my grandfather ever farmed again, although I remember a big kitchen, like that of a farmhouse. At one time – and certainly after I was born – he worked in a brickworks, as he had been doing at the time of my mother's birth. But what exactly he did between 1897 and 1905 when he died, I do not know.

Two of Ada's elder brothers joined the Army, because there was no other work available. Both became sergeant majors, but Harry, the eldest, fell into some (to me unexplained) disgrace, lost his stripes and became an alcoholic, or so I judge from the hushed whispers I heard. He died comparatively young. The other, Rowland, stayed in the Army till his retirement. A third brother, Justin, the one with whom Ada had most in common and whom she loved best, left his job as a fireman on the railway and went to fight in the Boer War. There was a tale that he and Rowland met unexpectedly in the middle of the veldt, but I cannot vouch for its accuracy. When the war was over he could not settle down in England, so he returned to South Africa, where he became an engine driver on the railways on the Rand goldfields. Like his sister, he was active in trade union affairs, in 1914 even spending time in prison as a result of his agitation in favour of better wages and conditions. In later years he never had a good word for Jan Smuts, who broke the strike my uncle was involved in; his attitude to Smuts was as hostile as that of English trade unionists to Winston Churchill after the general strike of 1926.

The younger brothers had better opportunities. One got a job in local government service under Crewe Corporation, ending up as 'the rates chap'. In a family of tall men, he was the runt, known to his brothers as 'Fag', but he outlived them all, dying in 1970 at the age of nearly ninety-one. A second brother could not afford to go to a training college for teachers, but qualified for his Teachers' Certificate externally. These two spent all their lives in Crewe, which they seldom left even for holidays. The youngest was the most fortunate; the others clubbed together to give him a secondary education, and he entered the civil service, becoming a tax inspector. Only one was a rolling stone, and he eventually ended up as a working engineer.

There was no women's army then for Ada to join even if she had wished, and she had no training in anything but domestic work. She was not content to remain the stay-at-home daughter, and it is doubtful whether the family could have supported her as well as May and the 'little brothers'. All I know is that between 1887 and 1896 she worked in a shop in Nantwich, a factory in Crewe, and – briefly and, she said, unsuccessfully – taught in a church school in Lincolnshire.

'Crewe Factory Girl': 1894

Just when Ada Nield began work as a tailoress in the Crewe factory where uniforms were made on contract for soldiers, policemen and railway workers, I don't know – perhaps in the early 1890s. But in an article in the *Common Cause* I found a later reference to that time. In this she told how 'desperate for money' she started to work as a learner in this factory, where she was told she would receive no wage for a week, but when, with the help of an older woman, she had learned the work, she would be able to earn eight shillings a week. In another factory she would have been a learner without pay for three months.

There were tailors in the factory, and Ada noticed that when the government inspector came round these men were given the job of sewing in the sleeves of tunics, work which was usually done by the women. When she asked the reason for this, she was told that the men were paid one shilling and five-pence an hour, while for the same work the women received only fivepence. The contractors' estimate was presumably based on male rates of pay, allowing the contractors to pocket the difference.

On 5 May 1894 a letter signed 'Crewe Factory Girl' appeared in the *Crewe Chronicle*, describing the kind of life led by the girls who worked in the factory. The reason for the letter was clearly stated: 'I have come to the conclusion, sir, that so long as we are silent ourselves and apparently content with our lot, so long shall we be left in enjoyment [?] of that lot.' The writer continued:

> To take what may be considered a good week's wage the work has to be so close and unremitting that we cannot be said to 'live', we merely exist. We eat, we sleep, we work, endlessly

13

work, from Monday morning to Saturday night, without remission. Cultivation of the mind? How is it possible? Reading? Those of us who are determined to live like human beings and require food for mind as well as body, are obliged to take time which is necessary for sleep to gratify this desire . . . Certainly we have Sundays, but Sunday is to many of us after our week of slavery, a day of exhaustion . . .

It may be said that we should utilise slack time for recruiting our bodies and cultivating our minds. Many of us do so, as far as is possible in that anxious state of mind we are necessarily in, knowing that we are not earning our keep, for it is not possible, absolutely not possible, for the average ordinary 'hand' to earn enough in busy times, even with overtime, . . . to make up for the slack ones.

A 'living wage!' Ours is a lingering, dying wage!

On 19 May a second letter appeared, headed 'A Living Wage for Factory Girls at Crewe'. The factory itself was not described, but the writer gave a detailed account of the finishing department in which she worked doing piecework along with other young women. With a normal working day of nine to ten hours, they earned on average only eight shillings a week. The letter ended with the expression of a burning sense of injustice: 'Why, because we are women, without pluck and grit enough to stand up for our rights, should we be ground down to this miserable wage?' At least this wholesale description did not apply to Ada Nield herself.

The two letters attracted the attention of a number of people, among them the secretary of the Crewe branch of the recently founded Independent Labour Party (ILP). Ada Nield did not accept his invitation (made through the *Chronicle*) to get in touch with him. She refused, she said, for personal reasons, but added that if her identity was ever revealed, she would gladly contact him and work with the ILP to the best of her ability 'in the effort to improve the conditions not only of the factory girls, but of all other workers'.

Other correspondents were not so favourably disposed towards the 'Crewe Factory Girl'. One letter accused the girls who, like 'Factory Girl', came from respectable homes, of working only for 'pin money'. This she hotly denied, demanding, 'Why should we, because we come from respectable homes and have respectable parents, be robbed of the fruits of our work by those who employ us? Justice is justice the world over, but if that is justice I am a Dutchman.'

Four articles, presumably commissioned by the editor of the *Chronicle*, followed in June and July, all under the heading of 'Life in a Crewe Factory'. In the first of these, the writer stated uncompromisingly that 'The influence of her life on the factory girl is demoralising and debasing, and downward in its every tendency . . . Improve conditions . . . and I venture to say that the factory girl will rise in social status in the same degree. I admit that we are an essentially noisy class of girls.'

In another article the daily life of the factory girls was described in detail, while the final one listed the various grievances in order, stating that the root cause of all these evils was the failure to pay a living wage. The work done in the factory was chiefly government work – orders for army and police uniforms; and there were some railway orders too, but they were better paid. Did the government know of the sweating? Couldn't it pay a living wage? Did the employer reduce the percentage of profit in proportion to the price received, as he reduced the amount paid to his hands? 'I believe – under the present social system – in an employer taking his fair and proper percentage of profit on the capital he expends, and no more.' The inescapable conclusion, said 'Factory Girl' with dangerous bluntness, was that 'either the Government or the employers are robbers'.

The remedy she proposed was that the factory girls and any other 'female workers' should organise themselves and join a union, not, alas, that of the tailors, who thought that women had no business in the trade anyway. 'Factory Girl' thought that this was a short-sighted, even selfish, view, and in the light of the undercutting she had already written about, it is difficult not to agree with her.

I do not know whether Ada Nield was too carried away by her own eloquent arguments, or too naïve to realise the effect

15

this exposure was likely to have on the management of the factory, whose identity must have become increasingly obvious, or whether she was fully aware of the probable consequences of her actions. In any case she was soon informed of them. On 28 July a letter from her headed 'Life in a Crewe Factory: a Storm' appeared in the *Chronicle*, reporting a not unsuccessful attempt by the manager to turn the other workers against 'Factory Girl'. Calling them all to a meeting he announced the closure of the tea-room and the sick club, telling them to blame 'our friend' who had been alleging unfair practices in relation to them.

The following week a further instalment described an escalation of the counter-attack when at another meeting, this time addressed by one of the employers who had come specially from London, she had been provoked into revealing her identity. In front of several hundred fellow workers, some of whom were hostile, some neutral, and none of whom dared to support her openly, she defended her case, speaking in public for the first time in her life and in a situation from which practised debaters would shrink. Needless to say, she thought later of many cogent points which she had forgotten to make. She did wonder why, if joining a union were as useless as her employer maintained, it should be necessary to warn his workers against it; but it was obvious that the main front of her offending was that she had 'blazoned' her grievances in the public press.

On 25 August she reported the final act in the drama: the sacking of a friendly tailor and of twelve girls who, though they were among the best finishers, had openly expressed sympathy with her; followed by her own resignation in an abortive attempt to prevent the dismissal of the other girls. This last letter was signed '(an ex) Crewe Factory Girl'.

In the same issue of the *Chronicle* there was a report of a labour meeting in Crewe, which was addressed not only by Eleanor Marx (referred to throughout as Mrs. Aveling), active socialist and daughter of Karl Marx, but also by Miss Ada Nield, now revealed as the 'Crewe Factory Girl'. This meeting was held under the auspices of the National Union of Gasworkers and General Labourers, the union which had opened its doors to the tailoresses when their male colleagues had refused to accept them, and of whose executive Eleanor Marx was a member. (It was the precursor of the Union of General and Municipal Workers.) The *Chronicle* reported a crowded attendance, and continued: 'Miss Ada Nield, the "Factory Girl" whose letters to the *Chronicle* have created considerable interest, not only in Crewe itself but all over the country, was received with hearty applause and delivered an interesting address.' The climax of this speech which, it was said, was punctuated by cheers and 'Hear hears', was the statement that 'there was only one remedy': combination on the part of the workers. She asked the public to make the factory girls' case their own and to see that justice was done to them. Mrs. Aveling, too, stressed the importance of girls and women combining: 'So few of the girls had stood by the noble girl who had spoken to them that night.' According to the reporter, there was an interjection at this point from a factory girl in the audience to the effect that they would have been sacked, which, replied Mrs. Aveling, proved the need for organisation.

By 1 September, the *Chronicle* was reporting action on the lines suggested by Eleanor Marx. W. S. Maclaren, the Liberal MP for Crewe, textile manufacturer and Secretary of the Parliamentary Committee of the Manchester Society for Women's Suffrage, had taken up the case, and had written to the company involved, now identified as Compton Brothers. He would ask the Home Office whether the prices paid to Compton's for uniforms were such as to enable the company to pay a living wage to its workers. Will Thorne, General Secretary of the Gasworkers and General Labourers Union, was also in communication with Compton's, and Eleanor Marx was to consult John Burns, MP and the editors of several London newspapers.

In a letter to the *Chronicle* of 22 September, Ada Nield commented on the interview between Thorne and Compton's, and in another on 6 October she once more repeated not only that she had a right to publish her views, but that she was the sole author of the offending letters – a sore point since the management refused to believe that she could have produced them unaided – and that she had no accomplices, such as a socialist vicar nor the ILP. One result was that she did now become a member of the Crewe branch of the ILP, but she made contact with them only after her identity had been revealed.

I have sometimes wondered what Ada Nield's family felt about all this publicity. My impression is that her father stood by her, and certainly she found a stalwart supporter in her brother Justin, who also adopted her political convictions.

Travelling Socialist Speaker: 1894-8

Ada Nield's local prominence at this time led to her election to the Nantwich Board of Guardians, who were responsible for the administration of the Poor Law in Crewe and the surrounding district. W. H. Chaloner describes her as the first Guardian who was also a member of the Crewe ILP, adding that most of her colleagues on the Board put cost before need. The resulting differences between her views and theirs may be illustrated from the *Clarion*, the socialist weekly founded by Robert Blatchford in 1891 and widely read by ILP members. On 30 March 1895 it reported:

> The Nantwich Board of Guardians have given us another taste of their capacity for doing nothing. At a recent meeting Miss Ada Nield, the Trades Council representative, moved a resolution to the effect 'That the Board should avail themselves of the power vested in them and acquire fifty acres of land to find work for the unemployed.' After a short discussion it was adjourned. At the next meeting it was proposed to appoint a committee to see what could be done in the matter.
>
> During the discussion one member stated that the distress was not exceptional, and now that the frost had gone, it would be easy for those who wanted to get work. He also stated that he objected to discussing these subjects as a matter of policy, a statement which he afterwards withdrew. The motion was lost, four voting for it, all the rest against.

Her experience as a Poor Law Guardian made a deep impression on my mother. Years later, in 1909, she was carrying on a forthright argument with the editor of the *Rochdale Observer* on the subject of the Poor Law Commission of 1909. The minority report, produced for it by Sidney and Beatrice Webb, advocated the provision for an 'enforced minimum of civilised

19

life', and my mother argued strongly in favour of this, while the *Observer*, objecting to the idea that the 'capables' should support the 'incapables', took the other side.

I know of little else in Ada Nield's life during this period, except that her membership of the Crewe ILP brought her into contact with the man she was later to marry, an ex-weaver from north-east Lancashire, George Chew. The *Clarion* on 25 January 1896 reported that 'The socialist light in Crewe continues burning uniformly and steadily. Comrade George Chew of Rochdale [where he was then living] has done useful work in forming branches of the ILP in Sandbach and Willaston.'

In February 1896, Julia Dawson, a prominent member of the ILP, and regular contributor to the *Clarion*, first suggested in her weekly letter that her women readers might like the idea of setting up and keeping a van on the road for thirteen weeks, when it could travel 'into small market towns and country districts . . . to introduce Socialism'. A Mr. Runstead had offered the use of his Soup Van, from which many of Liverpool's starving had been fed 'during the cruel frosts of last winter'. He was also prepared to lend a tent in which a boy could sleep who would look after the horse and make himself generally useful in making fires, washing dishes and so on. Preparations for the expedition started. On 30 May Julia Dawson burst into an ecstatic description of the van: 'The heart of woman could not wish for a prettier room to live in than the interior of that van!' Its walls were a delicate cream, its ceiling striped red and cream. 'Tricky little cupboards' had also been painted cream, and there were roomy lockers, a table on hinges, spotted muslin curtains and four bunks which also did duty as seats.

The van set out on 13 June, beginning with a public meeting outside Chester Town Hall, and arousing great enthusiasm along its route in Cheshire. On 15 August it was announced that the rest of the journey would be spent exclusively amongst the Durham and Northumberland miners. Three women were to travel in the vehicle, one of whom was Miss Ada Nield; and

Mr. Chew of Rochdale and an Oldham friend were to be in the tent and responsible for the odd jobs. (Knowing my father, I was astonished by this information, which I do not recall having heard before. How he coped with a horse I cannot imagine, nor do I believe that anything but a very strong personal motive could have persuaded him to undertake any domestic chores.)

By Saturday 29 August the Clarion van campaign had reached Gateshead, and on Monday night it was in the Bigg Market, Newcastle-on-Tyne, where 'the largest meeting yet held by the present Vanners' was held by the light of an electric lamp. The rain did not dampen the enthusiasm of the crowd. The following Tuesday the Vanners went to Swalwell, where a miners' strike had been going on for six weeks. A splendid meeting was held – which is hardly surprising, since the subject was 'Ought the miners to strike?'; I cannot believe that any speaker argued in the negative. By Friday they had reached Jarrow, where they had not intended to hold a meeting, but where one was requested and was very successful, the audience voting unanimously in favour of the political, social and industrial freedom of women.

At all these meetings Ada Nield's name was on the list of speakers, and by 19 September she was writing the Van Report to Julia Dawson, who commented 'Miss Ada Nield's Van Report is so full of love and gratitude to local friends and fellow Vanners for unlimited kindnesses, that it seems a shame to weed out all her pretty expressions and leave only the bare skeleton of facts'.

Further successful meetings were held at Jarrow, South Shields, Beldon Colliery and Sunderland, where there was an 'immense gathering' opposite the Red Lion Hotel, and 'great enthusiasm' was expressed. More meetings were held in spite of bad weather, and at all of them Ada Nield spoke; she had gone far from the day in 1894 when she was first compelled to defend herself in public. Since her only companion was ill from 14 September for nearly a week, she would have been the 'lone Vanner' but for the 'true comradeship of local friends'. She was persuaded by these same friends to address a trade union meeting on Sunday 27 September, and was 'strongly advised by all to devote more and more time to the Socialist platform'.

It was estimated that 6000 people had listened weekly when the tour ended on 23 September, after fifteen weeks' hard work. In the last week there had been rain and violent gales, which made an open-air meeting on 22 September impossible, while the next day not only did the weather prevent a meeting at Hartlepool, but the 'people are in such a deadly state of apathy and indifference' that the Vanners' best efforts apparently failed to make any impression. There were good numbers, a fair sale of 'literature', but no enthusiasm. The campaign as a whole though had been such a success that it was decided to run a similar one in 1897, when Bruce Glasier, accompanied by Ada Nield ('now Ada Chew, mark you,' added Julia Dawson), would be among the speakers. Ada Nield, who had married in a registry office in Nantwich on 13 April 1897, with her favourite brother Justin and a friend (Mrs. Powell) as witnesses, in fact did not accompany the van.

George Chew was originally from Rishton, north-east Lancashire, and came from a family of cotton weavers (when I knew my grandparents however, they kept a small corner shop). George and his two sisters had been sent to the mill as half-timers at the age of ten, as was customary. George, however, was determined to educate himself, and to that end he walked seven miles each way to evening classes in Blackburn several times a week. He won at least one prize there – a bound volume of Shakespeare which has only recently fallen to pieces. He hated weaving, and in one thing he was luckier than his sisters: being a boy, he was allowed to study instead of having to help with the housework. It was at this time he learnt to concentrate no matter what the distractions. His mother was an incessant talker, and George discovered how to read without paying any attention to other people's conversation, or even to direct questioning. This served him in good stead when he was at home, but in later life my mother and I were often irritated by his ability to ignore what we were saying, no matter how pertinent it might be.

I am not at all sure when he was able to leave the mill and become an ILP organiser, but certainly in his youth he must have been an idealist for I have been told that he went around disguised as a tramp to a number of workhouses to sample for himself the kind of accommodation provided for the casual wanderer. He had, too, a great admiration for John Bright, the Liberal reformer, and for the Rochdale Pioneers, the originators of the modern co-operative society, and this led him to live in Rochdale before he married. (Incidentally, none of this information came direct from my father: I never met anybody less interested in personal reminiscences.)

Physically my parents were very different. My father was short and always wore glasses, and his straight dark hair turned grey when he was in his thirties. My mother, with her bright hair, was altogether more striking. After they married they went together to Rochdale, where they rented a cottage in Shawclough, then a village just outside the town, but now absorbed by it. From here my mother went out on propagandist trips round the country. On 3 July 1897 an article by her appeared in the *Labour Leader*, the organ of the ILP, then edited by Keir Hardie. The article was headed 'From Scotland to Salop', but did not contain an account of what had obviously been a speaking tour of Scotland. She said that after her return from that country she paid her third visit to Liverpool, where she had intelligent and kindly, if critical, audiences. From there she went to Earlstown and St. Helens. 'If there is any place where the bright hope of our movement is needed, it is St. Helens . . . I am strongly tempted to call it hell upon earth.' However, there was a 'brave little branch of the ILP', amidst the rain, which pelted in merciless torrents.

From there she went to Rochdale, 'where there is a strong branch . . . But I have since come to live very near Rochdale . . . and will one day devote a whole article to it, and especially to this particular village where I live, for it and its residents are . . . a curiosity which affords me endless amusement and instruction'. This reference was to Shawclough, but if the article was ever written, I have been unable to find it, which I regret, for a description of a Lancashire village in the industrial belt at the turn of the century would have been of great interest. From here she went on to William Morris Labour Church in Leek, Staffordshire, where she felt she must protest against the signboard of a public house, 'which I felt to be an insult to my sex. Its name was the "Quiet Woman", and I was indignant to find that on the board was a woman – minus a head!'

Her comment on the Oldham of the 1890s was harsh: 'Those of you who have never seen Oldham pray you never may.' In Leicester she found more encouragement than any-where, but Birmingham was apathetic. Her visit there was fol-lowed by a week in Shropshire – not the rural county of the Welsh border, but the industrial area, where girls walked two or three miles to their work on the pit banks of Madeley, begin-ning at 6 a.m. and continuing work until 3.30-4 p.m. For this long day they were paid eight pence to a shilling.

On 31 July the *Labour Leader* published a second article from her about a speaking tour, this time mainly in the Black Country, in the 'depressing surroundings' of South Staffordshire, though it also took in Crewe, Long Eaton and Kettering. In Wolverhampton she was distressed to find that drink was sold in the working men's clubs. This reaction may sound priggish, but these were days when drink could ruin the lives of families on the edge of subsistence even more easily than today. Temperance had strong support among the working class, especially among the women, and also in the Labour movement. My father was brought up a teetotaller because of his family's experience with a drunken grandfather, and this was not uncommon. My mother was not a teetotaller, and in later years she would take the odd drink, but in my youth we never had drink in the house.

A third and last article in this series was headed 'In and Out and Round About', and appeared in the *Labour Leader* on 14 August 1897. This time Ada Nield had visited Dudley,

Stockport, Huddersfield and Derby. Of a temperance orator in Derby she wrote: 'Ah me! Shall I ever forget that man's awful voice on Derby Place? It was like the roar of a cannon and completely drowned the small piping voice of the Salvation Army band. Things are unequally divided, and that man has got someone else's share of vocal organs as well as his own.'

From here she went to Eccles, where 'The meeting ground is in the centre of a spot from which four roads diverge: a capital place to draw an audience but calculated to batter off the speaker's head. Trams to the right of you, trams to the left of you, trams behind and before you.' In Wallasey, however, the weather was the enemy. 'It was blowing gales and oh! so cold, as we stood on an open space near the sea shore.' She was very critical of the Manchester area. 'There is a terrible sameness about the flock of towns surrounding Manchester. Walkden, however, is not quite so dingy as Pendlebury . . . But oh, the listlessness, the apparent indifference of the people!'

Blackburn, on the other hand, seems to have made a better impression on her than almost any other town.

> At Blackburn there is a resoluteness, a level-headedness, and a reasonableness about the audiences, as well as the comrades, which is good to feel. Discussion classes are held on the immense Market Square at all hours of the day and night, and we have only to put in an appearance to be surrounded immediately by an enquiring audience. There was a time when a Socialist was bustled off to the station as the incarnation of wickedness, but Blackburn folk will never be found in the rear, and now are ready not only to listen, but to endorse . . . Approval of our statements was shown, to my joy, by the shawled and clogged women as by the men.

In the same tour she visited Hebden Bridge, 'buried between the high hills', Glossop, Accrington and Leek, where 'my kind friends again overwhelmed me with love and indulgence . . . Wages are much lower than formerly. Trade unionism here, I understand, is practically unknown.'

Since 1894, Ada Nield had become a vivacious public speaker who used no notes (she said later that she could not understand my being able to do so) but never hesitated for a word, and who had learnt through hard experience to project her voice in the open air. Her writing, too, had developed a relaxed, even racy style, while remaining as cogent as ever.

In one of the articles in the *Labour Leader*, Ada Nield had referred to 'those of us who are constantly on the road', but with the birth of her only child, myself, in June 1898, her peregrinations came perforce to an end for the time being. At the time I was born my father was working as a weaver again, and is so described on my birth certificate. Later he took up organising again – whether for trade unions or the ILP I am not sure. During this period we moved to Preston, staying there for a year, then for a time to Dunfermline, in Scotland. By 1900, however, we were back in Rochdale, living behind a tiny shop, where my parents sold 'fents' or cloth remnants, near Toad Lane and the original Rochdale Pioneers shop. The main building in the tiny square of St. Mary's Gate was a temperance club, and behind this was a rough gully where I used to play with the local children, rushing home every now and then for a 'sugar butty' – bread and butter sprinkled with sugar. The 'fent' shop was the beginning of the trading which occupied my father for the rest of his life. Later he opened a number of market stalls in the Lancashire towns (and Crewe), and a chain of shops in Rochdale. One of these, probably the first, was a Penny Bazaar. Later, however, he concentrated in the shops, as on the market stalls, on the sale of shoes and slippers.

Women's Trade Union Organiser: 1900-08

I knew that in the first decade of this century my mother had worked as a trade union organiser with Mary Macarthur, who became a well known public figure in this period. Turning to the quarterly *Women's Trade Union Review*, the organ of the Women's Trade Union League, whose secretary Mary Macarthur was, and which I found in the British Library, I began to discover something about this side of her work.

As Ada Nield herself had learnt from bitter personal experience, women were both wretchedly paid and reluctant to organise. It was to deal with both these problems that the Women's Trade Union League (WTUL) had been founded in the 1870s. In the year 1900 its honorary secretary and editor of the *Review*, Miss Gertrude Tuckwell, reported that Mrs. Chew, a well known speaker on labour questions, had accepted a post as one of the League's organisers. In every quarter thereafter, until 1908, there was a regular report of her activities, and in 1903, the year when Mary Macarthur succeeded Mona Wilson as organising secretary, Mrs. Chew was named sole organiser.

This work, of course, she carried out as a married woman and a mother, and people may wonder what part my father and I played in these activities, and in particular what my father's attitude was to his wife's outside work and his daughter's upbringing. As far as I was concerned, the answer was simple. When my mother began her work for the League, I was only two years old. The first time she went away for a few days I was left at home with my father and presumably some form of household help, but my mother was so stricken by the look on my face and the unbelieving exclamation of 'Mamma!' when I was brought to the station to meet her on her return, that she decided then and there that she would never leave me behind again. Thus from 1900 to 1905, when I went to school at the age of seven, it was understood that when hospitality was offered to the trade union organiser, it must include that organiser's child. The lamb always accompanied Mary. (As has been pointed out to me, this was only possible because my mother had no more than one child.)

I was not, of course, taken round to meetings, but must have been left behind every day in other people's homes. My recollections of the period are disjointed and very incomplete, and of course of no use in assessing my mother's success in her work. Nevertheless, I have retained a vague impression that it was a very uphill task, and this is borne out by many comments both in the *Review* and in the League's annual report. It appears that Miss Macarthur and Mrs. Chew divided the country between them. My mother evidently covered both Scotland and the North and Midlands of England. We went everywhere by train, of course, since travel by bus or car was still in the future.

We stayed in many homes and met many people in those days, but alas, only two families remain in my memory, and those both Scottish – the Guilds of Rutherglen and the Misses Husband of Dundee, the latter a couple of charming and intelligent women with whom my mother struck up a lasting friendship.

My father's attitude to this was simple too. He considered that the prime responsibility for my welfare lay with his wife. I have reason to believe that he never really wanted a child, but accepted my birth as something his wife had chosen. All through my childhood and youth it was she who made the ultimate decisions, and who dealt with the outside bodies which concerned themselves with my education. Where they insisted – to my mother's intense indignation – on having the consent of the father as the sole responsible parent in law to anything, he gave it without question. I do not wish to give the impression that my father was in any way indifferent to my well being, merely that he left decisions to his wife. I have no doubt that he was consulted, and when the time came for secondary education he was as keen as my mother that I should have the best available to a working-class family.

As for my father's attitude towards my mother's choice of work, it must be remembered that he had been brought up in the home of Lancashire weavers who took it for granted that the wife should go out to work, as well as looking after the home. Of course, wives did not usually go away for days at a time, but after all, my father had married my mother knowing quite well the sort of person she was and the sort of life she intended to lead. He agreed both to her contributing to the family income and to the way in which she did it. Moreover, his political beliefs precluded any objection in principle to the way she spread the gospel they both believed in.

As I grew older, I was struck by two main differences between my parents and those of my school friends. We were an extremely undemonstrative household; my father, as I remember, never showed physical affection either for my mother or myself. This was not unusual, however, in most Lancashire working men's homes, but still my father did not seem to feel affection easily. He never showed any for his parents or his sisters, and would have been content to drift away from them altogether if my mother had not insisted on keeping in touch. (She never got any credit from my grandmother for this, while she was certainly blamed for the fact that I was, in my paternal grandparents' eyes, shockingly over-educated.) My parents never addressed each other by name – much less used any terms of affection towards each other. Mother and I were not very demonstrative to each other either once I began to grow up, except in letters and in the pet names we had for each other.

My parents both had a sense of humour, but not the same one. My father's was more robust: he liked music halls. Mother's tended towards irony: she liked Jane Austen. However, both enjoyed George Bernard Shaw. When we moved back to Rochdale in 1907 my parents occupied separate rooms. Mother said my father snored.

When Mother wrote her sketches of life in working-class households, it was evident that she knew from the inside the Lancashire working man's attitude to his wife's spending of the weekly budget. My father never found any extra money over and above the weekly sum he handed over. If they ever had any outside expenses, like a meal in a restaurant, she was left to pay for it. I cannot, however, see my father in any other aspect of the working-class life she wrote about; the basis of her writing was generalised observation. Whether he ever read any of Mother's writings I don't know, but I shouldn't be surprised if he did not. He was never very interested in fiction, although I believe he read H. G. Wells and possibly Arnold Bennett.

Meanwhile my mother was busy with her work as a trade union organiser. From the reports in the WTUL *Review* of her activities, one gets an interesting picture of the number and variety of trades in which women were employed. My mother was busy organising weavers in Lancashire, Yorkshire and Scotland; boot and shoe operatives in Northamptonshire; felt-hat trimmers in Leicester; cigar makers in Nottingham; and hosiery workers in Loughborough. She visited Hull, Coventry, Carlisle, Leek, Cheadle, Bradford, York, Halifax, Worcester, Mansfield, Dunfermline and Dundee. In July 1901 she described the intolerable conditions in the egg sorting trade in Hartlepool, where the women worked with saturated feet and clothing. The egg breakers were covered with filthy slime, and there was a stench from the bad eggs, while the work was carried on in dark cells, with poor ventilation and inadequate sanitation.

In July 1900 she spoke at Wigan to the cotton operatives who were striking for the increase in wages which had been granted by employers in other districts in Lancashire. The report says they refused her advice (presumably on organisation and how to raise money), and the strike collapsed for want of funds. Again, in October, a hard week's canvassing for the Weavers' Union had discouraging results, and in December 1903 she commented that 'Earby has a sad record for Trade Unionism.

They only join when there is a dispute; then leave again. Earby has never been anything but a source of trouble to Colne Weavers' Association.'

It was much more difficult to organise women workers than men, for then as now most women had a double job to do; and there was even less equality in pay and household responsibility between the sexes than there is today. Women, like men, worked in the factory all day, but then they went home and worked there in the evening, so that it was difficult to get them to attend meetings. In Skipton in December 1903 a meeting was abandoned because 'the effort would be wasted on Friday night, when everyone was cleaning'. Yet trade union membership among women trebled from 1900 to 1914, according to B. L. Hutchins' *Women in Modern Industry*, so it is understandable that (judging from her own and Mary Macarthur's reports) my mother nevertheless felt her efforts achieved a good deal of success.

In Dunfermline in the autumn of 1901 the union was considerably strengthened in spite of the heavy rain which interrupted several meetings. In 1903 in Wolverhampton there was a large attendance of women at the inaugural meeting of the local branch of the National Union of Boot and Shoe Operatives, while in Stockport she won 150 new members for the Gasworkers' and General Workers' Union; and in Kettering the numbers of women in the Boot and Shoe Operatives' Union 'had increased considerably', and she had good meetings. In January 1904 there was a 'capital' attendance at Holcombe Brook, and in Heywood the workers were in the union almost to a man and woman. In February the Upholsterers' Union was said to be flourishing; in March there was a crowded meeting in Hyde, where the very successful union was an object lesson to trade unionists everywhere. In the same year Miss Macarthur noted that 'considerable success attended Mrs. Chew's visit to the Todmorden weavers, while her efforts to organise the women bleachers in conjunction with the local officials of the Bolton Amalgamated Society of Bleachers, Dyers and Finishers resulted in the addition of about one hundred and fifty women members.' A success which must have given my mother a good deal of pleasure was that in September 1905, she formed a strong branch of the Amalgamated Society of Tailors, in Crewe.

Returning early in 1906 to Leek, where she was well known from at least two previous visits, she set up a branch of the newly formed Union of Women Workers. This was a general union providing a central structure to furnish co-ordination and support for branches in different localities and trades; it worked alongside the differently organised Women's Trade Union League which linked autonomous (often isolated and short-lived) locally based unions. Mary Macarthur, brilliant and energetic secretary of the League, was instrumental in setting up the Federation, whose centralised structure she believed would be much more suitable for women workers. In March 1906 she noted approvingly in the WTUL *Review* that 'thanks to Mrs. Chew's splendid work the Leek branch is already over 500 strong'. It apparently went on from strength to strength: by June 1907 it had 2000 members, while the union had spread to Macclesfield, Congleton and Cheadle.[1]

Over and over again the reports mention the weather, that ever present hazard for open-air speakers and events in Britain. In November 1901 meetings in Bury were spoilt by fog and cold. In August 1903 there were good meetings in Brechin, except for the rain. Again in July 1904 meetings of laundry workers at York were held in spite of the rain, while in Kettering and Todmorden there was dreadful weather in November, but good audiences on the whole. In the same month in Bury there was a splendid meeting in spite of blinding fog. In August 1905 my mother was to finish a week in Raunds with open-air meetings on Saturday and Sunday. On Saturday 'rain descended all day', and the meetings which had been planned had to be abandoned. On Sunday 'a big crowd listened to us until the heavens opened and a terrible downpour scattered us in all directions'.

Mrs. Chew's quarterly reports were by no means restricted to recording facts, and were certainly not dull. Anyone who has visited the little town of Heptonstall in the West Riding, with its black stone houses and little closes, rising steeply up a hill above Hebden Bridge, will appreciate the following description:

> This is a place entirely out of this world, on the slopes of the other side of a mountain, the summit of which has to be climbed in order to reach the destined place. On a wild November night it is an experience likely to make an impression on the memory.

At least twice, to her great surprise and pleasure, my mother was given presents by the workers on whose behalf she strove. In August 1902 she was presented with a handsome shawl made in Alva, Scotland, and at the final meeting in Raunds in August 1905 'a handsomely framed picture of the strikers who marched to London in May' was handed her for 'services rendered to the branch'.

In 1898 Gertrude Tuckwell had founded the Potteries Fund Committee as an offshoot of the WTUL; its object, as stated in the report for 1903, was 'keeping a worker in the Potteries who shall report cases of suffering, and for the relief, where desirable, of the sufferers'. During my childhood and youth that worker was my mother. At first she paid weekly visits to the Potteries at a time when lead poisoning was common among workers on the 'pot banks'. Two of the sketches she wrote for the *Common Cause* were illustrative of this. Her reports are referred to though not published in the *Review*, but the WTUL secretary mentioned 'thirty new cases of suffering' in 1903, and fifty in 1904. In 1905 an article written by Rosalind Nash and headed 'The Compensation Rules in the Potteries' was published in the *Review*, and the writer illustrated her points by quoting from one of Ada Nield Chew's reports on a man who was found ill and suffering from wrist drop, a characteristic result of lead poisoning which leaves the hands useless.

November 1904. The poor fellow's hands are much worse, and he cannot feed or wash himself. His general health is also worse, for he frets and worries about his helplessness. A strong intelligent young man of thirty-four, to be as helpless as a baby! It grieves one to see him and the matter is worse in that he was always careful and clean while at work. He had seen three doctors in the infirmary that day, and is resolute in receiving electrical treatment, but unfortunately does not improve.

February 1905. Died a few days after my last visit. There was a post mortem and he was found to be full of lead. The death was certified as 'consumption' brought on by lead poisoning. There is no consumption in his family, and he was a fine healthy man until he got the lead. His widow is left with two children.

The amount of compensation awarded, said Rosalind Nash, was a mockery: four shillings and sixpence for men, two shillings and threepence for women.

My mother gave up her work as a regular trade union organiser in 1908, though even in 1911 and 1912 she was mentioned as giving assistance from time to time. She may have become tired of the incessant grind of constant travelling; and the campaign for women's suffrage, in which she had always believed as an essential preliminary to industrial and social progress for women, was becoming a very live issue. But I have a feeling that at least one of the reasons for her resignation may have been an uneasy relationship with her superior, Mary Macarthur. I cannot give chapter and verse for this for I was only ten at the time, but the persistence of this impression must have some cause. Incidentally, in the Gertrude Tuckwell papers in the Trades Union Congress Library, I could find no mention of my mother or her work, only of Gertrude Tuckwell herself and Mary Macarthur. As far as my childish recollection goes, Mother was amiably disposed towards Gertrude Tuckwell, to whom she referred (in the family circle) as 'Tuck'. I was taken aback, however, on one occasion when I met her former employer, to find that when I referred to the long years of association I was met by a blank stare and the answer; 'No, I don't remember her.' It is true that Miss Tuckwell was old by then, and I know from experience that it is all too easy to forget names from the past when one has lost all contact over a long period, but not usually when one has known them as long as Miss Tuckwell had known my mother; and this meeting took place only a few years after her death.

Mother continued her visits to the Potteries for a good many years. Her reports on lead poisoning were mentioned in later issues of the *Review*; in 1914 her 'admirable and devoted work' was referred to, while in 1915, although the winding up of the fund was discussed, it was felt that Mrs. Chew's services were too valuable to lose. The League amalgamated with the TUC in 1920, and what happened to the Potteries Fund Committee after that I don't know, nor can I be sure how long Mother continued the work, although it was still being mentioned in 1917. Once or twice, when I was older, she took me with her, and I remember the mean little streets of brick houses, and the barrenness of the kitchens, where the sufferers had nothing to sit on but hard wooden chairs. I discovered only recently that the use of lead in the glazing of pottery was not absolutely prohibited until 1947. How many generations of workers had suffered chronic illness before then?

In 1903 we had left the 'fent' shop in St. Mary's Gate and had gone to live in the Greave, a hamlet to the north of Rochdale, in part because my mother believed every child should be brought up in the country if at all possible. As far as I recall, there was a Victorian mansion on a hillock surrounded by fields, a row of three or four cottages where we lived, and a farm where I was allowed to help – or at least pretend to help – at hay-time. To reach the Greave you had to take a tram and then, from whatever direction you approached, walk over fields. Every Whit Friday there was a Sunday School procession to the Greave, followed by festivities, in which I joined illicitly, in the fields between the big house and the cottages. None of this exists now except in my memory, for as long ago as 1936 we found that a housing estate had been built on the site.

Mother had a lot of theories on various subjects, among them children's education. Although she was a socialist she disapproved of the State educational system of the day on two counts: that it 'forced' children by sending them to school too young, and that it was through infections contracted at school that so many infantile diseases were spread. She therefore had no scruples about keeping me at home until I was seven, and it is a fact that I escaped the common childhood diseases. However, our next door neighbour was the strongly disapproving headmaster of an elementary school. He informed the authorities of my parents' lapse, and they were threatened with a visit from the 'School Board Man', so something had to be done. Again, it was my mother's decision to send me to a small private school run by three sisters where I need only attend half-days. Here I went for five years until I was twelve, walking over the fields and through the streets, the first three in the afternoons, and the last two in the mornings.

Those years must have been extremely busy ones for my mother. For much of the time she was working away from home, while taking an active interest in her husband's business, as well as looking after a home and family. She did succeed in getting the help of charwomen, one of whom is described in the first of her stories about married working women, but even so I can remember coming home from school to find her scrubbing the outside privy, and whether or not we had a hot water supply I have no recollection.

But she always found time to read, and the three of us spent hours round the fire, each absorbed in a book. The novels of H. G. Wells and Arnold Bennett were always at hand. As far as I was concerned, the greatest virtue shown by my parents – apart from the constant love and support which I took for granted – was their willingness to leave me alone to play by myself or with neighbours' children, or to read whatever I liked without censorship. I learned to appreciate this invaluable quality through visits to a childless friend of the family who wanted to supervise my every action. I have read since that only children are apt to be bored; but I never was.

Even before we left the Greave, in 1907, when I was nine, my parents had introduced me to the theatre, and the severest punishment they could give me for misbehaviour was to forbid a visit to the Theatre Royal in Rochdale. Later, in my teens, I was taken to see plays in Manchester theatres as well as the Gilbert and Sullivan operas played by the d'Oyly Carte Opera Company. Grand opera I discovered for myself later, but I have always been grateful for that early introduction to drama.

During these years my parents were active in the Rochdale branch of the ILP, and my mother continued to speak to other branches as well as to socialist Sunday Schools and Labour churches, on such subjects as: 'Should Women Have a Vote?', 'Should Women Support Trade Unionism?' and 'My Work Among Women'. Neither my mother nor my father had any religious affiliations: my father was a conscious agnostic, having revolted in his youth against the religious observances of his family, and my mother was a natural one. They did not substitute socialism for religion however; I was sent twice to the local socialist Sunday School, but when I decided I would rather not go, no pressure was brought to bear on me.

Evidence of Mother's fervently held socialist and feminist views can be found in a series of letters in the *Clarion* during December 1904. In these she conducted an argument with Christabel Pankhurst, then secretary of the Women's Social and Political Union, about the proposed women's suffrage Bill, based on a property qualification, and supported by the ILP. She complained that the *Labour Leader* had twice cut out of her letters her main argument against this Bill that:

> Well-to-do women would, by means of this Bill, be enfranchised almost to a woman, and that their vote, given naturally in their own interests, would help to swamp the Labour vote. Miss Pankhurst does not deny this. She makes an attempt to confuse the issue by saying that 'wealthy men can already buy as many votes as they like, though not in the same constituency' – which is only partly true. It is true that they could not themselves vote more than once in the same constituency. It is well known that they can always provide their sons with votes – in the same constituency. And if this Bill becomes law they could add to the power of their class by registering their daughters in the same constituency.

Pursuing the argument in another letter she wrote:

> For Miss Pankhurst to say that the vote of the well-to-do women could not be used more stupidly than the working man already uses his is not an answer to my argument, but on the contrary, only strengthens my position; and her remarks about its being necessary for the Labour Party to champion this Bill before the Liberals come into office are, of course, without point to women like myself, who could not support a Bill based on property, even if the Socialists themselves were in office. A better way, it seems to us, is to work for the abolition of all existing anomalies, and so prepare the way for a Bill which would enable a man or woman to vote simply because they are man and woman, not because they are more fortunate financially than their fellow men and women.

No half-measures for Ada Nield Chew; it must be the whole loaf or nothing, and in the end her view, and that of those who thought like her, prevailed.

The names of the great socialists of the time were, of course, household words for me, for not only did we take the *Labour Leader* and the *Clarion*, but sometimes both my parents and certainly my mother met these men and women in the flesh. They talked of the MacDonalds, the Snowdens, J. R. Clynes and Robert Smillie the miners' leader (of whom mother thought highly), and of the Bruce Glasiers. There was also Julia Dawson, and the brilliant socialist speaker, Enid Stacy, who died young; and Mary Macarthur visited us at the Greave. After we moved back into the town there were others, mostly visiting lecturers, like Fenner (now Lord) Brockway and R. H. Tawney, gentle, considerate, and aware even of the youngest member of the family, who sat there silent.

Our daily newspaper was the *Manchester Guardian*, read by many people who did not share its Liberal politics; and A. P. Wadsworth, later editor of that paper, but when we knew him a reporter on the staff of the *Observer*, became well known to my parents after the Workers' Educational Association came to Rochdale. One of the first WEA tutorial classes was held in Rochdale in 1908, with R. H. Tawney as its tutor, and both my parents were members of this. Mother was also involved in a women's class formed in 1909 which started by studying the economic position of women, and went on to 'Home and Child Study' (this is recalled by her in a letter to the *Common Cause* on how to reach the married working woman, published 7 November 1913). The WEA also organised monthly meetings with songs, recitations, homily and discussion, while tea and cakes were provided at a cost of one penny. Its regular members, like my parents, no doubt valued the chance of social activities with the like-minded.

My parents, having had so little formal education themselves, were determined that I should have the best they could afford, which meant that I should attend the secondary school which had been opened (following the Education Act of 1902) on the premises of the Technical School at the foot of the parish church steps, in the middle of the town. I was to be a feepayer for £6 a year: there were only thirty scholarships, and these were for children from the local elementary schools. The entrance examination for feepayers was not so exacting as that for scholarship pupils, but even so it was clear that schooling restricted to afternoons, two of which were largely spent in sewing lessons, was not adequate preparation for a secondary education; my timetable, therefore, was changed to mornings, which were devoted to academic subjects.

In 1910, at the age of twelve, I duly entered Rochdale Municipal Secondary School, one of the type since generically known as a 'grammar school' although it was really nothing of the kind, being one of the early municipal ventures into higher education for brighter working-class children. The middle classes, like doctors' families, did not send their children there. I always feel indignant at the general denigration of this type of school. The time has come to replace it by a more comprehensive form of education, but it played an essential part in giving working-class children like myself the opportunities their parents had so signally lacked.

Here my mother soon became known to the staff not only as a political and social reformer, but also as a parent who did not hesitate to interview the headmaster on any matter connected with my education. She was the only parent to object to her child's taking an examination called the Oxford Junior on the grounds that young people should not be pushed. It was a completely unnecessary test, and was abandoned by the school the following year, but I was very embarrassed to be the only one not taking it, especially when everyone knew I wasn't being in the least 'pushed'.

On the other hand, when it was a question of school discipline, I received no sympathy from either parent; my teachers were always right. In spite of this I was aware that the staff thought my mother a peculiar person, and on her account I was the natural choice for Miss Strongmind in a topical play, and for the Labour candidate in a mock parliamentary election (run even in those far-off days on the system of proportional representation) in which I got thirteen votes. Some of it, however, must be laid at my own door. In class I was no trouble at all – I liked learning – but outside it I could be a nuisance, as when I conducted a campaign for girls as well as boys to be allowed to go on a holiday excursion. And again, following my mother, I became well known as a speaker in school debates. It was natural that these activities should be attributed at least in part to the sort of mother I had. We rubbed off on each other, so to speak.

My schooling, like my parents' various political and educational activities, was made easier by our removal in 1907 to Kilnerdeyne Terrace, which overlooks Broadfield Park in the middle of Rochdale. If you couldn't live in the country, it was a good place to be. There was a park in front, and at the back we had a garden full of bushes; and there was also an attic which my mother turned over to me, where later I gave parties and staged plays. We rented the house, as we did all our homes, but Mother succeeded in turning a bedroom into a bathroom and making other improvements. In 1908 Rochdale was arguing hotly about the benefits of water-borne sewage – the pages of the *Rochdale Observer* at that time are full of the arguments on both sides – and this when 'sanitary carts' still carried tubs of evil-smelling human excrement through the streets. As soon as it was possible, we had the new system installed.

We continued to have the help of charwomen and, since Mother had to go away for days at a time, more regular daily help in the house. The washing was done every Monday in a kind of glasshouse, originally intended I suppose as a conservatory, at the back of the house. Clouds of steam filled the air, and afterwards the damp sheets and clothing covered the 'maidens' or clothes-horses in front of the living room fire. I never liked coming home at lunchtime on Mondays.

Mother baked much of her own bread – with 'Mr. Allinsons' brown flour – in the oven beside the fire, which was also the only means of heating water in the back boiler. We lit the house with incandescent gas mantles, and the only machine power to hand was good old elbow grease. It is no wonder that in Mother's sketches and stories the burdens borne by married working women were ever present.

NOTES

[1] See F. Burchill & J. Sweeney, *A History of Trade Unionism in the Silk Industry in North Staffordshire.* I am grateful to Jill Norris for bringing this reference to my notice.

Women's Suffrage Speaker, Writer and Organiser: 1911-14

My mother had always believed that the mental abilities of working-class women were largely wasted in domestic drudgery and low-paid work. One of the people who had most influence on her ideas was the American writer, Charlotte Perkins Gilman, who argued that this drudgery could be ended by co-operative effort.[1] (Instead, the answer, though incomplete, has come largely through the development of technology.)

To most thinking women, especially those who, like my mother, were concerned with social justice, the securing of the vote was only a first but a necessary step towards the removal of the social and economic burdens placed upon women, which she believed retarded the progress of the human race. It might appear that her forthright opposition to injustice and oppression would have made her a natural militant, but she was a convinced opponent of the use of physical force in any context (including international relations), and therefore opposed to the methods of the Women's Social and Political Union (WSPU) (see Foreword, p. xxiv). As her argument with Christabel Pankhurst shows, she considered her ideas on equality distinctly limited; nor would she ever have been prepared to accept the dictatorship of the Pankhursts. Any organisation she chose to join would have to be run democratically. Because of this belief, she had become a member of the National Union of Women's Suffrage Societies (NUWSS) (see Foreword p. xxiv), though I have no idea when.

My mother's political energies in this period were increasingly devoted to suffrage campaigns, though always from a

Labour perspective. Some evidence survives of her activities at local level: for instance in 1911 a branch of the Women's Labour League was formed,[2] and as its Secretary she wrote to the local paper advocating the extension of the school clinic recently set up in Rochdale. (*Rochdale Observer*, 9 December 1911.) She and my father were by this time becoming disillusioned by the doctrinaire attitudes of some of their fellow socialists, and although their sympathies and votes were always with the Labour Party, my mother wrote in 1912 that she belonged to no political party. This was in a letter to the *Common Cause* (18 April) which stressed the need to attract the support of working women, who in turn would convince the men. Working women, she said, distrusted the suffrage societies because they were thought to be run by 'fine ladies'. The following month there was indeed a change in policy decided at a special meeting of the NUWSS, favouring support for Labour candidates in by-elections, especially where the record of the Liberal candidate on suffrage was unsatisfactory. Hitherto the union had been politically neutral in theory, while leaning towards the Liberals.

Mrs. Chew, Mrs. Annot Robinson and Mrs. Cooper, all Labour sympathisers as well as suffragists, were therefore among the speakers campaigning at a by-election shortly afterwards. On 20 June the readers of the *Common Cause* were told that on the previous Saturday evening, at Holmfirth in the West Riding, 'in a very few minutes there was a crowd of eight hundred listening to Mrs. Chew'. A letter from Mrs. Chew herself described the people of Holmfirth as slow and contented; they came to laugh *at* the speakers and ended by laughing *with* them. One comment she had heard on her own arguments was, 'Yon woman talks sense!'

In July 1912 there was a by-election in Crewe. This was of course my mother's old stamping ground, and though her parents were dead, some of her family and friends still lived in the neighbourhood. Nor was she forgotten by those who had worked with her in earlier days.

After the Crewe election came Midlothian, a constituency of

300 square miles and covering thirty to forty villages round Edinburgh. I have reason to remember this because, much to the disapproval of my headmaster, my mother insisted on taking me with her for a week. She said it would be a political education for me, but he did not consider this either necessary or particularly advisable. There was however nothing he could do, for I was fourteen and had passed the statutory school leaving age (then thirteen). So off I went, to stay in an Edinburgh boarding house and do my stint of addressing envelopes in the committee rooms at Dalkeith and Mid Calder. We travelled between these and the other centres of population mainly by pony and trap. Possibly there were other means of locomotion, but I don't recall any. I do remember, however, how pleasant it was clip-clopping along leafy lanes in what in retrospect seems always to have been fine weather. In the evenings meetings were held at which my mother spoke and I tried to sell copies of the *Common Cause*. That paper subsequently reported that the organisation was fortunate in having been able to secure the services of Mrs. Annot Robinson and Mrs. Chew, both immensely popular speakers in the Labour as well as the suffrage movement; and noted elsewhere: 'Following Miss Crompton came Mrs. Chew, whose experiences as a sweated worker always held her audiences tense with interest and sympathy.'

The next week's report mentioned that 'Mrs. Chew, who is always eagerly sought after by the organisers of Labour meetings, was addressing several meetings, one after another, in the open air'. The *Labour Leader* gave full credit to the suffragists for their assistance, and on 5 September a letter headed 'Women in Midlothian', and signed by Ada Nield Chew, told how the activity of the National Union was causing terror in the Liberal Party. 'The single taxers cannot get a hearing when we are about; and last night I heard of a Liberal indoor meeting having an audience of fifteen, while we had an outdoor crowd numbering hundreds.' She went on to describe the village of Juniper Green, where the 'working men have only a "but and ben" [a single storey, two-roomed house], and Loganlea,

44

which was one long row of miners' cottages. Addiewell, a mile away, was a 'dreary blot on the landscape'; the average wage was 21 shillings a week. 'Inside our committee room devoted women are doing the deadly drudgery work writing out canvass cards and addressing envelopes; others go up the stairs and into the closes doing still more difficult canvassing work. We shirk nothing. The Labour fight is our fight.'

Other by-elections followed in 1913 and 1914, at Lanark, North-East Durham, Leith Burghs, East Fife and East Derbyshire, in which my mother spoke and worked for the Labour candidates. Needless to say, none of the Labour men was elected, but the National Union calculated (according to Josephine Kamm in *Rapiers and Battleaxes*) that in six of the elections the suffragists' intervention had helped to keep the Liberal out.

During these years my mother was the NUWSS organiser in the Rossendale Valley constituency, near our home in Rochdale; she and another Labour woman, Mrs. Aldersley, worked it together. In January 1913 the *Common Cause* referred to their work in addressing meetings, organising societies and getting resolutions passed by trade unions and other societies. 'A continuous indoor and outdoor programme was being carried on by October, and this had met with striking unbroken success.' The columns of the *Bacup Chronicle* carried regular reports of these meetings, which were addressed by such prominent campaigners as the wealthy Liberal suffragist, Margaret Ashton, long active in the NUWSS; Margaret Roberton, the NUWSS chief organiser; the Labour MP for Blackburn, Philip Snowden (much later Chancellor in the first Labour government); and Helena Swanwick, editor of the *Common Cause*. Further evidence of their endeavours is to be found in the *Bacup Chronicle*'s reports of suffrage resolutions passed at various gatherings. It also carried, on 15 March 1913, a full account of a public debate on women's suffrage between 'Mrs. Chew of Rochdale' and 'Mr. R. H. Law of Waterfoot' (in Rossendale), in the course of which Mr. Law remarked, condescendingly, that

Mrs. Chew was a good speaker but she had a bad case. I was roped in in Rossendale too, delivering notices of meetings to the rows of terraced houses between Bacup and Whitworth. I remember Mother's irritation when she went canvassing only to find her arguments met by the apathetic response, 'I'll 'ave to ask me 'usbun'!'

As part of her organising work Ada Nield wrote propaganda articles in the local press. The Burnley reference librarian kindly drew my attention to one in the *Burnley News* (1 January 1913) entitled 'Woman's Suffrage from a Working Woman's Point of View'. In everything she said and did it was the working woman she was concerned for, and as a working woman she spoke. It was, of course, her origins and experience that made her so valuable to the NUWSS, most of whose members were middle-class. On the whole, my mother liked and certainly admired those middle-class women with and for whom she worked. In this article she emphasised the fact that neither trade unionism among women nor the suffrage movement could exist but for men and middle-class women giving freely of their time and experience. They in turn fully acknowledged their debt both to her and to the other working-class women among them. To her surprise too they sometimes admired her looks. She reported once that one committee member apologised for inattention to the business in hand by saying that she had been 'looking at the wonderful prettiness of Mrs. Chew'. On the other hand, she had no illusions about her lack of dress sense. On 5 September 1913 a letter signed A.N.C. appeared in the *Common Cause* urging that paper to give advice on dress to its readers, because many well meaning but stupid suffragists did not know how to dress. To illustrate this, she quoted a comment from a nameless gentlemen to the effect that 'You can always tell Suffragists by the way they are dressed . . . There's Mrs. Chew, for instance – her hat's never on straight!' How much easier it would have been today when she would not have needed to wear a hat!

But though she frankly admitted her shortcomings, she was always keenly aware of the difference in education and upbringing between herself and the middle-class women around her, and was fiercely determined to maintain her dignity. There were occasions when she felt that some of her colleagues were inclined to condescend to those who, like herself, could not afford to work on a voluntary basis, and then her pride rose up. Yet in later years I met with kindness from such people as Maude Royden and Margaret Ashton purely on account of their respect and liking for my mother. Fundamentally, too, she was extremely reserved. (Her fellow worker, Selina Cooper, recalled however that she had a fiery temper. I can confirm this, but she never bore malice.) Her reserve was recalled and regretted years later by a fellow suffrage worker, Wilma Meikle, to whom apparently my mother had written about a book she had recently published (*Towards a Sane Feminism*, 1916). Replying to my mother in a letter dated 11 January 1917, Miss Meikle wrote:

> I remember so well that Crewe election [in 1912, referred to above] when, though I admired and respected your reserve, I often wished that you would come out of it and let me know you better. Especially after I had spent most of polling day in a Labour committee room and heard your praises sung by a little group of Labour men who looked at me distastefully and told me that Mrs. Chew was the only one of us who really knew what she was talking about! One of them, I remember, had known you before you were married and was very proud of his old acquaintance with you!

At the time this letter was written, I was in the middle of a History honours degree course at Manchester University. Evidently one of the points made in the book concerned the value of a university education, which Miss Meikle, herself an Oxford graduate, seems to have depreciated. She continued on this point:

> I find it a little difficult to write about this because when I read your letter I found myself instinctively admiring the splendid way in which you had determined to send your daughter to the university . . . And I think it is a tremendous advantage to her that she does not belong to a family which stands apart from

the most urgent modern problems. In short, it is a great
privilege for her to have you for a mother!

The gulf in class and education which separated my mother
even from those who were her political colleagues must have
accentuated her natural reserve in such cases. Her personal
friends were mostly politically conscious members of the
working class like herself.

Her sympathy with working-class women and her intimate
knowledge of their lives informed the sketches and stories to
which she was turning her writing skills in these years. These
vignettes of working-class life, many of which are included in
this book, appeared both in the national political publications,
like *Common Cause* or the *Englishwoman*, and in the local
press. They share realistic settings and dialogue, and political
intent: suffrage arguments both spring from the situations
described and are explicitly woven into them. In 'All in the
Day's Work: Mrs. Turpin' for instance (see pp. 152 – 60), she
recounts in detail an ordinary day spent by the mother of six
children with a pitifully small income and only her own
hands – no machines – to do the housework. (I hear echoes
of my mother's own childhood in this sketch, as well as the
acute observation she brought to bear on working-class homes
she had visited.) Like the bedtime fairy stories which Mother
sometimes told me, Mrs. Turpin's story, and many of the
others she was to write, ended with a moral: Mrs. Turpin and
her like through their daily labour and their budgetary skills
worked miracles and continually demonstrated their fitness to
vote:

> She brings up her children on a sum which those housekeepers
> on a large scale [governments], with their advantages in buying
> in bulk, find totally inadequate to such results as she produces.
> The whole fabric of the State rests on the work she is doing, yet
> she is considered incapable or unworthy of expressing an
> opinion on affairs in which she is expert.

Other stories dealt with the legal disabilities under which
women then laboured. My mother deeply resented these, par-

ticularly the fact that the mother was not the legal guardian of her child; every document relating to that child had to be signed by the father alone. Nor had she any illusions about the mother's right to keep her child in the event of divorce, and once said passionately, 'I'd live with the Devil to keep my child!' She also considered that married women were treated unfairly in the courts, in which at that time not only judges but also magistrates were all men. Two of the stories here, both from the 'Workaday Women' series which appeared in the *Common Cause* in 1913, are fired by this resentment. One tells of a marriage in which the wife worked outside the home, except when she had three young children who could not be left or 'minded'. Even then her husband contributed as little as possible to the family income, and, perhaps to compensate for what he did give his wife, knocked her about. When the children were old enough to work, he gave her no money at all, and when they were all married and had left home he saw no need to change his habits, but expected his wife to keep him out of her own wage. Finally, and not unnaturally, she tired of it and applied for a separation order, but as she was earning twenty shillings a week and her husband twenty-one, she was granted maintenance of only one shilling a week. (I could well understand my mother's indignation at this woman's history, but having sat on the Bench myself, though not in her lifetime, I could see the magistrates' point of view, which was presumably financial and not punitive.) Another story was also about a bench of magistrates. In this a woman had lost an eye as a result of her husband's brutality. His reason for frequently knocking her about was that when he kept his wages for himself, she nagged at him.

> The magistrates are men. Possibly a woman's tongue may have stung them some time, and they were animated by a fellow feeling for the rascal before them. 'There was great provocation,' said they. 'Ten shillings and costs.'
>
> ('Assault and Battery,' *Common Cause*,
> 12 September 1913.)

In 'The Mother's Story' (*Common Cause*, 11 April 1913), she wrote about women from a colliery village built on a hill in the Potteries. The village was Kidsgrove (which she told me was pronounced locally 'Kitcrew'). She knew it, she wrote, 'as one knows vitally only one spot – that in which one's own life took root'. On this exposed hilltop the wind was often strong, and brought with it dirt and dust from the surrounding pits and slagheaps. To shut the door when it blew hard you might 'have to turn round and put your back against it and push with all your might'. And when it rained, water flooded in under the door by the bucketful. The usual cottage would have a 'house place' of four square yards, a door opening onto the street, and a little kitchen beyond 'with absurdly inadequate cooking apparatus'. The mother in this story, a widow, was earning eleven shillings a week by taking in washing. Her eldest daughter, a lead poisoning case, drew a miserable five shillings and fourpence a week in compensation for the wage (eleven shillings) she could no longer earn; and there were four younger children not yet earning. Perpetual steam exacerbated the girl's incipient TB, and when she married her young man – which meant that he too joined the crowded household, though bringing in a little more money, ('she *had* to get married to get kept,' said the mother sadly) – pregnancy and childbirth weakened her health still further. The writer's indignation flares in the last sentence (the moral again): 'We must stand all together, and refuse to tolerate a world where women's lives are so cheap.'

Some of the stories do draw on her own childhood experiences, for instance the group of sketches about Mrs. Stubbs, a farmer's wife in a farm on the borders of Cheshire and Staffordshire, full of salty humour and common sense. The farm in these stories must have been based on the one Mother had grown up in. But who was Mrs. Stubbs if not a sheer invention? My grandmother, whom I do not remember except as an invalid in a wheelchair, died in 1903, and from the impression I retain of Mother's memories of her, was by no means the same forthright sort of woman as Mrs. Stubbs. In any case one would think that the birth of thirteen children in sixteen years would have inhibited her other activities. Mrs. Stubbs had views on a number of subjects, among them being 'woman's sphere', not much heard of nowadays, but identified at that time by many suffragists as the German 'Kinder, Küche, Kirche' (children, kitchen, church). Mrs. Stubbs claimed that she could farm as well as her husband could, and when he asked why she didn't she replied, 'Becos' a've to be dowin' things as tha canna do – make butter, patch clothes, look after milk, egg and butter money, as well as nursin' the baby'. Again the moral concerned suffrage: Mr. Stubbs with his limitations had the vote, while she, who could do his work and her own, had not. 'If any o' my lads begin their ''wimmin's sphere'' at me they'll get a cleaut in th' ear'ole!' Mrs. Stubbs' views on this and also on militancy, ('settin' fire to 'eauses . . . damidge and destruction'), which was men's stuff and brought the vote no nearer, were of course those of her creator. But they were expressed in a way that brought them alive, at once carrying conviction as the voice of the individual but representative of working women, and, perhaps, talking a language more acceptable to ordinary women than the usual suffrage arguments and tracts. My mother had, and in these sketches made use of, a good ear for speech, and each character spoke in the dialect of the particular locality she was writing about. (She could also, if so inclined, shift into dialect in her own speech.) 'A Woman's Work is Never Done' (*Common Cause*, 24 April 1914) is a good example in which the Lancashire language of the two women presented is sustained through their whole discussion, on childrearing and women's place.

Besides writing these fictional accounts of suffrage arguments, based, as an editorial note in the *Common Cause* pointed out (17 October 1917), 'upon first hand knowledge of the facts used in them', my mother was also contributing letters and articles. In 1914 quite a lengthy discussion took place in the columns of the *Common Cause* between Mrs. Chew and Mrs. Annot Robinson on the subject of a possible solution to the economic dependence of the married woman with children. My mother disagreed both with the socialist proposals on 'the endowment of motherhood' (roughly what was later to be implemented as family allowance, or now child benefit, though more generously conceived), and with the middle-class suggestion that the wife should have a legal claim on the husband's earnings. Endowment, she said, would mould all poorer women in one pattern, as childrearers, whether or not their skills and inclinations tended that way; and risked condemning poor children to incompetent and unskilled care. On the other hand, to enforce a legal claim on the husband's earnings was absurd as a solution to poverty. It would not make a woman economically independent, and 'if she is on good terms with her husband she already gets the bulk of his earnings'. Middle-class women, she said, were themselves rebelling against the domestic tabby cat ideal, but still held it up as suitable for working-class women. Women were human beings first; they should take part in work which advanced human progress, and all work should be open to and shared by women. Not all women are fit for domestic tasks or baby tending, just as not all men are suited to engineering. Women are in charge of the development and guardianship of the race through collective care. Marriage and motherhood should not be for sale, they should be disassociated from what *is* for sale – domestic drudgery.

In another article she put forward her own solutions, which involved the collective care of babies, for whom understanding and trained care were as essential as for schoolchildren. There should be nurseries for all babies, in the charge of trained people who would not necessarily be mothers, and these should be available for all women of whatever class. Domestic training should not be essential for all girls, who should be brought up as human, not merely female. Married women should insist on their right to do paid work and should refuse to do domestic jobs expected of them simply because they were women. In Lancashire, she pointed out, there was no prejudice against married women's work; nevertheless women were slaves to domestic work there too.

Some of these ideas have never taken root; others are still live issues today. The right of a married woman to work outside her home is generally accepted, but frowned on sometimes if she

has children. I have often heard it argued that juvenile delin-
quency is largely due to the fact that working mothers are not
there when the children come home from school, and all my
life I have felt bound to defend my own mother's right to work
outside the home. Apart from the fact that I have never seen
any figures which prove that Lancashire children are any more
delinquent than those in other parts of the country, this argument always riled me personally. I first heard it put forward
one evening in a discussion at the WEA, at which, for some forgotten reason, I was present without my parents. I was about
eleven years old, and to my own and everyone else's amaze-
ment I heard myself protesting that it was not necessarily a bad
thing for one's mother to work outside the home; that mine
did, and it made life much more interesting for me. The grown-
ups who listened to my outburst were very understanding, but
my mother was horrified when she first heard of it. Her own
version of the argument as it must commonly have taken place
in those days may be read below, in one of her sketches for the
Accrington Observer under the title 'Men, Women and the
Vote'.[3] Published on 26 August 1913, it presents a scene on a
Devonshire hill on a brilliant summer's day. (It clearly stems
from a visit which Mother and I made to Torquay, after taking
part in the Suffrage Pilgrimage organised by the NUWSS in
1913. We walked only from Manchester to Stockport, travelling the rest of the way by train; then after the demonstration,
which culminated in the presentation of a petition signed by
many thousands of women, we went on for a holiday in Devonshire.) Here two couples, one from Lancashire and one
Cockney, are depicted arguing about suffrage and married
women's work. The Southerners are presented as ignorant of
wages and working conditions in Lancashire, bewildered as to
why a married woman might want to work, and prejudiced as
to the results of her employment. The Lancashire couple
defend their ways robustly. The wife stresses the importance of
having her own money for pride's sake and because it improves
the family income, and bristles at the suggestion that she
might not have much of a home as a result of being out all day;
while the husband counters the unfavourable infant mortality

statistics cited from 'Mr. Burns . . . the other day' by pointing out the close connection between poor housing and infant mortality. Burns[4] had 'quoted Burnley, where there is always a high death rate because there are more back-to-back houses than are in any other town in the country. But he forgot Nelson, only three miles from Burnley, where the houses are modern, and where the death rate is lower than in his favourite Battersea . . . Nelson mothers work in mills, just as the Burnley mothers do. So you see that tale won't wash.'

NOTES

[1] Charlotte Perkins Gilman's *Women and Economics* (1898) was widely read and discussed in Britain in the 1900s. Her attack on women's isolation in the home, her emphasis on co-operative and socialist solutions, and her assertion of the power of mother-love all accord with Ada Nield Chew's expressed views.

[2] The Women's Labour League was founded in 1906 to work generally for Labour representation in parliament (through the Labour Party), and particularly for Labour representation of women in parliament and on all local bodies. It also took on a wide range of social issues (e.g. school meals, education, women's work and health, infant mortality). Its close ties with the Labour Party, personal as well as political, were seen by some as undermining its commitment to women's suffrage.

[3] I am grateful to Jill Liddington for drawing my attention to these.

[4] John Burns, president of the local government board in London in the years before World War One, was an active campaigner on the need to reduce the infant mortality rate. Like many others he ignored a wide variety of causes linked to poverty and environment and focused on the shortcomings of mothers.

Businesswoman: 1915-30

I found less evidence of my mother's public career in the years after 1915, partly because the war swamped the campaign for women's suffrage, and also because her own energies were increasingly devoted to developing her business. But she took an active interest in the welfare of women and children, and the way in which this was affected by the war. On 2 October 1914 she represented the National Federation of Women Workers and the Women's Labour League on a deputation to the Rochdale Health Committee, to urge the local authority to establish health centres and a maternity centre.

In a letter to the *Common Cause* on 9 October she gave a graphic description of the effects of the war on the Lancashire factory towns, which, she said, had been very hard hit. The cotton operatives were extremely thrifty; they had a passion to 'mek a bit' (i.e. save) 'even if it's nobbut a 'awpenny'. They had a high standard of comfort, perhaps because the work in the cotton mills was so long and exhausting, as evinced by the comment of an outsider, 'How tired they all seem!' Indeed, their work left them chronically weary, and they felt a need for 'summat tasty', as a result of the hot humid air in the mills. Their incomes were not so large, however, even in times of full employment, that slack times could come and leave no effect. Whole families were at work, there were no idle daughters in normal times. The wages of the men were average and those of the women and children (half-time was not abolished until 1918) were higher than elsewhere, but they had little reserve capital, and their savings were soon exhausted. It was true that the elderly were usually 'not without money', for they had saved a little in the Co-op or the building fund, but it was very hard on them when this money, saved by work and thrift, had to be thrown into the general melting pot. Apart from this, the majority of the working classes, here as elsewhere, lived on what they earned from week to week. There was need for other work until it became practicable to resume cotton manufacture, rudely interrupted by the war, and this should be provided by the government and local authorities. 'Nearly all Lancashire towns very badly need more habitable and healthy houses.'

She followed up this concern for the sufferings produced by wartime unemployment by throwing her energies early in 1915 into starting a scheme for feeding babies under three and their mothers, which was eventually put in hand in spite of 'blank misunderstanding and maddening inertia'. It was on the same lines as the initiative taken by suffragists in Manchester, where Margaret Ashton had offered help to the Manchester Health Department; they had a grant from the local Relief Committee and suitable rooms on loan in different parts of the city, with free use of crockery and only heating costs to pay. Dinners were distributed from a central kitchen to various feeding centres in corporation vans. There were twelve centres, each serving daily forty-five to seventy dinners to mothers, and as many again to children.

By this time we had moved from Kilnerdeyne Terrace, though we were still in Rochdale. My father had opened a number of shops, including drapery stores for which Mother was responsible. In 1914 he found a shop with what seemed like adequate living accommodation at the top end of York-shire Street, one of Rochdale's two main shopping streets, and just before war broke out we moved there. Here we had a twin business, with shoes and slippers on one side and drapery on the other. There was a big living room over the shop itself, where we did everything but eat and sleep. The walls were lined with bookshelves which drew from my Lancashire grandmother, who had taught herself to read the Bible but nothing else the comment, 'Nowt but lumber!'

Apart from the fact that we had no garden and no view, except of one tree in the forecourt of the dentist's opposite, the chief drawback of this arrangement was that it gave full scope to my father's propensity for piling up boxes of shoes and slippers, and sometimes loose pairs, everywhere but in the living room. They lined the stairs and overflowed into the bedrooms; you could not escape them.

My mother was responsible for buying the drapery, but as we had help in the shop itself, she did not have enough outlet for her energies. She was a pacifist, but apart from her membership of the Women's International League for Peace and Freedom, she took no active part in opposing the war. She was now in her mid-forties, her independent earnings had dried up with the cessation of suffrage activities, and she had begun to worry about what she and my father would live on when they gave up work. Until he died, we had no idea how much he had been able to save and invest. So Mother felt she had to provide for her own old age – she would have done this anyway, since she had never in her life been dependent on her husband except at the time of my birth – and she looked round for an additional means of earning, one over which she would have control.

At one time during the war she opened a small health food store. This was a project in which she took a particular interest, since she was an almost lifelong vegetarian, less on the grounds of principle than of feeling. The war was not the best time for such a venture, however, for it was difficult to get the right stock just when you wanted it. On one occasion she had ordered and sold a special kind of non-dairy 'butter', which was a complete failure. Customers brought it back angrily, and I was packed off to Manchester to buy and bring back a more orthodox kind of margarine.

I think she broke even on the health food store, but she certainly made no profit, so after a year or two she closed it and looked round for a fresh opening. She knew most about drapery, so she finally decided to start a wholesale, mail order business; I cannot remember, however, the exact date of this. She ran it from Yorkshire Street at first, and our living room was gradually taken over by correspondence and parcels. She had to produce a catalogue, of course, and she took this to a local printer whose daughter I had known at school. I remember her saying in a surprised tone, 'You know, he's a Tory, but he's a very nice man!'

My parents were members of the Fabian Society as well as of the ILP. The Fabian Society is still in existence, though I am not sure how much influence it now has on political thought. It was founded in 1884 from the Fellowship of the New Life, a small ethical society, and its membership was only about 4000, but at that time its intellectual activity and output were enormous, largely owing to the ability and standing of its most prominent members, among them George Bernard Shaw, Hubert Bland, E. Nesbit, Sydney Olivier, and Sidney and Beatrice Webb. Its theories owed most to radicals such as Jeremy Bentham and John Stuart Mill, and its philosophy was not one of revolution but of gradualism and permeation – hence its name, which came from Fabius Cunctator, the Roman dictator who wore down Hannibal by a policy of retreat and evasion.

I don't recall that there was a branch of the Fabian Society whose meetings George and Ada Chew attended, but they read the literature put out by the Society and twice we went *en famille* to Fabian summer schools, held in Barrow House, Derwentwater. Once, I remember, G. B. Shaw, who was staying near by, was invited to attend a debate on the unlikely subject of 'A little Bit of Fluff'. My chief recollection of this is Shaw's pulverisation of the unfortunate young man who was asked to open the debate. It was most embarrassing to sit through.

But my parents were gradually drifting away from their political associates in Rochdale. The war itself and their own business activity would have meant less time for active involvement, at least for Mother, but as far as my father was concerned, a definite breach had opened up when he wrote a letter to the *Rochdale Observer* suggesting that socialists should vote for the Liberal candidate in the general election of 1910 as the best means of securing certain reforms. This was a cardinal sin, and he was never forgiven for it.

It is not easy to assess the quality of any marriage, even when one is a child of that marriage and therefore deeply involved at second hand. In such a case, too, the difficulty is compounded by a strong disinclination to delve into the intimate relationship of two people so close to oneself and yet separated by age and circumstance. In my teens, however, I began to be aware of a change that was taking place between my mother and father.

They had been drawn together originally by shared ideals and an intense faith in the philosophy of socialism as well as opposition to what they saw as the immediate evils of capitalism. Their common interests gave them plenty to talk about. This gradually changed after my father's split from his political colleagues. It was not that my mother disagreed with him over this: she too was becoming disillusioned; but it did remove one major interest which they had in common. My father was a man with a grievance, and even I became bored with it. Moreover, by this time he had a number of market stalls and knew a good many other men engaged in a similar business on both the wholesale and retail side. As his ideas became more conservative and his main concern the prosecution of his business, it was to them that he turned for conversation and discussion of all his day-to-day concerns. I remember Mother saying to me once, 'He never *talks* to me any more!' Things were not made easier by the fact that he was subject to fits of the sulks, during which nobody could engage in any conversation at all, since a black cloud hung over the house. When I was eight he told me in an uncharacteristic burst of confidence that I should consider myself lucky not to have a sulky temper.

He had always been a theoretical believer in the equality of women and in the right of a married woman to work outside the home. In his own family this was the recognised norm. In any case the wife always did the housework or paid someone else to do it, so the husband was not inconvenienced, and her financial independence enabled him to go on producing the housekeeping money (in our case never varying over years) and to leave his wife to provide everything else. This may sound a cynical assessment, but it was the way my father had been brought up, and in all personal matters he was extremely conservative.

According to his lights he was fairminded, and I only once remember his challenging the woman's right to equality. We were cycling home together from Crewe where we had been visiting relations, and for some reason Mother was not with us. I have no idea of the context, nor of the reason why he broke his invariable rule of not criticising Mother to me, but I remember very well his saying, 'After all, someone must be master.' Being about fifteen and with no discretion I later blurted this out to Mother, and shall never forget the stricken look on her face or her outraged cry, 'Oh no! He didn't say that!' Whether there was any sequel to this I don't know. If there was, it was kept strictly private; but I doubt whether Mother's sense of dignity would have allowed her to raise the subject. I am sure, though, that it changed her own attitude.

As I became older I myself became a divisive factor. My father and I could always talk about our shared interests, but we were not deeply attached as Mother and I were, and he was undoubtedly jealous of me. If, like most daughters, I had formed other ties and left home permanently, it would have been easier, but I came home for at least part of a teacher's long holidays, and both in Manchester and later in Burnley I lived at home. When Mother was away my father and I got on much better than when she was there, and of course she bore the brunt of this.

What made things worse was that he was an extremely inarticulate man. He was an unsuccessful speaker, and almost totally unable to write a letter. This led to difficulties when Mother sailed around the world in 1935 and was away for several months. I wrote to every port and once sent a cablegram, while he hardly wrote at all. Deeply hurt by this silence, she ceased to write to him and he became totally dependent on me for news. In one letter I wrote:

Two more letters from Shanghai . . . Dad was here when they arrived . . . and was obviously impatient to know what was in them. In spite of being 'so busy that he would like a fortnight instead of a week before he goes away', he postponed his departure to hear me read them aloud. I judiciously omit the parts which he would disapprove of too much, or that he would consider sentimental. Now that you don't seem even to have sent him a card, and I know – which you didn't – that he did make an effort to write to Singapore, I feel sorry for him. I didn't even tell him that C. and S. had received communications – I thought it might appear marked. Usually he receives all remarks on ship and passengers in dead silence, though he clearly listens intently. Today he looked up the town between Kobe and Kyoto and decided that it was Osaka . . . and at the end he said 'Very interesting. I read about that typhoon and wondered if they would be in it.'

Yet I have always believed that the one person my father ever really loved was his wife. Intellectually they drifted apart, and I am sure that she felt betrayed by the revelation of his fundamental attitude to women, but emotionally he was completely dependent on her. She was the only person in his life with whom he had been able, once at least, to create a totally satisfying relationship. In the twenties, and once in the thirties, we took family holidays.' Otherwise we went separately, or Mother and I went together. Only once did my parents travel alone together, to South Africa in 1932. Yet when Mother left Rochdale for Manchester, he went too; when she decided to make a definite break and live with me in Burnley, leaving him to live alone if he wished, he followed her. Mercifully, he died first. Some time after his death she said pathetically and almost in bewilderment, 'You know, I'm happier without him'.

A year or two after the end of the war my parents' tenuous connection with the Rochdale socialists – if any did indeed remain – came to an end when Mother decided to move her business to Salford, 'Chew and Co.', as she called it, had grown beyond the bounds of the Yorkshire Street shop, and I have a shrewd idea that she was also tired of living in the midst of retail slippers and wholesale drapery, so she leased a small warehouse in Chapel Street, Salford.

It meant leaving Rochdale altogether, for it would have been too arduous to travel to Manchester every day by train, do a full day's work there and come back to housework in the evening; after all, she was now in her fifties. And the Yorkshire Street shop was no longer much of a home. I don't know what discussions she had with my father about this, for by this time I was only at home in the holidays, but he was always inclined, even when amiably disposed, to take the line of least resistance and continue on it unless forcibly derailed. So it is likely that he simply refused to discuss the matter, leaving her to go ahead with her own arrangements until the removal became a *fait accompli* and he could no longer ignore it, after which, with no more discussion, he would simply fall into line.

So in 1921 my parents left the town which had been their home for almost the whole of their married life. Manchester was only ten miles away, but the move involved a much greater break with their former life than would appear on the surface. At first Mother even gave up housekeeping and took furnished rooms in Victoria Park. It would be a rest, she said. However, the idea was better than the reality, and she soon grew tired of living with a landlady, so after a few months we moved to a permanent home (the first house we had which was not rented) in Chorlton-cum-Hardy, on the south side of the city. From here Mother travelled to her warehouse every day by tram. One thing she was determined to do was to exclude my father's shoeboxes from her premises. At first it was touch and go until he found a suitable shop in Manchester, in a street now swallowed up by the expansion of the university.

For the next nine years she worked like one possessed. All too soon she would be sixty; somehow she must make enough money from her business to keep her in retirement. If anyone ever earned the profit from a business, she did. She had very little help. Not only did she write the catalogues from which most of her customers ordered their goods, but she packed her own parcels and took them to the post office. I remember how cross she got with the Manchester 'Whit Walks',[1] which blocked the streets when she was out laden with parcels. She taught herself to type and to keep accounts which would satisfy the tax inspector. She enjoyed drawing up the catalogues, now the only outlet for her literary talent, but it meant that she was working fifteen hours a day, including housework and shopping. In the evenings the incessant clacking of the typewriter was an irritation and a reproach to the other members of the family. 'Do stop!' we begged.

In spite of these long working days, Mother still found time to write occasional letters to the *Woman's Leader*, organ of the National Union of Societies for Equal Citizenship. One of these, published on 15 September 1922, returns to the subject of the endowment of motherhood, which she had earlier opposed so strongly in the *Common Cause*, and which had found an able and energetic protagonist in Eleanor Rathbone. In this letter she said,

> Some of us worked for suffrage not because we very much wanted the vote as a vote, but because we felt it was a step towards a larger freedom for women, towards opportunities for human development and race service denied them while dependent on men.

The money for endowment would still be earned largely by men.

> Personally, if I must be kept by men at all, I would prefer to delegate that privilege to one I know, rather than to a crowd of inoffensive male creatures, on whom I, as an able-bodied adult, even though of feminine sex, have no claim at all.

At no stage in her life would my mother entertain the idea of being paid for housework for her family and above all for motherhood, and although she was no longer active in any women's movement, her burning desire that the working woman should be economically independent had abated not at all. She ended: 'Do we seriously want to brand [motherhood] as an occupation and a trade – the more fruit-

63

ful the woman the better the pay? Is this really our idea of freedom for women?'

It should be remembered that she was writing in an era when the idea of over-population and the need to restrict rather than to encourage fertility had little support. In the 1930s they were still teaching us that the population of Britain was bound to decline before the end of the century; the only argument was about how much it would decrease. And of course we were not bombarded with statistics about the rest of the world as we are today.

On 15 February 1926 another letter appeared in the *Woman's Leader*, on the subject of separate income tax assessment and allowances for married women. After some explanation of the methods and responsibilities of obtaining separate assessments, she concluded:

> I am under the impression that few married women claim separate assessment . . . I cannot help wondering what other women with separate incomes do? Do they allow their husbands to pay their tax for them? – they handing over the requisite amount less allowance due? . . . One presumably does the right thing, being fair with a man even though married to him? Surely women do not want to 'eat their cake and have it too' as in your paragraph? It should, in my opinion, be a point of honour for women to shoulder the responsibilites of economic freedom, whether married or single.

This letter illustrates once again how political consciousness remained a powerful force for my mother even when she had almost ceased political activity. It is also a reminder of how inseparable her proud principles were from her politics, and of how both intertwined with her everyday life, even as a businesswoman.

I had effectively left home in 1920, when I took a teaching post in Newcastle upon Tyne, but in 1924 I decided to leave this with the double purpose of helping Mother in her business and giving myself a break from the school-college-school routine which had made up my life. However, it did not take long to discover that I was not cut out for a business career, and Mother offered to pay for the necessary training for any other career I might wish to take up.

There were, of course, far fewer openings for women then than now, and it had to be something with a pension at the end of it, Mother had had enough of insecurity for herself and was not prepared to countenance it for me. I did have one offer of an interesting organising post, but there was no pension. In any case, after careful consideration and with the option of trying something like the library service or secretarial work, I decided that teaching was, after all, not only what I was trained for but what I wanted most to do. Easier said than done, however. There was no shortage of teachers, and Heads looked askance at someone who had actually given up her post without first securing another; the general impression was that there was something wrong. So I was left high and dry, with a sense of failure which must have been as hard on my parents, especially my mother, as it was on me.

However, we still had our political interests. Mother, of course, had had the vote since 1918, though she complained that she had not yet been able to use it effectively, since in Rochdale the successful candidate was always a Liberal, while Chorlton-cum-Hardy was a safe Tory seat. I had a deeper sense of grievance, since women of my age had been deliberately excluded from voting except in certain circumstances until we reached the age of thirty, whereas men were enfranchised at twenty-one. To add insult to injury, we were said to be demanding a 'flapper' vote.

The chief interest we shared was the Manchester branch of the Women's International League for Peace and Freedom, which had come out of the Hague Conference of Women in 1915, with the object of supporting movements to further peace, internationalism and the freedom of women. This, of course, was right up Mother's street. Many of the English-women connected with the movement had been known to her through her suffrage work – women like Margaret Ashton, Kathleen Courtney, Ethel Snowden, Mrs. Swanwick and Ellen

Wilkinson, whose elder sister, Annie, was the Secretary of the Manchester branch. Under her direction a good deal went on in Manchester, and our membership served to keep Mother in touch with her old interests and some of her co-workers, while it gave me an outlet for some of my unused energies.

It was not enough, however. In February 1926 and growing desperate, I took a post as a teacher of English in a Berlitz school in Magdeburg, Germany. The Women's International League kindly gave me an introduction to one of their German members through whom I met the local branch, and who gave me much hospitality herself. Mother, however, would not rest until she had got me safely back to England and on orthodox lines again. She could see no future in teaching in language schools, and of course she was right. She sent me details of every possible teaching post advertised, and insisted on my applying for them all, and eventually a suitable temporary post did turn up, enabling me to return to England after only a few months (on the eve of the General Strike) and later to secure a permanent post.

Meanwhile, she continued with the hard grind of her own working day. Apart from newspapers and periodicals such as the *Women's Leader*, or *Time and Tide*, her chief reading and recreation were novels. If she did not get an hour for this every day she became really bad tempered. We did have holidays however. In 1921 my father bought a Ford car (an original 'Tin Lizzie'), and motoring holidays, on bad roads but without traffic jams, became a possibility. Then at Easter 1927, Mother and I went to the south of France, the first time she had ever been abroad. She was delighted to find that French hotels made excellent omelettes for vegetarians, unlike English ones which seemed to have no ideas beyond a boiled egg.

In the course of her work Mother built up quite a number of surprisingly intimate relationships with small shop-keepers – many of them women – scattered in small towns and villages all over the country. They usually learnt of Chew and Co. through advertisements in the *Drapers' Record*. They were all real people to her, and her only regret was that it was not possible for her to meet them, and that once she retired from business she would not be able to keep in touch with them.

Surprise has been expressed to me that a woman who had played such an active part in public affairs and had displayed such talent for writing should have been content with running a business. Three significant facts must be remembered. First, my mother was an adventurous and adaptable woman, who was always ready to strike out on fresh lines. Secondly, she had a firm basis to work from; this was not a shot in the dark, because she already had long experience in the retail drapery trade on which she could base her new enterprise. And thirdly there was her concern that I have already mentioned – the driving need to provide for her old age. The idea of dependence on me would have been anathema. She was not, of course, entitled to any form of State pension, which in any case, was pitifully small in those days. If ever there was a woman who combined a fierce sense of injustice with compassion for others and determination to 'stand on her own two feet', it was my mother, Ada Nield Chew.

So she decided to buy a house in Burnley, where I was teaching, and to remove there. If my father wished to come too it was near enough to Manchester for him to travel to and fro; in any case he had to spend time visiting his market stalls in other towns, and buying slippers, mostly in the Rossendale valley, next door to Burnley. She told him of her decision, and as usual he ignored it, until she – and most of the furniture – had gone. Then one day he turned up and settled down, without a word. He did, however, keep a room in his Manchester shop, where he spent two or three nights each week, in the muddle which was natural to him. Mother went there occasionally, but she made no attempt to tidy things up. It would have been resented, and was in any case a useless endeavour.

NOTES

[1] These were processions of church or chapel members in a body, entire congregations from Nonconformists to Catholics, which took place on practically every day of Whit Week in Manchester. Smaller towns managed with one day in the week: Friday was the day in Rochdale. This custom has now largely died out.

Retirement and the World Outside: 1930-45

My mother had always bitterly regretted that her own mother had refused to have a photograph taken, so before she retired she had a miniature of herself painted for me, which makes it odder still that she did not realise how I should have treasured written mementoes. In the miniature she seems to be looking into an uncharted but predictable future, for the prospect of old age and death is different in kind from any prospect of change and development in earlier life.

However, she was still active at sixty, and although for the first time in her life she was not working outside the house, her pioneering spirit had not left her. She must have been one of the first women in Burnley, outside the well-to-do, to have an electric washing machine and refrigerator, and she had no hesitation in 'going all electric' because it was so much cleaner. For many years she coped with the housework alone, but at length we persuaded her to engage domestic help.

In 1931 I went to the United States as an exchange teacher, and while I was there my parents took the opportunity to visit my Uncle Justin in South Africa. Later, in 1935, Mother embarked on a four-month voyage round the world on an American liner. One or two of her letters written on this voyage have survived, and they show that she had by no means lost her gift for shrewd and amusing characterisation and summing up.

Today, the ocean being moderately – not really *very* – peaceful, having had letters and the weather being quite cool I am feeling hopeful about eventually landing again – there have been many days when I could not hope, and just had to endure. . . .

The O.'s bought a boxful of something . . . and Mr. O. groaned aloud when presented with the bill, and was inclined to dispute it . . . Then O., who had protested about the amount of his wife's purchases, would have us all go to a china shop, where he bought . . . china to give to his married sons. Mrs. O. objected to that, and they very nearly had a quarrel – we three others feeling *de trop*. Finally he had his way, as a paymaster always does. Indeed he said to her in front of us, 'I'm payin', ain't I?' I felt sorry for her and him. She had provoked him, or he wouldn't have been publicly rude to her, for he is really a very kind man. Whereas she, who has to submit all her purchases to him, has to stand by and see him fling money away (from her point of view) whenever the fancy takes him. It's a false position, and yet, when a woman is independent, a man never likes it and is resentful. Moral: be a bachelor.

From Liberal and Tory safe seats, she had now gone to a Labour constituency, which returned Arthur Henderson, the Foreign Secretary in Ramsay MacDonald's Labour government. He lost his seat in the Conservative landslide of 1931.

The thirties were not a comfortable decade to live through. Quite apart from the great depression and unemployment, the international scene was at first discouraging and later alarming. First there was the invasion of China by Japan in 1931, and the failure of the League of Nations to do anything effective about it; and after that the growing power of the dictatorships was like a black cloud spreading over the sky. Hitler first took the Rhineland, then Austria, while Mother's return from her voyage round the world was marred by Italy's invasion of Ethiopia (or Abyssinia, as we called it then). Then, in 1936, the Spanish Civil War began.

My parents' time of active involvement in politics, national or international, was over, but I was deeply concerned with local movements in favour of collective security and Spanish Aid, and emotionally much disturbed. I cannot have been a comfortable housemate. My father, I believe, once remarked that he and my mother had thought when I was young that it would be dreadful if I were to grow up uninterested in politics, but now he wished I had.

He died suddenly in Manchester at the beginning of March 1940, before the worst period of the war, and my mother, at the age of seventy, was left to sort out his affairs. I doubt if he would ever have retired completely, and he had certainly taken no steps in that direction. She had to wind up one shop and several market stalls in different towns, and this occupied her during the disastrous summer that followed. Physically it was a very demanding task, for I have never in my life seen such an appalling muddle as that shop was in. Not only boxes of slippers, but endless unboxed pairs, with their strings inextricably tangled, filled every nook and cranny. I was amazed at the inexhaustible energy she showed during those months.

But the next few years were hard on everybody, not least on the old. Our car was sold for lack of petrol, and though we went away by train once or twice, it was not a success, for rheumatism and growing arthritis made strange beds (not as comfortable as they are now, or as her 'Vispring' at home) hard to endure. So she was restricted to the immediate neighbourhood of the house, and suffered long periods of solitude, for she had never been intimate with neighbours and this was a time when it was not easy to entertain friends. Luckily for us, Burnley was not a target for air raids. When a bomb did fall in the park opposite the house, smashing windows and bringing down a heavy fall of soot from the chimneys, I was at home, so she did not have to suffer it alone.

She managed the house and did the cooking until the day she died, and when the doctor told her her heart was weakening she said she was not afraid of death, except that she would no longer know what was happening to me. We did not discuss it further, because I was not prepared to face the possibility.

There was only one person left who shared the memories of her youth, and that was her brother Justin. He was making plans to visit us in 1946, but she did not wait for him. On the afternoon of 27 December 1945 she went upstairs to rest, and never came down again.

The women of this generation owe more than they realise to those of my mother's day. I hope this record, incomplete as it is, of her work for women in general and married working women in particular, will help both to enlighten and to inspire them.

THE WRITINGS

Letters of a 'Crewe Factory Girl' to the Crewe Chronicle

1 A Living Wage for Factory Girls at Crewe, 5 May 1894

Sir, – Will you grant me space in your sensible and widely read paper to complain of a great grievance of the class – that of tailoresses in some of the Crewe factories – to which I belong? I have hoped against hope that some influential man (or woman) would take up our cause and put us in the right way to remedy – for of course there is a remedy – for the evils we are suffering from. But although one cannot open a newspaper without seeing what all sorts and conditions of men are constantly agitating for and slowly but surely obtaining – as in the miners' eight hour bill – only very vague mention is ever made of the under-paid, over-worked 'Factory Girl'. And I have come to the conclusion, sir, that as long as we are silent ourselves and apparently content with our lot, so long shall we be left in the enjoyment [?] of that lot.

The rates paid for the work done by us are so fearfully low as to be totally inadequate to – I had almost said keep body and soul together. Well, sir, it is a fact which I could prove, if necessary, that we are compelled, not by our employers, but by stern necessity, in order to keep ourselves in independence, which self-respecting girls even in our class of life like to do, to work so many hours – I would rather not say how many – that life loses its savour, and our toil, which in moderation and at a fair rate of remuneration would be pleasurable, becomes drudgery of the most wearisome kind.

To take what may be considered a good week's wage the work has to be so close and unremitting that we cannot be said

75

to 'live' – we merely exist. We eat, we sleep, we work, endlessly, ceaselessly work, from Monday morning till Saturday night, without remission. Cultivation of the mind? How is it possible? Reading? Those of us who are determined to live like human beings and require food for mind as well as body are obliged to take time which is necessary for sleep to gratify this desire. As for recreation and enjoying the beauties of nature, the seasons come and go, and we have barely time to notice whether it is spring or summer.

Certainly we have Sundays: but Sunday is to many of us, after our week of slavery, a day of exhaustion. It has frequently been so in my case, and I am not delicate. This, you will understand, sir, is when work is plentiful. Of course we have slack times, of which the present is one (otherwise I should not have time to write to you). It may be said that we should utilise these slack times for recruiting our bodies and cultivating our minds. Many of us do so, as far as is possible in the anxious state we are necessarily in, knowing that we are not earning our 'keep', for it is not possible, absolutely not possible, for the average ordinary 'hand' to earn enough in busy seasons, even with the overtime I have mentioned, to make up for slack ones.

'A living wage!' Ours is a lingering, dying wage. Who reaps the benefit of our toil? I read sometimes of a different state of things in other factories, and if in others, why not those in Crewe? I have just read the report of the Royal Commission on Labour. Very good; but while Royal Commissions are enquiring and reporting and making suggestions, some of the workers are being hurried to their graves.

I am afraid I am trespassing a great deal on your space, sir, but my subject has such serious interest for me – I sometimes wax very warm as I sit stitching and thinking over our wrongs – that they, and the knowledge that your columns are always open to the needy, however humble, must be my excuse.

I am, sir, yours sincerely,
A CREWE FACTORY GIRL
Crewe, 1 May 1894

Editor's note: Our correspondent writes a most intelligent letter; and if she is a specimen of the factory girl, then Crewe factory proprietors should be proud of their 'hands'. We shall be glad to hear further from our correspondent as to the wages paid, the numbers of hours worked, and the conditions of their employment. *Crewe Chronicle*, 5 May 1894

2 *A Living Wage for Factory Girls at Crewe, 19 May 1894*

A fortnight back we printed a neatly written and admirably expressed letter from 'A Crewe Factory Girl', and we requested the writer to supply us with additional details about her work. She very kindly responds to our invitation in the following interesting letter. She writes:

In your issue of 5 May you were good enough to publish a letter of mine on the above subject, and also to invite me to write you further on our wages, hours of work, and conditions of employment. Before responding to the same I have waited in the hope that an abler pen than mine might take up my subject and say a word on our behalf. I conclude, however, that sufficient interest is not taken in factory girls and their wrongs outside their own sphere to call for any comment. Speaking for ourselves, sir, I can assure you that this question of prices paid for our work and the general inadequacy of the same in proportion to the work done is one naturally of keen interest, and forms the subject of constant discussion and complaint – entirely amongst ourselves, please take note, sir! Notwithstanding this general private discontent, we unfortunately as a body regard the existing state of things as inevitable, and have not sufficient courage, and do not know how if we had, to make a resolute stand against the injustice done us. I feel my position, sir, in this matter of giving information, to be one of peculiar difficulty. On the one hand, to be quite fair to myself and to those I am endeavouring to represent, I ought, and would like, to describe fully and explicitly the exact kind of work done by us, the exact amount of it, and the exact price paid for that amount, and to give my own experience without reserve. But on the other hand, were I to do this I should be making revelations which would lead to instant recognition by many people of the particular factory in which I am employed, and probably also, sir, to the identification of your correspondent, which I shall do well to avoid. And therefore, on that account I feel reluctance to reveal them, greatly as I value this opportunity which you, sir, have so kindly given me of emphasising – for it must already be known – the fact that we are suffering from a great evil which stands in urgent need of redressing.

However, I think that even within the limits to which I shall have to restrict myself I can make good the statements contained in my first letter. I must explain before proceeding further that I shall speak of the branch of factory work known as 'finishing' only. I have reason to believe that the other branches [of female employment] are not overpaid, but I shall speak only of what I know to be actual fact. With regard to wages. We are paid not by the hour or day, but a certain sum per garment. Wages, then, vary greatly. For instance, many different classes of work have to be done, and different prices are paid, not at all, however, in proportion to the amount of work to be done, for while one price may yield us as much as 3d an hour (occasionally), another will not yield us 1½d an hour (quite frequently), working equally hard for each sum. Of course, all classes of work have to be done, and we have to accept with gratitude (or otherwise) whatever sum someone – our employer presumably – thinks it right to give us. We are doing excellently when earning 3d an hour. We not infrequently work for 1½d an hour. An average of about 2d for the average 'hand' may be taken as fair. Occasionally we may get work which will yield us as much as 4½d an hour, but it is so very occasional that it may be passed by in silence – otherwise, of course, we should have no cause for complaint.

And now to take an average of a year's wage of the 'average ordinary hand', which was the class I mentioned in my first letter, and being that which is in a majority may be taken as fairly representative. The wages of such a 'hand', sir, will barely average – but by exercise of the imagination – 8 shillings a week. I ought to say, too, that there is a minority, which is also considerable, whose wages will not average above 5 shillings a week. I would impress upon you that this is making the very best of the case, and is over rather than understating. What do you think of it, Mr. Editor, for a 'living' wage?

I wish some of those, whoever they may be who mete it out to us, would try to 'live' on it for a few weeks, as the factory girl has to do 52 weeks in a year. To pay board and lodging, to provide herself decent boots and clothes to stand all weathers, to pay an occasional doctor's bill, literature, and a holiday away from the scope of her daily drudging, for which even the factory girl has the audacity to long sometimes – but has quite as often to do without. Not to speak of provision for old age, when eyes have grown too dim to thread the everlasting needle, and to guide the worn fingers over the accustomed task. Yet this is a question which some of us, at least, ought to face, ignore it as we may, and are compelled to do. The census showing such a large preponderance of women over men in this country, it follows that the factory girl must inevitably contribute her quota to the ranks of old maidenism – be she never so willing to have it otherwise.

And now as to the number of hours worked to earn – or rather to get – this magnificent sum. I explained in my first letter that we are subject to fluctuations as to the amount of work supplied us. In other words that we have busy seasons and slack ones. It follows, then, that in busy seasons, to total up to the yearly average I have given, we make good wages – and, of course, work a proportionately long number of hours – and in slack seasons bad wages.

Now, sir, our working day – that is, in the factory –

consists of from 9 to 10 hours. Take out of this time (often considerable and unavoidably so) to obtain the work, to obtain the 'trimmings' and materials to do it with, and then to get it 'passed' and booked in to us when done, and then calculate how much – say we are getting 2d an hour – we shall be able to earn in an ordinary working day in the factory. It will be plain that in order to average this wage we have in busy seasons to work longer than the actual time in the factory.

Home-work, then, is the only resource of the poor slave who has the misfortune to adopt 'finishing' as a means of earning a livelihood. I have myself, repeatedly, five nights a week, besides Saturday afternoons, for weeks at a time, regularly taken four hours, at least, work home with me, and have done it. This, too, after a close hard day's work in the factory. In giving my own experience I give that of us all. We are obliged to do it, sir, to earn this living wage! It will be unnecessary to point out how fearfully exhausting and tedious it is to sit boring at the same thing for 14 or 15 hours at a stretch – meal times excepted of course.

But we are not asking for pity, sir, we ask for justice. Surely it would not be more than just to pay us at such a rate, that we could realise a living wage – in the true sense of the words – in a reasonable time, say one present working day of from 9 to 10 hours – till the eight hour day becomes general, and reaches even factory girls. Our work is necessary (presumably) to our employers. Were we not employed others would have to be, and if of the opposite sex, I venture to say, sir, would have to be paid on a very different scale. Why, because we are weak women, without pluck and grit enough to stand up for our rights, should we be ground down to this miserable wage?

With regard to the conditions of our employment, those of which I can speak leave nothing to be desired. In the particular factory in which I am employed, we work in greatest freedom and comfort, and I should like to add, that as far as I personally am concerned, from those in immediate authority over me I have never received anything but consideration and courtesy.

In conclusion, sir, I am aware that in writing these letters to you I am probably doing what I was reading of the other day, namely, 'butting my head against a stone wall'; but, as the writer I am quoting went on to say, 'How can one be sure it is a stone wall, or one made only of paper, unless one does butt one's head against it?' Now I am not quite sanguine enough to think that the wall against which I am butting my head will give way at least with my solitary 'butt'. Nevertheless, sir, I am determined to butt my head against it. Indeed, I feel it to be personally degrading and a disgrace upon me to remain silent and submit without a protest to the injustice done me.

And if the wall is of stone, sir, and the only remedy lies in the radical one recommended by the minority report of the Labour Commission, then will you allow me to urge upon your readers, upon those of my own sex who though not yet having the privilege of voting themselves, yet have influence with those who have, to use that influence intelligently, in the right direction? And to those of the opposite sex who do enjoy this privilege, to send only those men to Parliament, of whatever political creed, who stand pledged to do all in their power, with the utmost possible speed, to relieve the burden of the oppressed and suffering workers of this country, not least amongst whom are the factory girls of Crewe.

Crewe Chronicle, 19 May 1894

3 *Life in a Crewe Factory, 9 June 1894*

I make my bow to the readers of the *Chronicle*, and beg to re-introduce myself as the 'Crewe Factory Girl' who has on two former occasions drawn their attention to the 'living wage' which she and her fellow-workers are at present enjoying. I ask them now, first, to make acquaintance with factory girls themselves, as the writer, who is one of them, knows them to be. Secondly, I ask them to come with me (in imagination) through the factory doors, and view for themselves the life of the factory girl therein. It has on several occasions been the privilege (?) of the writer to see visitors of high degree conducted by the manager through the ranks of the workers in the factory of which she writes, all admiring evidently the apparent comfort and happiness of these factory girls. The writer has wondered on such occasions if the visitors' opinions would have differed had they known the internal working of this phase of life on which they were looking as it is known to those who live the life. The visitors are shown some of the work done by these rows of women and girls. Are they informed of the price paid for it? No doubt a week's wage of one of these girls is quoted to them (I have of course no proof of this) but not, I venture to say, of the 'average ordinary' hands of which I have spoken exclusively hitherto, but of experts, of what I can best describe as the 'clique', known amongst ourselves as the 'favourites' (I hope to explain that fully). Are they informed of the hours worked to obtain that sum? These visitors look only on the outside of things, from the employers' point of view. A band of happy girls, apparently working in greatest ease, whose comfort is the careful consideration of their employer. Now these visitors are only those of the employers, and are only a privileged few. The factory doors are closed on the general public, who know nothing of what takes place therein. But I, the factory girl, throw wide these doors. I invite the public, one and all, to come with me as my visitors. I will give them not the superficial view which the manager's visitors get, but a thorough good look into everything, from the factory girl's point of view. Thank God for the public press, which sheds its strong white light on all the dark corners of the earth! Like John Ploughman [pen name of another correspondent], I am thankful, too, that we have a good local paper in the *Chronicle*, which fearlessly publishes the opinions, however varying, of all classes of thinkers; and lends its powerful aid as willingly to the weary factory girl as to the peer of the realm.

When my readers have accompanied me and seen things for

themselves, I am confident that my opinion will be theirs, namely that the condition of the factory girls is bad in nearly every particular, and really needs the helping hand of the Radical reformer. I unhesitatingly and emphatically affirm that the influence of her life on the factory girl is demoralising and debasing, and downward in its every tendency. And this, before I have finished, I will prove. I am aware that I cannot do so without revealing the identity of the factory of which I speak. I do not fear. What I have said so far has been proved to be irrefutable – surely receiving no contradiction may be taken as proof – and what I have said with regard to wages, especially, will apply to at least one other factory in Crewe (I know it to be a fact). And what I have to say now is only what these eyes and ears have seen and heard, so that I do not need to fear the consequences. When my readers and I have had a look into things, I will respectfully submit some ideas of my own for the improvement of the condition of my class. When I have finished, I hope that Mr. Editor and any of my readers will criticise my notions, and suggest any of their own which may prove to be better than mine. I shall not have space to-day to do more than make an introductory and explanatory sketch of the factory girl herself. That visit to the factory must be reserved till next week. I promise that it shall be an accurate, faithful and thorough one. All the dark places shall be made light.

Now we factory girls are aware of the public opinion of us. That we are regarded as quite the lowest class of female workers. As a noisy, cheeky, idle, ignorant, shallow class of girls. I do not wish to obtrude myself unnecessarily, but a little personal experience here in explanation and proof of the assertion I have just made may not be out of place. It is a fact, then, that I have myself, on more than one occasion, heard my class spoken of, and by those whose opinions I have valued, in such terms of contemptuous scorn, of such sneering sarcasm – milder language will not express my meaning – that the blood in my veins has boiled with indignation. I resolved, whenever opportunity served, or to make such opportunity for myself when possible, that I would vindicate, with all the energy and power of conviction which intimate knowledge of the subject, and experience of the kind I have just quoted may be calculated to give me, the social position and general character of the class to which I am not ashamed to belong. There is no better way of doing this than by showing the life she lives, which tends to make the factory girl what she seems to be, and in a measure is.

As to her social position – improve these same conditions of her life and I venture to say that the factory girl will rise in the social status in the same degree – I admit that we have faults. I admit that we are essentially a noisy class of girls. I use the term 'essentially' advisedly, because I intend to prove in that visit to the factory next week, that on certain occasions it actually is essential to be noisy, if we must obtain a wage of any kind, whether 'living' or 'dying'. Unfortunately, however, but not unnaturally, our noisy propensities do not end when the necessity for them ends, and we are noisy everywhere – as we sit at work, in our general progress about the factory, and even outside, for we rush through the doors like a pack of wild Indians, hustling and jostling, and yelling and hooting at each other, and generally annoying everybody who comes in contact with us.

It is quite true, also, that we are an exceedingly 'cheeky' class of girls. But 'cheek' too, I shall show next week, is a necessary qualification for the obtaining of that living wage which we enjoy. It is well known amongst ourselves that to be at all shy is fatal to success in the particular line of life of which we are the ornaments. It is an interesting study to some of us when a somewhat quiet, shy girl enters our arena, to watch her gradual development into one of ourselves – as we are obliged to be. The writer is an example of the kind. She, however, has learnt the inevitable lesson – by painful degrees! – and is now well-known amongst her cheeky comrades as one able to hold her own.

I flatly deny that we are idle. There are exceptions, of course, but as a class we are hard-working and industrious. Anybody who carefully followed me through my second letter will understand that the factory girl absolutely must work. I shall not attempt to defend us against the charge of ignorance. To take an intelligent public through the factory as I propose to do, and show them that we meekly suffer oppression of all kinds without even a wish to alter things; and even show a spirit of resentment against any attempt at change for the better; and then to pretend that we are not ignorant would be an absurdity. Ignorance is no crime, however, and we shall improve. I shall have to admit that we are shallow, too. And we always shall be shallow as long as we are voracious readers of 'penny dreadfuls'. I can hardly contain myself when speaking of those awful 'novelettes' – I see such fearful effects of their baneful influence – in place of reading of a broader, more substantial kind; and in our hours of leisure parade the streets in gangs (please excuse the word, I cannot just think of one of a more polite kind), talking empty twaddle with the equally silly of the opposite sex, instead of taking a lively interest in the doings of our fellow-men and women in the great world around us, and ourselves taking a part, however humble, therein.

Well, we have virtues too. And I think when the public have been with me next week, they will agree with me that it is a wonder that we have. It is terribly hard to be good in a factory. Indeed, the grinding of the mill is so acute and never-ceasing that I am afraid some of us have given up trying to behave like Christians. I have myself wondered often, like John Ploughman, what the next life would be like after the training we are receiving here. Yet there are many evidences of generous impulse and self-sacrifice shown daily amongst these factory girls which go far to prove what I am persuaded is true – namely, that if the condition of the factory girl's life were improved, she herself would improve. The writer, in her experience of factory life, has met with many such instances, and owes a debt of gratitude to some of her fellow-workers which she can never repay. I have now introduced the factory girl; next week, if I possibly can – certainly as soon as I can, I will ask my readers to accompany her to work.

Crewe Chronicle, 9 June 1894

4 *Life in a Crewe Factory, 23 June 1894*

To-day something special happens. I not only plod to the factory myself, but I take a whole army of *Chronicle* readers with me. To-day the doors swing wide to admit them as well as me. Imagine yourselves therefore, my readers, within a certain factory in Crewe. Some of you will know it before your visit has ended. Please remember that we are in the 'finishing' department, for while many of my remarks and much of my information will apply to life in a factory in all its departments (of female employment) it is in the finishing department where my life is spent, and naturally it is here where I bring my visitors. With the room itself we are not concerned. As I have implied before, it is a comfortable room, light, clean, and commodious. It is the life lived in this room with which we have to do. I have explained to you before that as 'hands' we factory girls are of several grades. There are the average ordinary hands who, while able to do work of nearly every kind, chiefly take what is known as 'best' work. Do not mistake me. I mean best work, not best paid. There are hands below the average called 'common' hands; these take 'common' work. That is work not requiring much skill. The price paid for it otherwise yields the finisher quite as much as that paid to best hands for best work.

But these are not quite all the hands, dear readers. There are a few more, and with these I want to make you specially acquainted. These are the 'favourites'. What kind of girls are they as a rule? As a rule they are not girls at all, but married women. In one or two cases at least married women with husbands in full employment; in one case in particular, reputed to have private means. I am not concerned with that fact, if it be a fact; but in making a faithful representation I am bound to notice it, because you will understand that the knowledge of it exerts an influence – and that not for good – on the life of the girls who have to compete – if competition it can be called where favour is shown, and that all on one side – with this woman in the struggle for daily bread. In one or two cases at least these women are grandmothers. Amongst these favourites are a few girls – or unmarried women, to be quite correct – who are experts; who take absolutely the best kinds of work, that is, the work requiring most skill. Now that you have an idea of us 'hands', look at a certain spot in this room where a table or kind of counter is situated. Behind this counter two gentlemen stand, whose business it is to 'pass' our work, to give us work to do, to see that we do it, to book it 'out' and 'in' to us, to bring it back to us from other men, who pass it after it has been pressed, for any alterations, and to look after us generally (these gentlemen often appeal to us for sympathy in their hard task).

I shall want you to accompany me to my side of that counter presently, and I shall detain you there longer than at any other spot in the room; for it is there that the factory girl struggles for daily bread; where all that is bad in her nature is brought out and fostered; where lessons are taught and practices prevail which make upright, honest, honourable dealing between factory girl and factory girl, between woman and woman, and comrades, an impossibility. Let me now explain two rules which are sometimes supposed to obtain amongst us. One is that we shall pass our work (which has been finished the previous day or brought with us from home) in turn as we arrive at the doors in the morning. To understand that you must know that the doors are opened to us ten minutes before 8 o'clock (the hour we begin work), and those of us who choose to come early and to stand waiting outside the doors get the first chance to pass when we get in. Our first business then, if we do not see a comrade on the way immediately preceding us, on arriving at the door is to enquire who arrived last, and to follow that one in passing.

There are a few enterprising girls, and also married women, who make a point of arriving at the doors not later than 7.40, and sometimes as early as 7.25, and these, of course, pass first every day.

To make you understand the full importance of this rule I must explain the other. When this work is passed it is booked in to us, and the other rule is that we shall get more work out in rotation as we have passed. This rule of coming early to the door is not so closely observed when we are doing work of a steady, even-paying (mind I do not say adequate) kind. I remember one time when an order was being executed; which was acknowledged by all to yield us better 'pay' than anything else we get, and which only comes our way occasionally. Only a certain amount of it – not enough for us all – came each day for us to do, and you can imagine that while that order lasted we were most of us early risers. I remember some very keen competition amongst us at that time. I myself formed one of a number of about forty round the doors at 7.35. I daresay you would do the same, dear reader, if by so doing you could get a chance to really get what you earned – for once in a way – to get as much in two hours as you otherwise would get in four.

Please take in consideration the fact that these rules do not exist for all of us – not for the favourites, for instance, who as a rule, are exempt from them – and are entirely at the discretion of the two aforementioned gentlemen to rigorously enforce; to relax; or to ignore altogether, as they may see fit. Now that you are getting acquainted with some of the conditions of our life, come with me to this counter and share with me what I find there. Let us first suppose it to be a tolerably busy season.

Our struggles now at this table will not be very fierce. We shall probably have one garment ready to 'pass', shall have another or more 'out' to be doing, and of course we shall be able to take our turn for another. Let us take our work, and occupy any vacant place we may see, and wait our turn to pass. All that we shall have to do now will be to look sharply after our turn, and insist on passing in that turn. Should we be at all lax in this respect we might have to stay here all day, for our turn will be frequently disputed, and if the disputant is one of ourselves (not of the clique) it is a match between us, and the one with the most 'check' wins.

I have seen girls of a meek, submissive nature stand waiting here to pass for hours at a time — and some even a whole day. Should our disputant be a favourite, however, it is an extremely 'cheeky' one amongst us who undertakes to combat — most of us know the utter futility of entering the lists against one of these.

When we have passed we shall have to look closely after our turn again in getting work out, and shall only have to see all the specially good 'jobs' — which pay best — whether of the best or common class, given entirely to the favourites, while we, the rank and file, take whatever is left for us — and are duly grateful for the favour shown us.

Our life now (in a busy season) will be spent chiefly in work. Are you prepared, my reader, to come and work hard with us 9 hours in the factory, and then to come home with us and begin again, and sew till you can sew no longer, from sheer fatigue — such fatigue as some of you, I hope have not felt — and then to rise early again with some of us and do a little more before it is time to wend our way back for another day of it. This is no fanciful picture; nor does it refer peculiarly to myself; there are girls here in your midst who know by bitter experience whether that account is a faithful one. And the employers know it too, deny it as they may.

And now let us take the slack season. I think I shall be quite within the mark if I say that it exists more or less for half the year, so that you will see that we are bound to consider it fully. Come with me now to this counter. These rules we have considered will not be of much use now, because it is extremely probable that we shall have nothing to pass, and therefore cannot take turns to get work. As we may have to stay some

time at this counter we shall provide ourselves with some knitting, crotcheting, or a 'novelette' to read, to wile away the
tedium of waiting. If we have not been wary, and taken the
precaution to secure an early seat, the probability is that we
shall not find a front seat vacant, and as you will find it very
necessary that we should have a front seat, we shall watch our
opportunity, and on its occurring, at once seize it. Perhaps you
are mystified at our having a 'seat' at this counter. Well, my
reader, we may have to wait here half a day, and the probability is that you, as well as the factory girl, will grow tired
of standing; and much as I regret having nothing more elegant
in the way of a seat to offer visitors, when this opportunity
for which we are watching occurs, I shall be obliged to ask
you to jump – I am afraid you will have to jump, for it is
a pretty high counter – up with me on our side of this
counter.

We shall not be the only girls there! Don't feel ashamed of
sitting perched up in a row like – rabbits in the market. That
feeling will wear off with a little practice. Well, we are sitting
on this table. We shall not have much room to move our limbs
as our comrades are wedging us in on each side and in front,
and I daresay we shall get a little cramped, but we shall be able
to watch what is going on, nevertheless. At any rate we must
not dismount, or the place we have just secured with such difficulty may be lost, and we should have to begin over again. You
will understand that it is the ordinary and common hands
which are gathered round this table; the favourites will not be
under the necessity of making themselves seen and heard in
order to get served.

I fear after all that we shall not be able to finish our visit to-
day, because I want to go fully into what takes place at this
table in slack seasons, and there are also several other things
about our life in this factory which I want to show you, so that I
am afraid I shall either have to keep you waiting on that table
till next week, or if you object to that, shall have to beg you to
pay me another visit. I have not shown you the most important
things yet, nor said half that I wish to say. The doors will be

open next week, and the factory girl in attendance, if you will be so good as to come again.

Crewe Chronicle, 23 June 1894

5   The Wages of Crewe Factory Girls, 23 June 1894

To the Editor of the CHRONICLE

Sir, – Please allow me to reply briefly to 'One Competent to Advise', who writes in this week's *Chronicle*. With his advice I am not content. I have no doubt that parents and friends of working girls will value it for what it is worth. It is the statements and insinuations contained in the letter which may be calculated to mislead the uninitiated to which I feel it my duty to reply. This gentleman compels me to again emphatically assert that this 'movement' has originated with myself alone. I repeat that I alone am responsible for originating this 'controversy', and no 'portion' of workers at all, skilled or otherwise. It is odious to me to have to keep thrusting myself constantly before the public, but in self-defence I am obliged to do so. Be it known to this gentleman and the public then, that I, the originator of this controversy, though not on any account claiming to be an expert, am yet an average hand, and am able to do and take work requiring skill; and any alterations in my work are the exceptions, not the rule. As to the experience required to understand the conditions of the trade, I, the originator, being what I profess to be, a factory girl, am not yet old enough to lay claim to the experience this gentleman considers necessary. I think, however, that *Chronicle* readers will agree with me that a lifetime's experience may not be necessary to enable people to understand whether they are getting honest value for honest work. As this gentleman says, it is best known to ourselves why we are unable or unwilling to earn a decent living; and I think those who read my article on factory life in

91

to-day's *Chronicle* will also get an idea of the reason. At any rate, by the time I have finished with this subject they will, I hope, understand as well as those who 'best know themselves'.

I should like to say also that I think this gentleman will find that when these things are understood a little better by those whom they concern most that it will be chiefly the more skilled portion of the workers who will be found in sympathy with any effort at combination. One statement made by this gentleman is very misleading: that quick and well-trained girls in times of full employment earn from 18 shillings to 21 shillings per week. I defy him to prove it only in very exceptional and occasional cases, which it is not fair to take into consideration in dealing, as I am, with my class in its entirety. And if this sum is by chance earned sometimes, the reason why is no doubt 'best known' to this gentleman. With the remainder of his letter I shall probably deal in due course at a later stage of this 'controversy'. Thanking you for space, I remain, sir, yours sincerely,

A Crewe Factory Girl
Crewe Chronicle, 23 June 1894

6   *Life in a Crewe Factory, 30 June 1894*

My readers will remember that we are considering the slack season, and are sitting on the table in very close quarters. While we wait and at the same time keep a close watch for the supplies of work which will arrive at intervals from the machinists – while we wait, I say, let me have a little conversation with you. Now we, who are sitting on this table, are the ordinary hands, and are probably capable, good workers, able to do any kind of work which may come. It is very probable that we have had nothing to do for hours. Let me talk plainly, and say that it is quite possible that we have been idle the whole of yesterday, and have to look on the possibility of to-day being a repetition. Some of us are girls who live in lodgings; some of us live at home, and may have fathers and brothers who, for reasons which need not be discussed, may be unable to keep us, or, I take it, we should not be here. It is a plain, hard fact that the week is passing; and it is another fact that if we do not get something to do soon, when pay day comes we shall find ourselves unable to pay up. Now I submit to you, and I maintain it whether you agree with me or not, that we girls, whether we live in lodgings or live at home, have a wish, at least, to be honest and independent, and are just as anxious to get any work which may come, as any of the 'favourites', whether they be married women, widows, or experts who as 'hands' are of value to the employer. That is as it presents itself to us, as we sit on this table waiting for work. But we know for a fact, that the more respectable we appear to be, the less noise we make, the less we parade our private affairs, the less chance we have of getting anything to do. I ask you is that knowledge calculated to elevate or debase?

Some work is coming, however, as is evident by the commotion round the table, and the arrival in our midst of the favourites, who very probably were in their places doing work which they already have. Now the work has arrived, get as far on the table as you can – if you do not someone else will – and being a natural human being, ask, as everybody else is asking, for a share. While you try, adducing particular, and, to yourself, convincing reasons why you in particular should be the favoured one, watch it handed over your head to someone far behind, nearly out of sight, who had not even had the need to speak. Do you feel like the typical gentle English girl now, my reader? I ask you is it calculated to call forth and nurture the attributes of pure womanhood, first, to sit where we are sitting; and secondly to sit here hours and see this done time after time? I have seen a favourite who had as many as three garments out come up and get served before girls who sat here waiting and watching, and whose turn it was had justice been done. It is only fair to say, too, that I sat here and saw and heard that countenanced by those in supreme authority.

Do not suppose that we see it done without protest. We

spend our time on this table in one long protest. Sometimes those gentlemen and ourselves are not very polite towards each other. While we are waiting for another supply of work let me add another word. I told you last week that the favourites are of various kinds. Amongst them are widows who have children to maintain, and women who have sick husbands, and other pitiable cases which I could mention. Now I have spent hours on this table, and I say to you that never do I remember one complaint made, one protest uttered, or one word of any kind said by these anxious and capable girls who sit here waiting for work, when such work is given to any of these women whom I have just mentioned. I unhesitatingly declare that if the choice were given us we would prefer to suffer ourselves rather than take work out of the hands of these, who need it so badly. It is only when favourites who are in good circumstances who come to this table and get served two or three times before we get served once, that we raise our voices in protest. I have seen it all; have felt it all; have thought a great deal about it all; and I say to you that with such influences I cannot see how we can be angelic and good-tempered.

But another supply of work is coming. Let us now suppose that the favourites are pretty well supplied; that is not often the case, however. Now my reader, let us gird on our armour of 'cheek', and prepare for battle. All our comrades are doing likewise. When the work arrives – before it arrives – let us shout for it, beg for it in as loud a voice as we can; above all let us make ourselves as noticeable as possible, and be as persistent as possible, as then we may get served to 'get out of one row'. If we sit still, never speaking, or speak in a quiet voice, we never shall be heard or noticed, and consequently never shall get served. Sometimes the clamour made by the girls begging and fighting against each other for daily bread, not pocket money, can be heard in all parts of the factory. When the season was very slack indeed I have seen the youngest hands literally fight and scramble for garments, for which 2d is paid.

Imagine the scene, my reader! A table with at least 50 girls on and round it. Lay a dozen garments, probably not worth more than 7 shillings in all to us. These girls all clamouring, with arms outstretched, for a share of it, say a shilling's worth, for which when they have it they will have to do at least one and six' worth of work. Do not laugh. My heart swells now as I write and think of those scenes, as it has done many times when I have been an actor therein. I say to you with all the energy and emphasis which I can convey, that you are not men, you are not women in the true sense of the words; you are not true to your manhood, to your womanhood, if you can look on such scenes as these without a wish – without a manly and womanly determination – to find some way of altering things.

Before we leave this table let me say a few more words. Think over what I have told you. Don't you see how in the existing state of things it is impossible for us to act quite fairly and honourably towards each other? We have to take advantage of each other, as it were. Can you wonder that girls, not only in slack seasons but in busy ones, and the intermediate ones which are neither busy nor slack, take advantage of any accident which may arise which enables them to get served out of their turn or a second time before others who they know have not been served once? It will thus happen sometimes that one girl, through a series of accidents, will make a good week's wage; and another, equally capable, may get next to nothing. Did we stick to all that is perfectly upright and honourable, one half of our time, we should not get a third of a living, to say nothing of half. Does that tend to elevate or demoralise?

I think now that we may leave the table. Suppose we walk about a little to ease our cramped limbs, while I tell you of other things pertaining to our life here. Out of any price paid for any garment we have to find all the materials required, such as thread, silk, twist [for buttonholes], needles, wax. I will quote one week's wage in a busy season. I earned 14 shillings. I worked at least 14 hours a day for five days and about 12 on Saturday for that sum, and out of it I had to pay 1s 1d for materials.

One reason why common work in so many cases pays the finisher as well or better than best work is that the materials required are not so costly. We get these materials at the office window at one certain time in the forenoon, and another in the afternoon, only. If we are not gifted with foresight or are not of a provident disposition, what we require in the meantime is borrowed from a good-natured comrade. When getting these materials, we of course always have to take the money. I remember one time when an order was being completed which required a peculiar colour of silk, which cannot be used for any other colour of garment. While the order had been in progress the silk had been sold to us in skeins – two for 2½d I think it was – and we were not allowed to use any other kind of silk. Just before the order was completed, however, this silk gave out, and for some reason – which was not explained to us – no more was obtained; and we were compelled to buy reels of machine silk at 1s 8d a reel. We naturally arranged amongst ourselves to divide a reel between two or four of us, as the case might be. But I submit to you that we were not treated quite fairly in being obliged to buy even five-pence worth of silk out of one week's wage in order to finish about two garments. . . .

I am open to conviction in this; but I think also that when a certain time for supplying these materials is fixed, and girls stand at the window waiting to be served, they should hardly be kept waiting six minutes or longer while the young ladies who would serve them are finishing whatever they are doing. This is not a frequent occurrence, but I think it should not occur at all. When we whose time is of such value (when we have work to do) to us are kept frittering that time away here, it does not influence us for good in any way, unless by cultivating the virtue of patience. I have myself, on more than one occasion, after waiting five or six minutes, deliberately left the window and gone again before the hour has expired, to see if it would then be convenient to attend to my wants.

Another item I want to mention to you. Every Monday morning a boy comes round with a bag and a tray of numbered checks. We each are compelled to buy one of these checks – the one on which our number is inscribed. Some cost two-pence, some three-pence. If we pay two-pence, we have the inestimable privilege of a seat in the tea-room and a mug of tea every afternoon. If we pay three-pence, we have, in addition, the privilege of some hot water at lunch- or dinnertime. Now, there are a number of us who never take this tea. I am one of them. We thus pay two-pence for simply nothing at all. Personally I have two reasons for not drinking the tea. First because I do not like it, secondly because I do not consider that I need it, and I object either to drink tea which I do not like, or to drink tea which I do not consider that I need, and I object also to pay for what I never get. I ought to say that during my experience no attempt has ever been made either by myself or others to get this rule relaxed at all. But you will not be surprised at that when I tell you that I have myself seen girls get their work 'stopped' (that is, none is to be given to them for a stated period) for raising objections or for refusing to pay in very slack times, or when they may have been 'out' (away from work) for any portion of the week. I hope to revert to this matter of tea-money next week.

Another slight item in our life. Those of us who for any reason, laziness or otherwise, do not manage to arrive before the doors are locked, are allowed to come in at half-past-eight or nine o'clock on payment of a penny. I understand that this fine is added to the funds of a sick club which exists. Another small matter and then I must reluctantly take leave of you. Our week is reckoned from Wednesday to Wednesday. On Thursday morning a boy comes round to inscribe in a book the sums to which we are entitled. We sometimes have quite a variety of small sums ranging from a half-pence to 1s 6d to reckon, and you will not be surprised to hear that we make a mistake occasionally. Should we do so, however, a rule has recently been established which compels us to wait a day longer for our money. Thus, we who are in disgrace shall have to wait till Saturday, instead of getting paid on Friday, like our comrades. I have never experienced this myself, but I have seen and warmly sympathised with my fellow-workers who have. I remember at least one case quite recently, only the other week, when it transpired that a girl actually had made no mistake; but for some reason not clear to us the young lady who manages these things for us did not see fit to pay the girl till Saturday. You will understand that while this is not a matter of vital importance, yet it causes inconvenience, and is not looked on by us with favourable eyes.

I must now thank you earnestly for your visit and attention. I hope to address Mr. Editor and yourselves next week on this subject generally, and to submit to your judgement some suggestions for the improvement of the condition of the factory girls. In conclusion, may I say that if you are not clear on any point, if there is anything else about our life that you would like to know, or any question you would like to ask, if you will address me through the Editor in the columns of the *Chronicle*, I shall be happy to enlighten you on anything I know.

Crewe Chronicle, 30 June 1894

7 *Life in a Crewe Factory, 14 July 1894*

I propose today to sum up, review and comment on further where necessary, what I have already said on the above subject, and to submit the only practicable form of remedy from the evils from which we suffer which presents itself to me. Before proceeding to do this may I say that I have in my mind an ideal of what life in a factory could and might be, but I am bound to confess that at present my ideal, though not fanciful, is yet impracticable and somewhat beside the point, and therefore for the present useless. Perhaps at some future time, if you, sir, will so far indulge me, I may sketch out my ideal and the means of its realisation in your columns. Now for my summary.

First – I began by showing you that we are not paid fair value for the great bulk of the work done by us – in short, that we find it utterly impossible to realise a Living Wage. I wish to return to this point presently, for herein I recognise the root of all the evils from which we suffer; and in my opinion no substantial benefit could accrue to us – indeed, until this root is plucked up and destroyed, I do not see how any practical reforms in any other direction can be attempted for the evils of other kinds which exist in a great measure originate in, and are part and parcel of that root, and it were therefore almost impossible to attack the one without the other – in destroying the root we shall necessarily affect its offspring, which if not resulting in the like destruction of the offspring, will at any rate render the ultimate destruction of such easier of accomplishment.

Second – I tried to show you that we are unable to live rational human lives – that one half of our time we live the life of a slave or beast of burden, and the other half a comparatively idle, dependent life. This is a result of the root of all the evils, and I do not see how we can attempt to alter it till we pluck up the root.

Third – I next, as well as I was able, made a sketch of the factory girl herself as I know her to be; and tried to show that many of the faults of which she is accused are the natural result of the influences of her life. That point we may now leave, I think.

Fourth – That an evil of 'favouritism' exists to a fearful degree amongst us, not only in the factory in which I work, but in at least one other factory in Crewe, as I know for a fact.

Fifth – That married women are admitted into our arena. On that I will speak further.

Sixth – That the present system – or rather lack of system – in dealing out such work as there is, is an unjust and unfair one. This to a great degree is a result of the root of the evils, and in attacking and destroying the root we shall probably destroy this evil also.

Seventh – That materials for the due performance of our work are bought by us out of our living wage. I have comments to make on this presently.

Eighth – That the sum of two-pence per week or 8s 6d per year is extracted from us, in some cases, for absolutely no return at all. On that, too, I have further comments to make.

Ninth – Minor oppressions of various kinds I have shown you which are easily traceable to the root and will probably cease to exist when the root is destroyed – at any rate if we can destroy the root we shall have a chance with these.

To sum up then in a very few words: The general conditions of our life from wages downwards are bad – rotten throughout. This is a summary of the account with which I have from time to time supplied you, and as it has never in the slightest degree been contradicted, I take it that it stands proved a faithful account. That being so, I think you will agree with me that reforms are badly and urgently needed. Let me now comment on some of the points which I have just enumerated, and suggest what means of improvement I can wherever possible.

With your permission, sir, I will leave the first and most important point – the root of the evils, till the last, and will begin with the fourth – 'favouritism'. This is a very real evil, and I say should not exist at all. It is a pernicious, debasing practice, alike to the favoured and the unfavoured. It fosters the bad in the nature of the favoured one, for if she be already of an unhealthy disposition it adds to and makes worse what already exists; and if she be of a naturally healthy disposition, it also debases, for she knows and feels that in a manner she is robbing others of their rights, and this can never be satisfactory or influence for good, a girl of good heart. Of its effects on the unfavoured it is needless to speak. I say then that this practice of making favourites should in the best interests of all be entirely done away with. It may be said that this would be unfair, in that the good workers would be placed on a level with the bad. I say, no. The favourites are in many cases by no means the best workers. Skill and execution are not necessary qualifications for the rank of 'favourite'. Then place all on an equal footing, so that we can first respect ourselves, and secondly can respect our fellow workers. I say without hesitation that the good workers would soon be found in their proper position *viz.* the front ranks, not because they are 'favoured' – a degrading thought! – but because by their abilities they merit that position. As it is, no encouragement is given to girls who have [a] sense of honour to excel in their work, and this can only have a lowering effect. The only way of bringing about a change in this respect is the one I shall presently propose as a means of attempting the destruction of the root of the evil.

Point 5. Married Women. These chiefly constitute the 'favourites'. Now I think it unjust that women who have husbands working should be allowed to come, and in a manner take their means of subsistence from girls who are dependent for a livelihood on their earnings. Without going into the obvious neglect of these wives and mothers of other duties and solemn responsibilities – and how much might be said on the evils arising from that not only to themselves and families, but in an indirect manner to the community at large! – which in this case might be considered somewhat personal, it is manifestly unfair that married women in receipt of a husband's wages, for no valid reason, should be allowed to come and in some cases actually take precedence of girls who in many cases exceed them in ability and capability. You will understand, sir, that I am here not necessarily referring peculiarly to myself. What, then, shall we say about them? I do not say 'Make a clean sweep of them!' – though I confess to a leaning that way – even if we had power, because conscience tells me that we in turn should be a little unfair. But I do say this, and will maintain it in face of any opposition – Place them side by side with these girls in fair, open, above-board competition; give them an equal chance with these girls and no more. And the only way to effect this that I can see is the same which I shall propose for the plucking up of the root.

Point 7. The system of selling us materials. Now I say that as we are compelled to buy these materials, we have an undeniable right to know the exact, original cost of such, and any percentage which may be allowed on the wholesale buying of the same is ours by right, and ours only. In my opinion anyone who buys these materials for us and not only does not sell them to us at cost price but who also does not give us the full benefit of any and all reductions, is robbing us, neither more nor less. Now I do not say, sir, that anybody is doing this, but I do say that we have no certain knowledge to the contrary. And I say that we ought to have – that it should be made perfectly clear to us that we are getting full value for the hard-earned money we pay. This might be done without much trouble by posting up in a conspicuous place the bills for these materials, so that we could see for ourselves that we are paying only what is just and right. If we are, there can be no objection to this suggestion.

Point 8.   The tea-money. Out of this money a tea-woman is paid, I understand, 18 shillings a week. How many factory hands earn that? Does the work done by them not require so much skill? Gas has to be provided, and of course the tea, sugar and milk. I do not know the exact number of hands employed in this factory, but I believe it is upward of 400 girls, and something like 100 men and boys, who also pay two-pence a week for their tea. Now, sir, we all pay two-pence a week, and those of us (a considerable number) who also require hot water at lunch or dinner pay an additional penny. Does it take the whole of the tax levied on us for the providing of these things? I personally – quite recently and quite voluntarily – have been solemnly assured that it does. Let us now consider those who pay this two-pence who do not take the tea. Suppose we allow for the moment that the assertion just quoted be true. It is clear that the tea for which we pay, if made at all, as we are now supposing, is either consumed by others, or is thrown away. Now is it fair, just or in any sense right that we should be obliged to pay for tea for others to drink, or to pay for tea to be wasted? And now we will suppose that the tea for which we pay, but never take, is never made, which is far the most likely and reasonable supposition. Where, then, do our contributions go? Whom do they benefit? Have we not a right to know? I consider that if somebody obliges me to pay 8s 6d a year, that somebody is equally obliged to not only show me what equivalent for the same he may consider I get, but to give me some equivalent which I myself can appreciate substantially. In short, sir, I do consider, have always considered, and shall always consider, so long as we continue to pay it, that I and others are being robbed of two-pence every Monday morning.

And now as to those who pay the two-pence and drink the tea. I do not consider these fairly treated, and neither do they. I say in this case, as I said of the materials, that if we are obliged to pay this money nobody has a fraction of right to one farthing over what it costs to provide us with the tea. And, here again, I make no assertion that anybody is making any profit out of our money. Still, here again, we are not clear that it is otherwise. And we ought to be clear. The suggestion made in the other case will do equally well here; an exact account of the income and expenditure might from time to time be posted up where we can see it. I can see no possible objection to this. If those who manage for us have a right to get this money from us, nobody will deny that we have an equal right to know for ourselves, to our own satisfaction, exactly how our money goes.

But I do not recognise the right of the employer, or those who represent the employer, to demand this money from us at all. I say that we should have liberty to say whether we will have tea or not. It is a custom, I know, in some factories, simply to provide hot water at a charge of half-pence per week (and we pay a penny for exactly the same luxury – why?). This seems quite fair to me, and I do not see why it might not be applied in the factory about which I speak.

And now, sir, to come to the root. This living wage of ours! I intended, and would have liked to have spoken on this at some length, to have traced it to its origin, its subsequent growth as affecting all branches of the trade, and other trades as well, but I have already said so much, and so much still remains that is important to say, that I think to make myself sufficiently clear, I must confine my remarks to the factory in which I work. In doing so I shall probably answer my purpose quite as well, and you, sir, and your readers, will easily apply what I shall say to whatever else it may fit for yourselves. Now the work done in this factory is not of the 'civilian' class. It is chiefly Government work – orders for army and police clothing. Railway orders also, but those are recognised by us as being generally of a better paying class than those of the Government. Now I wonder if the Government of this country know (or care) that those on whom the real business of executing their orders falls are 'sweated' thereby? And is the Government so frightfully poor that it cannot afford to pay a living wage to those who make the clothing of our soldiers and policemen? I have told you before that one class of garment (even of Government work) will pay so much better than another. Now if the Government – or anybody else who gives orders for any class of work – (this will apply all round) can afford to pay a decent price for one class of work, it follows that they can for another. And if, as the employers tell us, these orders are in so many cases contracted for, and executed for such ridiculously small sums, who has the benefit? The Government? And through the Government the tax-payers? If so, it is clear that the few suffer for the apparent benefit of the many, which is manifestly unfair. But in undertaking these badly-paying orders does the employer reduce his percentage of profit in proportion to the price he pays his hands? Or does he first take what he considers right, and then give what remains to the workers? Now I believe under the present social system – in an employer taking his fair and proportionate – I emphasise both these words – percentage of profit on the capital he expends, and no more. To anything further than that I do not recognise his right. It is clear then in this case either that the Government, or whoever else may give orders of an inadequately paying class, is robbing – what else can we call it? – the employer and his hands, or else that the employer himself is the – robber. And may I say here that thinking over these things at different times, one form of remedy – or rather of alleviation – for one's sufferings has been – I confess that I have not much hope of ever seeing it come into operation – that when these wretchedly-paying orders are undertaken, first the employer in his percentage; next the manager, assistant manager, and all the ladies and gentlemen under them who get a living wage all the year round, no matter what kind of orders may be in process of execution, should have their wages reduced in exact proportion to the price paid the factory girl, and of the saving effected thereby the factory girl should receive her due share. What is there unfair in this? The labourer of whatever class is worthy of his hire. If it is fair for one class of workers to be reduced it surely is for another.

Now how shall we set about plucking up this root? Ask the employers to kindly consider it? Utterly useless! As things are at present, at least. We might as well look up beseechingly at the moon, and expect it to come down to our aid. We are now in an entirely disunited, disorganised state, and are consequently entirely at the mercy of the employers; and while we remain so, we shall, in my opinion, never get the slightest alleviation of this grievance. I propose then, as an ultimate, and not necessarily remote, means of remedy, that we, that is the factory girls of Crewe, and any other class of female workers who may like to join us, first organise ourselves into one strong united body, and further, that we affiliate with some already existing union of workers, and thus, when the time is ripe, shall we not only speak with an effective voice ourselves, but shall also have the help of other workers in the redress of our grievances, and on our part shall in turn be able to help others. I am of the opinion that a merely local union of factory girls alone would be of little or no use. We should never be sufficiently strong either to speak for ourselves or to maintain ourselves in case of need. Personally I look with favour on the Tailors' Union (I am not sure if that is its proper name) as peculiarly suitable for the admission of tailoresses; but I understand that tailors, as a body, absolutely refuse in this way to hold out a helping hand to their suffering sisters, their reason, I believe, being that women have no business to be in their trade at all. I must say that I think this a very short-sighted, not to say selfish, view; and I am rather surprised that such an intelligent body of men as I know tailors to be should take such a view as they do. However, there is no help for it, and we must make the best of such means as we have, and affiliate ourselves with a union of workers who are not so exclusive. I know the Independent Labour Party have interested themselves in this question; and through their good offices it is now possible for us to organise ourselves and to affiliate ourselves with another body of workers – I am sorry that I forget the name of the union – and for anything I know to the contrary this will answer as well as anything else. When we are thoroughly organised, and not till then, I propose that we unitedly, earnestly and determinedly set about the redress – or at any rate alleviation – of our grievances; that we try every means which will then be at our disposal to get these things righted.

And now let me say that I strongly deprecate a strike as a means to this end. I would resort to a strike only as a very last resource, when all other means had failed; in such a case only, in my opinion, would a strike be justifiable. And until we are organised thoroughly, and independent of charity, such a course as a strike would be the height of folly.

Will you now, sir, if you can possibly spare me sufficient space, allow me to address my fellow-workers. I know they read my articles, sir; I have seen them in the act. My fellow-workers, then – you all know, and most of you acknowledge that what I have been telling the public is true – every word of it. You know that we cannot earn enough from eight in the morning till six at night to keep us in independence the year round. Now I tell you that we have an absolute right to a living wage; and the reason why we do not get it is that somebody who has money and power is taking advantage of our weak, unorganised, dependent state to rob us of our right. It is also well known to you that the prices paid for our work grow visibly less and less, and I tell you that this will continue, and things will grow worse and worse, unless we take steps to alter them. Now nobody can do this for us. Many people can help – are helping; through the powerful aid of Mr. Editor we have already enlisted the sympathy, and shall have the help of all sensible and right-thinking men and women. But this is of no avail unless we first help ourselves. Each one of you has a part to play. Do each your own part, not only for your own good but for the good of others.

In one of my letters I likened this great grievance of ours – low prices for our work – to a stone wall. Now I alone may butt at this wall till I smash my head, and it will never move an inch; but if you individually, and all of you collectively, come with me, and we go at it with one or more if necessary strong, united, persistent 'butt', in all probability the wall will fall. Each one of you then bravely do your own part.

I now beg, sir, to express my deep gratitude to you for the help you are affording the factory girls. I respectfully submit to you and *Chronicle* readers these the only practical suggestions of which I can think for the improvement of the condition of my class. I hope that you and my readers will give me the benefit of anything else, or anything better which may have suggested itself to you. In conclusion will you, sir, allow me to say that any influence I can in any way and at any time use for the furtherance of the above object with both voice and pen I shall use unhesitatingly and gladly.

Crewe Chronicle, 14 July 1894

8 *Life in a Crewe Factory, 14 July 1894*

To the Editor of the CHRONICLE

Sir, – May I comment briefly on the letter from 'A Lancashire Woman' on the above subject in the current issue of the *Chronicle*. I believe she is actuated by a real desire to help factory girls out of their troubles, and I accordingly thank her for her suggestion. I have no personal knowledge whatever of domestic service, but I quite agree with 'A Lancashire Woman' that it may easily prove a more desirable, and less morally dangerous means of earning a livelihood than factory work. In my own case there are peculiar and quite insurmountable obstacles in the way of my adopting that means of bettering my position; but to any of my class *who have nothing against such a course*, I would concur with 'A Lancashire Woman' in advising them to adopt her suggestion. Let the experiment be tried, by all means. I do not see, however, how the reduction of our number would materially benefit the remaining factory girls. Our greatest grievance – inadequate return for work done – would be unaffected by it, and therefore would still await redress.

Please let me reply also to 'Another Factory Girl' who criticises my articles in the same issue. May I first, sir, inform my fellow-worker that though I claim to be a lady, yet I am also a factory girl, and am not ashamed of that fact, the latter being (as must be well known to 'Another Factory Girl') the name by which I am invariably known in the *Chronicle*. I should be glad, if she should ever have occasion to refer to me again, if she would do so by that name. I look with very dubious eyes on her own signature, sir. If she is what she professes to be, and stands side by side with me in daily 'competition' at that table on which the public kindly spent some time with me a fortnight ago, she knows, as I then showed the public, that the work is not by any means served out in strictly 'numerical' order. She knows, too, that she is not adhering strictly to facts when she says that what appears favouritism consists in the employer handing work (the 'employer' does not 'hand' work at all) to those most efficient in its execution.

I wonder if she is a 'favourite'? I myself have on occasion been regarded by my fellow-workers as somewhat of a favourite, and if I chose I could easily ingratiate myself into the ranks of the regulars – I know the way. But the idea is revolting to me. I want to stand side by side with my fellow-workers in real sisterhood and comradeship, and this I can never do if I step beyond them into the select band of 'favourites'.

With regard to the second part of the letter, I am at a loss to understand by what process of reasoning she arrives at the conclusion that the tea-money is my 'strongest point'. Those who comprehend me, or who do not wilfully misunderstand me, know that my strongest point is, and has ever been inadequate return for work, and this is a matter quite separate from the tea-money. What a charming picture this is – the tea-money and the great benefits accruing to us therefrom, looked at through the spectacles of 'Another Factory Girl'! I however, as will be seen elsewhere, am in the habit of looking at it through spectacles of quite another colour, and it is therefore no wonder that for me it wears a different aspect. May I ask 'Another Factory Girl', sir, whether she has observed that the 'cook' of whom she speaks has other duties than those pertaining to the factory hands, such as the daily cleaning of the office, and the daily preparation of and attendance on the office tea. And could she inform me if the ladies and gentlemen in the office contribute their share to the expenses of this 'cook'? I am naturally interested in that point, and moreover, consider that I have a right to information from somebody. As I deal with the whole of her letter elsewhere, I need not occupy your valuable space, sir, in replying to detail here. I am confident that you and *Chronicle* readers will take a deeper view of things than that taken by 'Another Factory Girl' without my aid. Thanking you for space,

I remain, sir, yours sincerely,
A Crewe Factory Girl
14 July 1894

9   Life in a Crewe Factory: A Storm, 28 July 1894

To the Editor of the CHRONICLE

Sir, – If I may, I should like to give *Chronicle* readers an account of some rather startling events which took place in the factory in which I work on Friday last. For some time previously there had been distinct and audible rumblings, especially every Friday, when copies of the *Chronicle* were so much in evidence, but on this particular Friday, sir, the climax was reached, and the storm burst in full fury. I myself was, of course present, and I think I will first give a faithful account of the doings of the day, after which, with your permission, I will comment thereupon, and finally will again address my fellow-workers. You will understand that I am unable to do this in any direct way, only through the medium of the *Chronicle*. Now for Friday last. We had only been at work about an hour when we became aware that something special was about to happen. In the finishing department tables and chairs were removed to make an open space. The machinists were then fetched from their room, and any of us who were in the tea-room or anywhere else were informed that a meeting was about to be held and were requested to attend forthwith. When we were all duly assembled the manager ascended a kind of platform and proceeded to address us. I listened very keenly, and as nearly as I can give it the address was as follows:

He (the manager) had been desired by the employer, who had visited the factory the previous day, to call that meeting together. He had called it here (in the finishing department) for two reasons: First, because it was more conveniently arranged – there was more room – and secondly, because it was from this room that the necessity for it had arisen. He need not say what had caused the necessity for the meeting – that was well-known to all. Some of them had been with him long enough to remember what sacrifices had been made by the employers in times past for their comfort. However, 'base insinuations' and statements had been made by one of the newspapers that profit was being made out of the materials and tea-money. (The manager was here greatly agitated, and the next sentence was very emphatic.) He denied these statements. Not one farthing of profit was being made out of them. However, as a consequence of these 'base insinuations' he was desired by the employers to inform them that the tea-room would be closed. A pause was made here, evidently for some expression of opinion by us, but as for the moment we were all quite overcome, strict silence was maintained!

110

The manager proceeded to tell us that there was a supply of tea in hand, and next week we should have tea as usual without paying, because we had already paid for it. After then the tea-room would be closed. He also desired to inform the late risers that in future they must arrive at eight o'clock or stay out altogether, and no more penny fines would be taken from them. Having now recovered a little some of us found voice and asked what we were to do for dinner if the tea-room was to be closed altogether. And just now I observed one of the persons with whom I made *Chronicle* readers acquainted mounted on a form, and she being one who dines in the factory at this point was most eloquent. The answer was received that we should all have to suffer for the one who had written the letters, and that we must 'thank our friend for that' (meaning the writer of these letters). The manager then dismounted, and the meeting broke up.

Chronicle readers are aware by this time that as a class we are not very far-seeing, and accordingly many of us now proceeded in somewhat strong language to call down all sort of blessings on the head of the unfortunate one who had been the cause of this deprivation. During the morning great excitement was evident everywhere, and I observed congregations of girls assembled at intervals in the machine-room. I, being a finisher, was now too far away to hear what was being said, but I understand that the object of the meetings was to devise some means of finding out and expelling the wicked girl who had written the letters. I am sorry, but not surprised, to say that I myself several times heard some rather creditable methods of doing this, which were more forcible than elegant proposals. And I think it only justice to say that these disgraceful propositions have not been confined to those of my own sex who are employed in this factory. And I can vouch for the truth of this statement because what I have just hinted at has been said to me – and before this particular Friday. During the morning a petition to have the tea-room remain open was addressed to the employers and submitted for the signatures of those of us who desired to sign. I have no knowledge whether this petition has since been forwarded to the employers. So much for the morning.

Now for the afternoon. A short time only had elapsed when we again became aware of something else in the wind! It transpired that a few brave spirits had arranged to assemble outside the office door (the office is situated midway between the machine and finishing departments) to interview the manager. Their object was to inform him that the tea-money, as was shown in the letters, was not the only grievance possessed by us. There was the 'favourite' question to deal with, he was informed, and the unfair way in which the work was distributed; about our having to rise at such unearthly hours to come and stand waiting outside the doors in a morning; and about a few girls, well-known to all of us, having a special gift this way, and as a consequence getting the work every day before we who were of a more sluggish disposition could get a chance. Oh! it was an exciting meeting, sir. The two gentlemen who have us in charge were desired to attend, and we closed round these two and the manager, and what some of those plucky girls said would have warmed the hearts of *Chronicle* readers.

To go into the details of this meeting would, I am afraid, take up all the columns of the *Chronicle*, and good as you are to me, sir, I can hardly expect that, so I shall have to content myself with just quoting one statement made by the manager and giving the results. I am rejoiced to say that the meeting had results of a practical nature. The statement made was as follows: The manager knew of two or three girls who were then surrounding him who were in a league, and had all been concerned in the writing of the letters. (I shall have something to say in reply to this statement presently.) Now as to the results. As a preliminary we were informed that if we were not satisfied we had better leave. But this was not our object as we tried to show, and finally the following new rules were made and approved of by us: That in slack times we should stay out a day occasionally while the work accumulated, instead of coming in and wasting so much time, as at present; that turns should not be taken from coming early to the door; that no work should be placed on the table before eight o'clock; that we should take turns in strict order as we placed our work on the table; finally, that if on one day we did not all get served, those who did not should be the first to be served on the following day.

This last rule is worth all the trouble, for it has frequently been our fate – it has to be somebody's when there is not supply sufficient for all – to get no work one day and then on the next to see some who had some the day before, before me, and yet more, before us. We came back very much flushed and dishevelled – for it was rather a crushing meeting – but triumphant. But that was not the last meeting, sir. We had hardly been seated a minute when we noticed several of the married ladies consulting together, and finally marching off in a body to the meeting-ground. You will not be surprised to hear, sir, that on seeing this we girls could not restrain our laughter, and a hearty outburst was the result. I should like to take this opportunity of assuring the married ladies that we were not laughing in derision, as they seemed to think and naturally resented. But it was not that – the situation was really funny, sir. Well, we girls naturally wanted to hear what the favourites had to say, and the meeting being an open one we accordingly filed off again. We had not now got the front place, and were not near enough to hear everything distinctly, but I heard the manager say with reference to one of the married ladies who is an invalid that he would see that she had in the future what she had had in the past – all the light and best work, and he was sure that she was a very cruel, hard-hearted girl who would grudge this. I did not hear of any other result of the meeting which is of any moment.

And now let me comment on some of the transactions of this eventful day. First with regard to the statement made by the manager which I have quoted above. I desire to inform that gentleman and anybody else whom it may concern that there is not a single girl in the factory or out of it who knows or can prove the identity of the writer of the letters. I take it that nobody can prove I wrote the letters unless I, as the writer, had told them so, and I hereby emphatically declare that no girl or woman in Crewe can say that I have ever done so. Nor have I ever hinted in the slightest degree to any of my fellow-workers that I am the writer. It is therefore impossible that any of them can have been concerned in the writing of the letters, and what the manager says he 'knows' is what he suspects, and is suspicion only. I make this statement as an act of justice to my fellow-workers. I am grieved that suspicion should attach to anyone through my agency in writing the letters.

And now as to the meetings and the results arising therefrom. With regard to the sacrifices made by the employers for our comfort – I have throughout done them full justice in this direction. Now as to the 'base insinuations'. How can what I have said be construed thus? If you will refer to my letter you will see that I made no assertion whatever that profit was being made out of the materials or tea-money. But I did make the assertion that we had no certain knowledge to the contrary. And I repeat that assertion. The manager has denied this, as I have shown, but you will forgive me if I want more than mere denial – I want proof. I asked for proofs, and they have not been given, and until they are given I must take the liberty to maintain my position. Why should they be withheld? Why not treat us like thinking, reasoning beings and satisfy us on this point? We are not complaining in an uncharitable spirit, but surely we may expect to have a little charity shown us. Why not indulge us and give us proofs?

And now as to the decision come to by the employers to close the tea-room. This will necessarily cause great inconvenience to those who come from a distance and dine in the factory, and also to the women pressers, whose work is very laborious, and who need refreshment. But, sir, I am entirely at a loss to understand why this drastic measure should be taken at all, and certainly do not see how I am responsible for it. I never contemplated being the means of depriving my fellow-workers of comforts to which they have become accustomed; and further, I deny that I am the means, or am the one to whom thanks is due (as stated by the manager) for this deprivation. If my fellow-workers will only exercise a little common sense they will surely see that it is the employers whom they have to thank, and not me. What I said, and shall say, is that we should have liberty such as is enjoyed in other factories, to have tea or not, as we please. Why not show us why this is impossible in our case? And supposing it is to be proved impossible, why not adopt my suggestions both in this case and that of the materials, and show us just how and in what way our money goes?

And now about the fines at the door. I made no comments whatever on that point – I simply stated that such a fine was imposed. I learn, however, that although the weekly contribution to the sick club is one-pence or two-pence, it cannot exist without these fines, and consequently will now cease to exist. I do not know if this is a serious matter at all to us. I suppose if it is it cannot be helped now.

And now as to the afternoon meetings. With the results of the first I am pleased and appreciate, and am grateful to and congratulate the energetic girls who were instrumental in bringing about these results. With regard to the case of invalids, etc., which was discussed at the meeting of married women, I ask *Chronicle* readers whether, throughout the course of my articles, I did not accord these cases justice and consideration? I declared before, and again declare that we girls do not grudge a fair share or more of the light work in such cases as these. But, sir, that is not what we complained about. What about the 'favourites' who have husbands in full employment? Please let us be treated as if we possessed at least a grain of sense.

As a general comment may I say, sir, that though we have been trying to lop off some of the branches, and have succeeded in lopping off one or two, the great root of all the evils – inadequate return for work done day by day – is there, stubborn and unyielding as ever, and about this nothing has been said.

If you can kindly give me space, sir, I will now address my fellow-workers. My fellow-workers: It did my heart good to see

115

some of you last Friday, and stimulated me to persevere in the effort to eradicate as far as possible the evils from which we suffer. I hope great things from you, and I want to show you how we can accomplish great things. We all appreciate even the minor concessions – which are only acts of justice towards us – which you plucky girls obtained for us last Friday. But you know the root is there still. This is the root: The fact that if we work hard 9½ hours a day we are still unable to get enough to maintain ourselves. You know that as a result of the present rate of payment there is not a girl amongst us who, when there is work to do, does not have to work after factory hours. Now we need not do this if we are all resolved not to do so, and set about it in the proper way. And remember that in asking for a fair day's wage we are only asking for our own – our right. But we shall never get this great evil remedied by asking the manager. The only effective way has been proved to be to ask in a body, with one voice, through an authorised representative, with means at our command to give these appeals weight. Now as I told you before the only way of doing this is to organise ourselves. Don't you see that we must do this ourselves? That part nobody can do for us. The willing help, Mr. Editor, of the few earnest men who have made it possible for us to organise – have given us the means of doing so – and the sympathy – and sympathy helps – of all the sensible people of Crewe cannot materially benefit us unless we ourselves are willing to do our part.

I am not quite sure, and have not time now to ascertain, but I believe the Co-operative Hall, Market Street, is at our disposal on Tuesday evenings at 7.30, and help will be given us in the way of organising, and our part is to attend and join. I am very glad to be able to tell you that the members of the local branch of the Amalgamated Society of Tailors have met and discussed the position of the tailoresses, and as far as they are concerned have resolved to give us admission to this Society. If the branches in other parts of the country prove themselves as intelligent as that of Crewe and neighbourhood we shall have the protection and help of this powerful organisation. At present we await the decision of other branches. But we need not be idle meanwhile. We can be forming ourselves into a body, and then shall be ready for an existing organisation to take us in. Let me urge upon you therefore, those of you who wish to help in plucking up this root (remember when it is plucked up we shall all reap the benefit) to do your part by attending and joining. I know some of you have already done so. Come again, nevertheless, and help by your countenance those who have not. Come in a body. Do not be afraid. Some of you showed last Friday that there is mettle in you. Come and show it again in this way. Do not be deterred because others are reluctant; probably if you come somebody else will. Do not be deterred because you are thinking of getting married, and therefore you may not reap any direct benefit yourself. Don't you see that that is rather a selfish way of looking at it, and that if you do not get the benefit (and in an indirect way you will) you will help to confer it on others by joining? In conclusion let me assure you that my object in trying to show how we may set about plucking up this root is that you as well as myself may have the benefit arising therefrom. I would also like to say that I make these remarks to all the tailoresses in Crewe, and not only to those with whom I am myself associated.

I beg you will allow me, sir, to publicly express my heartfelt gratitude to you for the reforms which through the agency of the *Chronicle* have already taken place, and for the hope of bringing about greater reforms in the future. I should look on it as a favour if you would also let me say that the sensible ones amongst us appreciate thoroughly the powerful aid which you yourself, sir, have given us by your remarks on our grievances.

I remain, sir, yours sincerely,
A Crewe Factory Girl
28 July 1894

Life in a Crewe Factory: A Hurricane, 4 August 1894

To the Editor of the CHRONICLE

Sir, – The storm of Friday, the 20th, was followed by a hurricane on Thursday, the 26th inst. As the full blast of the hurricane fell on the head of one individual, and that one of your correspondent, you will not be surprised to hear, sir, that my recollections of what took place while it lasted (an hour) are of a somewhat confused nature, and the feeling it has left is a decidedly sore one. I think, nevertheless, that I need not ask you to let me use the *Chronicle* for the purpose of justifying myself, and of stating and replying to whatever I can remember of what was said during this hurricane. Let me explain! When we returned from dinner on this particular Thursday we found that one of the employers had come down from London. We were immediately requested to assemble ourselves on the meeting ground described last week. It is utterly useless for me to try to give a precise and orderly account of this meeting, so that I shall have to ask you, sir, to let me give as clear an idea as I can, and to leave the rest to the imagination of my readers. The employer began by referring to my letters. I cannot regard the whole of his remarks on them as anything but a long series of insults and sneers against the girl who had written them and the Editor who had published them, and as such sneers deserve nothing but contempt I shall not particularise or comment upon them.

Now I played a prominent part in that meeting, sir, and I think to make *Chronicle* readers understand what took place during the meeting I had better explain two small matters. One is that from what transpired it is evident that the employer had come down with the express purpose of compelling the writer of the letters to reveal her identity, if she possessed any sense of honour at all. The other item I want you to notice is that for some reason I myself had from the very beginning been suspected by everybody in the factory to be the writer of the letters.

To return to the meeting. What first brought me to the light

118

of day was a question from the employer as to whether any of us were dissatisfied with the existing state of things. No diligent student of the *Chronicle* needs telling whether I am dissatisfied. Accordingly I acknowledged this to be the case. This was just what was wanted. The manager immediately descended from his high estate (alongside the employer) and fetched me to the front – was so kind as to assist me. I was invited, I remember, by both the employer and the manager, to take up my position between them and to address the audience. But this I resolutely refused to do – not feeling able, as a matter of fact. I stood, then just below them – quite by myself. I was naturally very much agitated. Before I proceed I want to ask you, in justice to me, to look calmly on both sides. On the one the employer, whom we only see occasionally; the manager, who, though better known to us, is yet an awe-inspiring personage in our midst, both of whom, as I can testify, had addressed audiences before, both prepared for this afternoon's work; upwards of 400 girls and women, all knowing, though not daring to say, that what had been made public was true, many of them strongly in sympathy with the writer of the letters, others, for some reason, very bitter against her; and a number of men and boys, all intently looking on. That is one side. This is the other. One girl, who though she had used her pen occasionally, had never in her life faced an audience before, now suddenly brought face to face with one, without any preparation whatever. Are the two sides equal? I put it, sir, to you and *Chronicle* readers whether it was fair to come down suddenly with the express purpose of finding out the author of the letters, and of holding her up to ridicule before those for whom she had written. Had I known of the intention of the employer I, as the 'Factory Girl', would have come prepared. I should not have stayed away. By no means. But I, too, like the employer, should have prepared myself, like him I should have had notes in my hand, to refresh my memory and to keep my ideas clear, and I should have done my level best to have defended the position I had taken up.

Before I resume my narrative I want to accord justice to my

119

fellow-workers. It is a fact, then, that though not one of them bore me out in anything I said – on the contrary went entirely against me and their own consciences (as they assured me later), yet they did not take advantage of the many hints which were given them to laugh me scornfully down, and the vast majority of them treated me respectfully, both then and later. Perhaps I may say here that my heart is full of gratitude to them for the kind things they said to me afterwards.

And now to resume. The employer proceeded to interrogate me in the most merciless manner. Out of my confused recollections I distinctly remember telling him that he was not treating me in a gentlemanly way, and after further reflection in cooler moments I do not withdraw that statement, and shall never withdraw it. The impression I received and conveyed to him has deepened a hundredfold since. I remember also acknowledging myself to be the writer of the letters, and emphatically declaring that I was not ashamed of having written them. I remember too, and very keenly, what led me to do this. One reason was that the employer persistently referred to the writer as 'she or they', and made it evident that he suspected more than one; and the other reason was that he repeatedly said whoever wrote anonymously was ashamed of what they wrote. Now, sir, I am not invulnerable, and I could not withstand that attack. Hence the declaration quoted above. Perhaps I may say that though I could not withstand that last sentiment expressed by the employer directed against myself, still I do not agree with it, and strongly disputed it with him.

The employer's next course, on my acknowledging myself to be the writer of the letters, was to subject me to a searching cross-examination as to who had helped me – suggested several means of help which I had probably availed myself of, finally suggested that you yourself, sir, had probably had a great deal to do with the composition and arrangement of the letters. Of course I denied all this, and a great deal followed which is all very personal indeed, and has nothing whatever to do with the point at issue. I think I will not say anything more about the meeting itself, except that the employer told my fellow-workers in concluding that he hoped they would not let what I had done make any difference in their treatment of me – that they would not show me any disrespect. I was very much astonished to hear that, sir, and am still greatly puzzled about it. If any *Chronicle* reader can give any enlightenment as to why such a caution should have been deemed necessary, I shall be glad.

And now, sir, with your permission I will state and reply to whatever I can remember of what was said during the hurricane. A great deal was said about the tea-money, and profit being made out of it. Well, we have at last obtained the long asked for information, and despite the denial of the manager the previous Friday, it was acknowledged that there certainly is profit made out of it. Such profit, however, we were informed, has been expended in 46 (I believe) sets of china, sugar basins etc., for the use of the annual tea party (on no other occasion). The tea party itself, it was acknowledged, is also in some degree provided for out of this tea-money; and also gifts made by the manager to very needy cases amongst us, which we have all been aware of, it now transpires, are provided for out of our tea-money. I believe the yearly amount of profit was given, but my mind was in too great a state of confusion by that time to get a clear idea of figures. My reply is that I do not know whether we have ever been consulted about these things – not in my time – but I certainly think that as we have a share in paying for them we ought to be consulted in the matter of buying china, etc., with our money. And about making presents. I do not think we should have any objection to five shillings or ten shillings being given occasionally to deserving cases which are well-known to us all, but I think it should have been made known before this from what source the money was drawn. Honour to whom honour is due. And it is clear also, as I remember pointing out to the employer and also to the manager, who interviewed me later in the day, that we who have not been taking the tea have been paying more than others towards the tea party. I cannot see justice in that. I do not remember what reply they gave me – it was not clear, I think.

121

But I personally should give my 8s 6d a year the preference of the tea party. I could easily get a good tea for that, and could treat myself to an entertainment as well, and should besides have the privilege of selection, which I have not in this case.

I also obtained a portion of the information for which I asked in one of my letters – whether the ladies and gentlemen in the office contributed their share towards the expenses of the 'cook'? Of late there has been only one gentleman in the office – the manager – and he was kind enough to inform me that he did not take tea in the office, but that the two ladies – his daughter and her assistant – did not pay for their tea. My answer to that is that they ought to pay – that they have no right to drink tea at other people's expense. On the unanimous vote of my fellow-workers, the decision come to by the employers to close the tea-room was at the close of this meeting rescinded. Accordingly this week the boy has again visited us with his money bag and checks. Some of us have refused to buy the checks. Our names have been recorded in the office, for what purpose we are not aware. The fines at the door were also reinstated on the unanimous vote of the factory hands. A balance sheet of the funds of the sick club, and the addition of the fines, was read out to us, but I have not the slightest idea of it which is of any use. Something was said, too, about the system of 'favourites', and the employer asked me what I meant by it. I informed him that I had explained it in my letters. I did not feel able to repeat my explanation verbally, and he persisted that what I considered favouritism consisted in the work being given to those best qualified to do it. Now I have shown that this is not the case, and I am willing to submit and leave it to *Chronicle* readers whether I, who see it every day, know anything about it, as well as the employer, who does not see it at all. A great deal was said, too, about the prices paid for our work, and the employer assured us that he gave us the best price he could afford, and that if the Government or others would pay him more he would in turn pay us more, and that sometimes he was actually a loser after vouchsafing to us a somewhat more munificent price than usual. Well, sir, I am a little dubious about all this. I do not quite believe all I am told! But my reply is that if this is true then the Government or who-ever else pays these ridiculously low sums for the clothing of soldiers and policemen ought to be made to pay more, and the sooner they are made the better, so that those who do their work can live by the work they do.

The employer asked me, I remember, what the remedy was for this? I have plainly shown throughout that I do not expect to get this evil remedied by merely asking him. The only remedy that I can see is for the girls themselves to unite, and in a body to set to work earnestly and intelligently, and not only to ask but to demand their right – a living wage. If this course is so certain to prove ineffectual, as the employers assure us, why are they so careful and persistent in advising us not to adopt it? Where is the need for the advice if what they tell us be true? Is it their overwhelming desire for our welfare which influences them in giving us this advice? Whose interests are they considering? Ours or their own?

Reference was made to the number of hours worked in busy seasons. The employer did not think they were excessive com-pared with the hours of other workers. I say in reply to that that it is time the hours of other workers were reduced if that is the case. Reference was made also to my having been kept waiting at the office window when getting materials. The employer could not promise that it would not occur again. An excuse was made in that the young ladies are sometimes adding up columns of figures. My answer is that I can see when they are adding up columns of figures, and it is not only on such occasions that I have been kept waiting. This is a very small matter, and I do not wish to dwell on it. If the young ladies are not truly lady-like enough to object to keeping girls waiting unnecessarily I have nothing further to say, and my fellow-workers and I must submit to what we cannot alter.

Nothing whatever was said about the system of selling us materials, and we have still no certain knowledge that profit is not being made out of these as out of the tea-money. I had not presence of mind to make any enquiries about this matter.

Finally, sir, the one great objection of both employer and manager, to which they persistently referred, was that I had 'blazoned forth' (the employer's term) our grievances in the public press. I ought, they said, to have made my objections to them. As an illustration they asked me repeatedly whether, if anything were wrong at home, I should write to the newspaper about it? My answer is no, most decidedly I should not, for two reasons. First, because I am quite sure that you, sir, would not lend me the columns of the *Chronicle* for such a trivial purpose; secondly, because I should object to have my private affairs 'blazoned forth'. But the cases are not parallel. What I have made public concerns not only the 400 employed in the factory in which I work, but also those employed in several other factories in Crewe, and indirectly every inhabitant of Crewe, and therefore is a fitting subject for the public press. I ought to have appealed to the employer as to a father, he tried to convince me. I say no, sir. I do not look on the employer in the light of a father, nor does he look on me and my fellow-workers with fatherly eyes. No father would have treated his child as the employer treated me on Thursday last, if proof is necessary. So that I may be excused, I think, for applying to other sources for help in my need.

This is all I can remember of what took place on Thursday last which is of any consequence. If there is anything else which I have forgotten to which I ought to reply, I shall be glad if anybody will point it out to me. If you will allow me, sir, I should like to inform my employer that I shall be glad to meet and answer anything he may wish to ask me, and to defend myself to the best of my ability, either in the columns of the *Chronicle* or personally. I should, however, greatly prefer the former, for my pen obeys my will far more readily than my voice. And if the latter I must stipulate that I have due notification of the intention of the employer, and that we have an unbiased arbitrator present to see fair play between us.

The employer now knows whom he is combating. He very tenderly assured me that he had read all my letters, so that he will no doubt read this one also. I should like now to make a very emphatic and, I hope, final declaration. During the time that my letters have been appearing I have heard several people, men and women, some employed in the factory, some outside, accused, in conjunction with myself, of complicity to a greater or lesser degree in the production of the letters. My declaration is as follows: That no other single person in the factory or out of it has had anything whatever to do with them in any way whatever. The writer is herself now known, and she alone is responsible for what has been made public.

I remain, sir, yours sincerely,
A CREWE FACTORY GIRL
4 August 1894

10 Life in a Crewe Factory, 25 August 1894

To the Editor of the CHRONICLE

Sir, – Please allow me to acquaint *Chronicle* readers with some events which have taken place in one of the Crewe factories since the disclosure, on July 26th, of my identity as the writer of the letters on 'Life in a Crewe Factory' which have appeared in the *Chronicle*. On Saturday morning, 4th August, a private meeting of some duration was held in the tea-room by the married women, at which the manager was present. One of the two men who have charge of the finishers kept guard at the tea-room door. On seeing and hearing the girls express amongst themselves their natural interest in and amusement at the proceedings this gentleman left the door, and came round expostulating with some warmth. The object of the meeting was kept secret. Whether what I shall now relate was an effect of any discussion and resolution arrived at at that meeting I shall leave my readers to judge. The following Monday was Bank Holiday. On Tuesday morning almost as soon as we had begun work a tailor employed in the factory was summarily discharged. I want to ask you, in justice to this tailor, to consider his case on its merits as I will show it to you, and to give your verdict, which I do not fear, as to whether his dismissal was a justifiable one.

He had been in the employ of the firm a number of years. He was acknowledged by them to be a clever and careful workman, and a most useful and capable man. But it is also a fact he was known to hold advanced views on things in general, and what is also worthy of notice he has never been heard to express any disapproval of the letters on factory life which were published by the *Chronicle*. On the contrary, he has been suspected, and I myself have heard him accused, of assisting me to produce those letters. I have repeatedly and emphatically denied this, both publicly and privately, but seemingly without the slightest effect in convincing those in authority that what I say is true.

I shall also be obliged to confess that this unfortunate tailor has without doubt been guilty of speaking quite frequently, and without showing any disrespect, to the writer of the letters. I am aware that some excuse was found for his dismissal; but I think in view of what I have just shown, that the public will not need much convincing as to what was the cause of that dismissal.

During this same Tuesday morning rumours of impending changes were rife in the factory, and one of the men who pass the finishers' work hinted very strongly to several of the girls that they were about to be discharged. I, on hearing this, and after the dismissal of the tailor, at which I naturally felt indignant – though not, I am sorry to say, surprised – thought that the discharging of a number was probably the method which was to be adopted as a means of getting rid of me. As I hinted very plainly in my second letter, I expected that if ever I were identified some means would be found of compelling me to leave. But I never thought that I should be the means of bringing misfortune on a number of innocent girls. On hearing these rumours, therefore, I naturally felt anxious to prevent the discharge of other girls if possible, and accordingly I told the manager that I wished to leave. He did not express any desire to retain my services. On the contrary he told me that he was expecting an order for my discharge on the following morning. Unfortunately it did not occur to me just then to enquire what reason was to be given for my discharge. I can only suppose that the reason was that I had written the letters to the *Chronicle*.

I left, then, on this Tuesday afternoon. On the following evening it came to my knowledge that 12 girls (besides myself) had been discharged. I understand that these girls naturally asked the reason for their discharge, and that the answer was 'Slackness of work; and the discontented ones must go'.

I will now state the case of these girls, and will ask for your verdict, which again I do not fear, as to the validity of the excuse just named. The girls, with the exception of one or two married women, are absolutely the most capable and experienced finishers which were employed by the firm. This is proved by what it is impossible for the employers to deny – that the girls have been in the habit of taking all the best kinds of work, and have displayed skill and execution in the performance of it. One has been in the employ of the firm thirteen years, another eleven years, five or six four or five years, and the least term of service is two years. With three exceptions they are girls who had given in their names as desirous of organising at meetings held for that purpose. They are of the girls who, as I stated in the *Chronicle* of July 28th, had courage enough to interview the manager with a view to getting a re-arrangement of the rules relating to the distribution of work. And this is their reward! It is worthy of notice, too, that these girls are of those who, on that memorable day when we were suddenly confronted by the employer, afterwards openly expressed regret at not having confirmed my statements, and approval of my conduct in maintaining my position. They are girls, too, who have shown a special fondness for the *Chronicle* of late, and I myself heard an insulting remark made by one of the men who pass the work, to one of the girls who has since been discharged, as she stood side by side with me at the table on which *Chronicle* readers were entertained a short time ago – a remark relating to the reading of the *Chronicle*, of which, sir, this poor girl had evidently been guilty that morning (which was Friday August 3rd).

I could tell, too, of a rather spiteful thing which I saw played on a girl for this same offence. Several of the girls have no fathers, and are entirely dependent on their own exertions for a livelihood. They have devoted the best years of their life to the employer who has just now discharged them, and are consequently now only qualified as tailoresses. I do not see how the discharge of these girls can be regarded as anything but cruel in the extreme. Are any of the offences which I have just enumerated worthy of dismissal after years of faithful service? And is it in accordance with reason to discharge the most valuable hands because work is slack?

We girls, as I have shown, have all had some experience, and have seen many slack seasons (more than the present one) but have never before seen experienced hands discharged and inexperienced ones retained. As to the charge of discontent, may we, then, not have the privilege of exercising our reasoning and thinking faculties? Are we required to be human beings, or machines? The discontent which as beings possessed of an average amount of sense it would be a disgrace on us not to feel did not prevent the due and satisfactory performance of our work, which is the only thing for which the employer pays us, and therefore I maintain that he had no right to discharge us on that account. I understand that the tea-money which had on the previous day been paid by some of the discharged ones, was on their discharge returned to them. This was as it should be, and I am glad that it was done. I should like to say, however, that during the years we have been working in the factory we must have paid a considerable sum, which could easily be calculated, towards the purchase of the china, sugar basins, etc. I would respectfully suggest, now that we have been discharged, either that the money we have paid be returned to us, or that our share of the china be distributed amongst us. It is quite clear that our money has bought a portion of it, and I think it would only be right to put us in possession of what is indubitably ours.

I would like to say that the proof − for which we have a perfect right to ask − that no profit is being made out of the materials supplied to the factory hands has never been given us; and in view of the fact that the same quality materials can be procured in the town of Crewe at a considerably less price than that charged in the factory; and in view of the additional fact that hands employed in the factory are in the habit of taking justifiable advantage of the knowledge of the former fact to procure materials from outside sources surreptitiously – in view of these facts, and of that of proof to the contrary being withheld, I am afraid we shall be obliged, however reluctantly, to come to the conclusion that it seems very probable that profit is made out of the materials, as out of the tea-money.

It would be satisfactory to have some information as to the way in which this profit is expended. We need not doubt that it is returned to the factory hands in some useful way, but it would only be kind to gratify our natural curiosity as to what particular benefit is conferred on them by this profit.

I have now shown the results, sir, to my fellow-workers and myself of the faithful representation of the undeniable evils from which the factory girls of Crewe are suffering, which have appeared from my pen in the columns of the *Chronicle*. I ask *Chronicle* readers whether this result is warrantable, or is anything like fair, to say nothing of generous treatment, from employers to employed? Why should we be discharged, and our means of earning a livelihood taken from us, for simply showing what cannot be denied, that the conditions of the life which we, not the employers, have to live are bad and detrimental to our moral welfare, and for proposing and adopting an ultimate means of improving those conditions – for attempting to protect ourselves as employees by uniting in one common interest? The employers and their representatives have repeatedly told us that they have no objection to our forming a union – that the most powerful organisation in the world will never obtain us anything more than we have. Why, then, on meeting nights, should men employed in the factory find it necessary to pass and re-pass the doors of the meeting-room, and also should have such a fit of curiosity on these particular evenings as to closely watch all who enter the room from a spot in the close vicinity of the doors which I could name? Why, I ask? Why should girls be frightened so effectually that they dare not acknowledge that they have joined, or would like to join a union of factory girls which is forming? If combination on the part of the girls is destined never to affect the employers in any way, then why not let the girls alone, and let them amuse themselves, if they choose, in this way? I cannot see why the employers and those under them should concern themselves about these matters so much in the privacy of the factory, as I have seen and heard them concern themselves.

We factory girls have been informed by those who were in authority over us, that it was the determination of the employers to 'put down their foot' on those letters in the *Chronicle*. Presumably this frightening the poor is the method adopted by the employer of putting down his feet. Why not come out and let the strong light of the public press shine on his doings? Why not put his foot down on the letters in the only open, straightforward way? He has been invited time after time to submit his case to the public. I will answer for the public that they would give him a fair hearing, as they have given the factory girls a fair hearing. On the day on which I had the pleasure of an interview with the employer, I remember asking him why he did not meet me on my own ground – in the *Chronicle*? His reply was that he did not deign to notice such communications as mine. I remember its occurring to me at the time that such a statement was a little ludicrous and contradictory in face of the meeting which was then being held. But I certainly cannot help thinking that it would be quite as dignified on the part of the employers to write to the press as to 'deign' to frighten the poor girls in the factory.

In conclusion, sir, if you will allow me, I should like to inform my late fellow-workers that through no fault of mine I am no longer one of them, yet in sympathy – warmest, deepest sympathy – and recollections of sufferings borne side by side with them – I am still with them, and shall always be with them. Anything which I may be able to do at any time in any way towards the effort to improve the conditions of their life, I shall do most gladly. And I would beg them also to be resolute in doing their part by uniting themselves, which is the only way to accomplish anything substantial. Thanking you for space.

I am, sir, yours sincerely,
(An Ex) Crewe Factory Girl,
25 August 1894

11 Messrs Compton's Clothing Factory, 22 September 1894

Sir –

With your permission I should like to comment on the statements made by Messrs Compton in an interview with Mr. Thorne, an official of the Gasworkers' Union, published in the current issue of the *Chronicle*. I read those statements, sir, with deep interest, with sincere satisfaction, and, if I may say so, a little amusement. I am glad to hear Messrs Compton reiterate their kind permission for their work people to organise in a union, for which permission I have always given them credit. I should be obliged if they would confirm their statement by instructing their subordinates to allow my late fellow-workers their liberty to exercise their right to this privilege without fear of its becoming known that they are doing or have done so, and without incurring the ridicule of those in authority.

I am very much pleased to hear that Messrs Compton have now no animosity against any of the dismissed girls. This is a change of feeling which does them credit. Messrs Compton have an undeniable right to discharge any number of hands they please when they have not work for them to do, but one point still puzzles the ordinary mind, sir, why in this case it was found necessary to do what had never been done before, namely to discharge capable and experienced hands – against whom there was no animosity?

I am rather at a loss to understand why Messrs Compton should announce that, if the girls applied for work, 'no objection would be made to them'. May I ask what possible objection could be made to us? What have we done for which we ought to apologise? Please allow me to ask also, sir, whether Mr. Wadkiss, the tailor who, after years of faithful and more than ordinarily effective service, was on the same day and apparently for the same reason (whatever that was) summarily dismissed with us, may now also apply for work? Is there any animosity against him? Personally I feel that it would hardly be fair to reinstate us and to leave the poor tailor out in the cold. Is there any objection to his returning with us? I have a keen and grateful remembrance, sir, of generous warm-hearted sympathy openly and unhesitatingly given me without fear of consequences, by Mr. Wadkiss, at a time when I sorely needed it. I am bitterly grieved that he should suffer through any action of mine.

Let me now say a few words on the remainder of Messrs Compton's remarks which concern myself alone. I fully discussed and debated the point referred to by Mr. Compton with that gentleman on the day on which he kindly paid my fellow-workers and me an unexpected visit during which he politely referred to my letter writing to the papers. I am sorry that he is still sore on that point, sir, but I still adhere to the opinion I expressed to him then, that I have a right to make public any knowledge I possess, with the sanction of the Editor to whom I submit my information. I have a profound respect for the public press; I look upon it as the most powerful agent for good this country possesses; I am thankful that it is a free press, open to employed as well as to employers; and I am thankful that the *Chronicle* was open to me and willingly extended and still extends a powerful helping hand to oppressed factory girls.

As to complaining to the firm, I may as well confess, sir, that if I could begin at the beginning again, and were positive that the statement made by Mr. Compton were true – that I should not have been discharged – I should still prefer to exercise my undeniable right to write to you. And Mr. Compton will admit, that when he invited me to complain to him, I was not backward in doing so, so that he will give me credit for honesty of purpose. If I exercise my right to complain in any way which pleases me best, Mr. Compton will forgive me, and being a gentleman, will allow a lady to use her prerogative of having her own way.

And now, sir, may I state a comment on some beneficial results of my letters which I briefly referred to last week. It will be remembered that in one of my letters I asked for proof that no profit was made out of the materials supplied the factory hands. I asked to see the bills for the materials; because, as I had to earn the money to buy them I considered and still consider, that I had a right to know where every farthing of my money went, in this way as in the tea-money. In the latter case, it will be remembered, I was informed that my two-pence weekly went to buy china (which I do not possess) and to provide me with a tea once a year which, I admit, was a good tea, and which I enjoyed, though I did not know at the time that my money had helped to buy it. This was satisfactory in so far as I knew what was done with the profit, but in the case of the materials, while I was in the factory no proof was given that profit was not made.

The other week, however, considerable reductions were made in the charge for materials in the factory. Reels of silk for which I paid 1s 4d, I understand are now one shilling; skeins of thread which formerly were 1½d are now one penny; and a halfpenny in every two yards of two kinds of twist (for buttonholes) is allowed. These are reductions which anybody who has had to buy to use them will appreciate thoroughly. I calculate that at the very least it will mean an extra 10 shillings a year in the pocket of each girl. That will go a long way towards providing her with a much needed holiday once a year.

I rejoice with my late fellow-workers in this most appreciable concession, and if I had written for nothing else, my letters would be worth this alone, but I hope you will pardon me if I say that I am not satisfied yet. If I were working in the factory I should still want to know whether the present reduced price is the original one or whether it is only a reduction of profit. In the case of the reels of silk, I believe they can be procured in the town of Crewe at a less price even than that now charged in the factory, and it is only reasonable to suppose that the shop-keeper wants to make a little profit by which to live, which does not apply to Messrs Compton. So that I should not be satisfied yet. And I cannot help wondering, sir, whether Messrs Compton have suddenly obtained the materials at a greatly reduced rate? Or whether the price formerly charged was with the addition of profit on the original? If the latter, whom did the profit benefit? Was it returned to us in some appreciable way, as in the china and sugar basins, or what became of it? I hope I am not of an insatiably curious disposition, but these thoughts certainly occur to me, and if I were working in the fac-tory, I should want to know something about these points, and if I wrote to the *Chronicle* and you, sir, recognised the justice of my enquiries, I should still consider that I was acting within my rights in publicly making my wishes known.

Now, sir, it stands proved that profit was made out of the materials and tea-money, despite the emphatic denial of the manager. I ask if for that reason alone, to say nothing of the wretched prices paid for the work and the vicious system of favourites, I was not justified in writing to the press? And what might not the girls effect if they would all organise and stand shoulder to shoulder in a resolute body? I wished to-day to have referred to the Truck Act, and its application to the deduction for materials, for tea-money, for the sick club, and for breakages of machinery, which I understand is also a practice in Messrs Compton's factory. But as I should like to go into it again as well and as fully as I can, and have already, I am afraid, occupied considerable space, I think I had better leave it to-day, and will beg you to favour me again, sir. Perhaps next week, if you can give me space. It is a subject well worth the attention of my readers.

Thanking you for space, I am, sir,
Yours sincerely,
Ada Nield
Crewe Chronicle, 22 September 1894

Sketches and Stories

The Charwoman (A True Story)

I have known Mrs. W. nine years. She introduced herself to me, at the same time asking if I could give her some sewing to do for my small daughter. At that time her husband was a stoker at the Gas Works, earning £1 a week, and she had six children, not one of whom was old enough to work. She confessed herself unable to make the £1 keep all eight of them, for they were all 'hearty' and 'his' work was hard, so of course he needed 'something tasty'. So she made garments for anybody who would give her any to make; and took in as much washing as she could squeeze in, along with the multifarious jobs which 'doing for' eight of them entailed. About this time I went to live outside the town, in a hamlet containing only nine houses, all told. To reach our habitation, after leaving the country highway, it was necessary to cross three fields, no light journey in the winter months. The supply of women's labour in this part of the country is scarcely equal to the demand; consequently charwomen could not be lured into taking a long and disagreeable journey before beginning a hard day's work, and I fear I should have been compelled to do my own charring if Mrs. W. had not come to my aid. She suffered from disadvantages as well as I. She had a houseful of children whom she had to see off to school, and dinner to prepare for them all before she could go out to work, which made her so late that most posts were closed to her. So we agreed to put up with drawbacks on both sides, and for several years she helped me over different places in that part of my life which is occupied with housekeeping.

In all that time her spirit of cheer and goodwill burned with

135

a steady flame, and never once did it even waver. She much enjoyed telling me how she had contrived a tasty bit for 'him' and a nourishing dinner for the children out of next to nothing; or that she had done the baking last night before she had finished the washing. So that now there was a pan full of bread again. 'But it won't last long,' she would say with a cheerful laugh. She would explain that 'do what she would' she found that all her husband's wages went on food (2s 6d each per week on food!) and that she had to 'do a bit' to provide the rent, coals, light and clothes. She was an inveterate frequenter of jumble sales, and would give me glowing descriptions of the wonderful bargains she had picked up for a few pence; and no woman in the town knew better than she where 'bits' could be 'picked up cheap'. She never once regarded it as a hardship that she should have to help to earn the money to keep the house as well as to look after it; but was always buoyed up with the prospect of a good time coming when 'our Mary' would be old enough to earn. And then the others would soon follow. That was the best of having them so quickly – they were all ready to work at once. The only bit of her life which she was ever disposed to look upon as a hardship was when her husband occasionally got drunk. But even this she took in true philosophical spirit, evidently looking upon it as an incident in the possession of a husband as inevitable as the acquiring of children. And I always had the feeling that the dressing down she never failed to give him, so soon as he had recovered sobriety of outlook, more than repaid her for the pinching (of herself, never of him or the children) which his indulgence entailed on her. She would tell me with a twinkle in her eye, how she had 'laid it on' – that the money he had spent would have bought 'our Tommy' a pair of trousers or 'our Jim' a pair of boots (she did not tell him that they would get the trousers and boots somehow, or their mother would know the reason why); and how he had quailed before the storm of her logic and reason, expressing his deep contrition in abject submission, and giving her a solemn promise that it should never happen again. She would look at me and smile sceptically as she reported this oft-repeated promise, but these confidences were never given in a complaining spirit; on the contrary, they were reported as cheerfully as all the rest of the happenings of her varied life. Even the coming of another child, and the ninth mouth to feed, never clouded her serenity. She worked cheerfully up to the day of its birth, and then brought it with her when she came back to work.

Then the long-looked-for day came when Mary was old enough for half-time, and later for full-time, [work] and soon she was earning as much as her mother could earn, and never was mother so proud and pleased. And this brought the day when her willing service for me came to an end. For she was a true home-maker and home-lover, and had never been under any illusion as to the loss to her husband and children of her wage-earning outside.

But those years of mutual help created a bond between Mrs. W. and myself, and she often comes to see me, and has never failed to inform me of fresh developments in the family fortunes. In this way I have learnt of the continued improvement following the entry of each child into the labour market (she has now four old enough to work). In the old days she could never afford anything new for herself, and was always dressed in secondhand bargains picked up at jumble sales; but of late she has been so smartly dressed that I have had difficulty in recalling my old-time friend; and she tells me proudly of the cost of 'our Jim's' new suit, or 'our Mary's' new dress. The increase of family income was quickly followed by migration from the cheap and nasty house which had been their home in her charring days; and she duly came to tell me about the acquisition of the new suite for the new front bedroom, of which she was now the proud possessor.

A few months back she came full of excitement and brimming with news. What did I think? Her husband was going to Australia. I gasped. 'Oh, how will you like that?' I asked. 'Oh, I'm not going – not yet,' she replied. Then it all came out. They have a relative out there who had kept writing to tell them to come, but now he had promised not only to help them to get work, but had actually sent passage money for the husband and eldest boy. So the two of them were off on a date not too far distant. 'But what will you do?' I asked. 'Oh!' she replied as cheerfully as of old – for all the world as if a woman could ask for no better fate – 'I shall go into a smaller house and shall start working again.'

At various stages of further development she has come to report progress. They had sold the suite, and the extra bed, and all the furniture which could be dispensed with, because of course 'he' and the boy needed a lot of clothes and 'all sorts of things' which the money thus obtained had procured for them. Next they had moved into a smaller house. Next the husband had sailed, and she was left to face the world with her six remaining children, three of whom were still too young to work. But such is her unfailing optimism, she confided in me that when she has got a sufficient amount of work she does not expect to be much worse off, because 'he' always had to have better food than the others, and lately the boy had expected to have everything the father had; and then the younger children who work had not seen why they should not share equally and she had been hard put to it to keep the peace. And now without any bad example to undermine her influence, they could all rough it together. She once more feels that the ship is under control, and has never a doubt of her ability to navigate it safely to its journey's end. Nor have I any doubt, either.

And the journey's end? She looked forward without misgiving but with positive eagerness, to taking her children to the Antipodes in twelve months' time, or as soon as any sort of home is ready for her, and never doubts that the new life will be all that her fancy imagines it.

The old country is afraid to trust such gallant women as she with a vote. The Commonwealth is wiser. And though she will add one more to the growing list of my friends who persist in placing the high seas between themselves and me, yet I cannot but rejoice that she is going where she will be estimated a little nearer to her true worth than she is in England.

Common Cause, 21 September 1911

Making It Stretch (A True Story)

It was breakfast time Friday morning. Mrs. Worth's brow was puckered into a frown as she rushed about performing her usual morning jobs. It was nearly time for her husband to come in for breakfast, and before he left again she had a disagreeable job to perform. He did not receive his wages till Friday teatime, and the dreadful fact was that she was spent up, and had not one farthing with which to buy the dinner.

True, the little shop at the corner would trust her till night, and she debated with herself which was easiest – to ask at the shop or to ask her husband. But she knew that the only way to get along at all was to pay her way as she went, and then out of next week's wages there wouldn't be a penny to pay for this week's debts. And her husband was so rich! If only she had four shillings a week all for herself! Little Franky wouldn't have to be wearing those thin vests in this cold weather; and Lily could have a good warm frock for school! She sighed as she thought of all the comforts she could get for the children if only she had an allowance *all for herself* as her husband insisted on having for himself. No, she must get the dinner out of him somehow.

A little later he and the four children – aged respectively nine, seven, five and three – were seated round the breakfast table. The children breakfasted on bread dipped in bacon fat. The man of course had most of the bacon. Mrs. Worth's breakfast was made of what remained, and she took it in the intervals of attending to the wants of the others.

Now for the plunge!

'Bill,' said she, 'lend us a shilling. I'm spent up.'

Bill snorted. 'What, again!' said he. 'You're always spent up. Twenty-two shillings a week to do as you like with, and never a Friday comes but you're on to me for some more. Sometimes it doesn't wait till Friday, and you're spent up on Thursday or even Wednesday. If I'd nothing else to do but

139

spend the money somebody else earned, I'd see if I couldn't make it do.'

Mrs. Worth fought with a rising lump in her throat.

'Well now, Bill,' said she with ominous quietness, 'you've said that to me a good many times lately. I'd like you to try, and to show me how to do better. I'd be only too glad to learn. So suppose you try, just for one month. You keep all your earnings and spend them all – except your own four shillings, which of course you'll spend on yourself as usual – and you'll be able to keep it intact when you haven't got me to ask for any of it. Of course, I shall keep doing my work just as usual, and I'll help you with advice; but I don't spend it – you do that.'

'All right, it's a bargain,' said Mr. Worth gaily, as he rose to go back to work. 'Here's your shilling, and to-night I'll keep the lot. I'll bet I shall have more than four shillings for myself next week!'

Mrs. Worth indulged in many a quiet chuckle as she went about her Friday's cleaning. After tea that night she said: 'Are you going to do the buying in, Bill? If you are, it's time to be off.'

'Why, what's wanted?' asked Bill.

'Well, I always buy as much flour and groceries as will last the week on Friday nights.'

'Well, how much is that?'

She produced pencil and paper. 'Flour, fifteen pounds, 1s 7½d; butter, one pound, Irish, 1s 2d; margarine, 6d; bacon, 9d; cheese, 5d; lard, 4d; soda, 1d; washing powder, 1½d; starch, 1d; blue, ½d; blacklead, 1d; donkey stone [for whitening doorsteps and windowsills], 1d; rice, 2d; vinegar, 1d; sugar, 7½d – 7s 4d altogether. And half a pound of tomatoes for the children's breakfast – 7s 6d. I'll fetch them – or are you going?'

Mr. Worth indulged in his favourite snort.

'No,' he said; 'paying's enough. Here you are,' handing her the exact amount.

Before she was ready to go, the rent man called.

'Four and nine, Bill,' she reminded him. It was produced.

Whilst his wife was out Mr. Worth was obliged to answer another knock at the door. Trade Union this time. Another fourpence gone.

Yet another knock. On other Friday nights Mrs. Worth had left books and money ready on the table, and the people simply came in, recorded the transaction, took the money, and left, without any trouble to Mr. Worth. To-night the books were there as usual, but the men looked to Mr. Worth for an explanation of the omission of the money.

Well, who was this man? Insurance against death, eh? The man informed him that all the family were insured – six of them – sixpence.

Mr. Worth paid it, asking himself angrily if it was a necessary drain on his pocket. He reflected, however, that any of them might die any minute, and he knew his wife had not saved anything – for was she not worrying him for money every week? – so how in the world would they be buried if the insurance man wasn't paid? He prepared to go out, and was just ready when his wife came in with her load of foodstuffs.

'You'd better leave the money for the chips for supper, Bill,' said she.

He flung the twopence down on the table, and left without a word.

Saturday, breakfast time.

'There's milk money this morning, Bill,' Mrs. Worth reminded her husband. 'It's one and tuppence.'

'Couldn't you do with less milk than that?' he growled. 'What do you do with it?'

'We drink it all at breakfast, tea and supper,' she answered. 'I often grudge the money, but when you remember that there's six cups a day to be filled at least twice a day, and some of them filled twice (Bill himself always had three cups) and that milk's so good for children, a pint a day's not much.'

He produced the money.

'And there's to-day's dinner. Shall we have some kippers? They're cheap.'

'Let's have 'em then, for goodness' sake. How much?'

'Threepence ha'penny.'

141

It was forthcoming.

Dinnertime.

'I shall want the money for to-morrow's meat, Bill, and for potatoes and cabbage, and some apples for a pie; there's your two papers to pay for.'

'Well, how much?'

'Meat, three pounds at 4½d, 1s 1½d; twelve pounds potatoes, 6d; cabbage, 2d; and papers, 2d. Willie and Maggie both want a pair of stockings, 6½d a pair; 3s 0½d altogether.'

'Can't you mend their stockings?'

For answer she brought out two pairs of stockings and held them before him silently. Even his masculine eyes could see that it was beyond even feminine skill to mend what did not exist, and there were literally no feet and very little leg left to the stockings. But his stock of money was going at an alarming rate, and he clung tenaciously to what remained.

'Well, what have they on? Won't those do?'

She called the children and took off their clogs. He produced the money.

A knock at the door.

'It's the clothing club man, Bill,' she explained, producing the card and looking to him for the money.

'How much?'

'A shilling.'

It was produced. When the man had gone: 'I never in my life saw a woman with so many clubs and so many ways of spending money. What's he for?'

'Well, we're paying for your boots now. How could I buy anything which costs a lot of money at once if I didn't buy it that way? I try to pay him more than a shilling if I can, and we shall have to pay him more than that because the children want new coats for the winter; but I made up my mind to give you as easy a time as I could this week, so am only asking for what we *must* have.'

He went off to the football match. A man needed a bit of distraction. To work all the week to get the money, and then to have his head worried off about spending it! He came home for tea, finding bread and butter cut, and the teapot ready for filling.

'What's for tea?' he asked. 'It's hungry working standing outside all afternoon.'

'Some fried fish?' she suggested. 'Pickled herrings?'

'Aye, pickled herrings,' he agreed. 'Let's have something tasty.'

She told the eldest child to fetch them. 'Father'll give you the money.'

'How much?'

'Twopence-ha'penny.'

After tea he went out again, and did not return until eleven o'clock, when he found his wife sewing. He was feeling much refreshed by his evening in congenial company, and inclined to be good-humoured.

'What in the world are you doing?' he asked. 'Never saw such creatures as women. They're never right unless they're making work. There's no need for 'em to be always at it – but they will be. They like it. Well, no accounting for tastes.'

Mrs. Worth had not had the stimulus of contact with congenial minds, and was in no mood for levity.

'Well,' she said bitterly, 'I do like to see the children with decent clothes on their backs, and just now Albert Victor's only got one shirt. If I'd been spending the money this week, I might have been tempted to spend 10½d on buying him another; as it is, I've washed it out since he went to bed, and now I'm mending it. Couldn't do it before because it wasn't dry. And I'll bet Mrs. Matchett (next door neighbour) notices it isn't out drying next washing day, and will know I haven't another to put on his back.'

Mr. Worth got the paper to read whilst finishing his supper of bread and cheese. His wife's conversation was becoming daily less interesting.

Mrs. Worth managed until Monday at teatime without asking for any more money. Then, after her husband had eaten up the remains of the meat which had served for Sunday's and Monday's dinners, she said:

'We shall have to have something for dinner to-morrow, Bill. It's baking day, so I'd better make a potato pie.'

'All right. Potato pie'll do grand.'

'It'll take at least fourpence ha'penny for meat, or else you'll say you have to smell at the meat and make up with potatoes. And we shall have to have some more apples; and if I had a jar of jam I could make a jam roll for pudding after the potato pie. When you are baking it's best to do it all at once to save the fire, and I've had to burn so much to-day with having to dry all the things inside, that I shall have to save at some other end; and that reminds me, the coal-man comes on Tuesdays, so I shall want the money for coal. I *can't* manage with less than two bags a week. And now it's a shilling a bag. Everything's going up – only wages!'

Mr. Worth snorted.

'How much?' he asked.

'Meat, 5d; apples, 2d; jam, 4½d; coal, 2s. Oh there's the yeast for making the bread, 2d; 3s 1½d altogether. And you'd better put a shilling away for the gas bill. It's to pay in three weeks' time and it's 2s 10½d. I always have to save up a bit before it's due.'

Now Mr. Worth had separated his own 4 shillings from the 22 shillings which was his wife's, and which he was now spending for her, and he found that he had not enough to supply her present requirements from the legitimate fund. So he was compelled to dip into his own perquisite to the tune of 2½d. And this was only Monday! And yet she seemed only to be getting necessaries. Oh confound it! If a chap must work all day, and then worry all night about spending his money, life wasn't worth living.

Wednesday morning, breakfast time.

'I could have eaten a bit more bacon, lass,' said Mr. Worth. 'One slice between two of us!' (He had not noticed that his wife had not taken her usual share.)

'Well, if you'll buy some more!' said she. 'But there are only two slices left out of the pound, and there's to-morrow morning and Friday morning yet!'

He wished he had not spoken.

'Is there nothing left?' he growled.

'Out of a potato pie divided by six?' she asked. 'Pork and onions? Liver and bacon? Stewed meat and onions? Broth?'

'Which is cheapest?' he asked.

'Oh, broth,' she replied. 'But you know you are not satisfied with broth and nothing else.'

He could not deny it.

'Well,' he said irritably, 'what would you do?'

'I should very likely get a taste for you and broth for the children,' answered his wife.

'Well, *how much*?'

'Bones and vegetables for broth, 3d; liver and bacon for you –'

'Let's have some pork,' he interrupted, 'it's tasty.'

'Well, pork, 4½d; 10d altogether. And a quarter of suet for a meat pie to-morrow – a shilling.'

He produced it.

Tea-time, same day.

'Why is there never anything good for tea?' asked Mr. Worth. 'You might get one a bit of fish or something. How would you like to be working all day, and then come home to bread and but – margarine? Yes, you've actually put margarine on *my* bread!'

'Well, the butter's all gone,' she answered.

He commanded his eldest daughter to fetch him some chips and fish.

'This everlasting mither about food's enough to drive a chap mad,' he said after tea.

'Bill, Franky'll have to have some new clogs. Look here.'

The dilapidated clogs were examined by the father. He swore under his breath.

'*How much*?' aloud.

'Two shillings. And Albert Victor's'll have to be mended. I'll take 'em when I fetch Franky's. Albert Victor'll have to wear his best shoes while they're being mended, and I shouldn't wonder if he ruins *them*!'

Mr. Worth went out. Thank goodness a chap could get out sometimes and forget his troubles.

Thursday morning.

'I shall have to have 3½d for meat to put in the suet pudding, Bill,' said Mrs. Worth. 'And the potatoes are nearly done – two pounds, 1d.'

The 5½d was produced.

At tea-time Mr. Worth spent the remainder of his week's wage – his wife's share and his own combined – on a relish for his tea.

Friday morning.

'What shall we have for dinner to-day?' asked Mrs. Worth. 'Oh damn the dinner!' answered her husband.

He reflected, however, that he would soon be turning his job over to her (thank goodness!) and as he had a few pence left over from his last week's allowance, he might as well spend it on the dinner.

'We may as well have a bit of fish; 5d will do. And there's Franky's clogs. They'll be about 10d, I expect.'

Now Mr. Worth did not possess 1s 3d, so he said, 'Franky's clogs must wait.'

At tea-time the same day he put down 22 shillings on the table, and said, 'Here you are, lass, you can have your job back; I've had enough.'

'Nay,' she replied firmly. 'You took it on for a month, Bill, and you'll have to do it for a month. By that time you'll know enough as to how I spend your money to prevent your wondering about it any more. You'll have to stick to your bargain.'

Mr. Worth spent less on himself during the next three weeks than he had ever done!

He has never since asked his wife what she does with the money. Indeed, he avoids the subject.

But he still keeps four shillings a week for himself.

When asked how he could reconcile this with his conscience, he replied, 'Nay, she must do as she likes. I married her to manage, and she must manage.'

Common Cause, 5 and 12 October 1911

The Pottery Worker (A True Story)

In one of the 'Five Towns', a portion of England made familiar to book-lovers by Arnold Bennett, is a long street. Every house in that street is just like every other house, and the next street is like it, and so is the one after that. Nearly every street is like it, and so are most of the streets in the other four towns. And as the towns merge into one another without a break for nearly seven miles in length, the general effect of dreariness and monotony is not lost for want of iteration.

Mrs. Evans is not conscious of her surroundings as constituting a grievance, however, for her mind is constantly preoccupied with weightier matters.

It was February, and a cold rain penetrated through her thin jacket, and through her still thinner shoes, as she hurried to the 'pot bank' to begin her day's work.

Her meditations were nearly always on one theme; and that is how to 'keep a roof over the children's heads', to get them enough to eat day by day without the help of the 'parish', which is the deepest disgrace she knows. Was it only thirteen years – it seems a hundred – since that good-looking lad – Bill Evans – came a-courting her? Ah! he was different then from the husband of later years! But conscience pricked. *Was* he so different? Was he not even then notorious for losing jobs? True, he had always a satisfactory reason, which she, poor fool, had believed then, before she knew any better.

He could not stand the foreman, or somebody had wanted to 'put on him', and they would find 'Bill Evans didn't take things lying down'. They did, and the result·was that eventually nobody would give him a job, which he took as a special distinction, and quite sufficient reason for loafing about expatiating on his martyrdom to anyone who would listen, whilst she went to work. He had always liked a 'glass', and, of course, when he had nothing to do, he got into bad company, and

147

liked more than one glass. Those were dreadful days!

Her mother minded her babies (she had three, and five in the churchyard), and at this time she had nearly all her meals at her parents'. But even so, they had got into debt, and the landlord had 'sold them up', and she had seen all her little household goods knocked down at auction. Then they had all come to live with her parents – and there were continual 'rows'! For her father was in the habit of 'speaking his mind' to his son-in-law, and the latter considered himself a much injured individual in having to 'pig among this lot', as he put it.

This horrible life lasted two or three years, and then Bill took himself off. He had gone off several times, threatening never to come back. He knew she was 'soft' where he was concerned, and that he'd make her squirm with a threat of leaving her – in those days! But now he really went; and for a time they were quite comfortable, with her father's and her brother's and her own wage. Then her father fell ill, six years ago now, and the doctor ordered him to the workhouse infirmary. This was a staggering blow, but owing to the demands of herself and others on them, the old folks had not been able to save, and they had to submit. Her father died – at the workhouse! Her mother had never looked up properly since, and the disgrace was a bitter pill. Later Bill turned up and said he was going to turn over a new leaf. Mrs. Evans' brother, aged fifteen, asked her why she had not shown him the door, and told her that if she was going to 'take up with that wastrel again,' he (her brother) was 'cutting off'. But her mother had an old-fashioned idea that the house and all its contents belonged to the man of the family by natural right, and told her she'd have to put up with him – she'd made her bed and must lie on it.

Mrs. Evans herself is a more modern product than this, and had a sneaking idea that if she 'had had the pluck of a mouse' she would have sent him off with a flea in his ear. But she never had any pluck where Bill was concerned! And he had said that he was different now, and it was such a hard job to keep them all now that father was gone!

Alas! for her hopes. Bill stayed a few weeks and actually got a job, and brought her a week's wages. Then one night he came across an old pal who 'treated' him. Next morning he was too tired to go to work. Tired men not being in request his name was 'Walker' again. For a few months he hung about and did a few odd jobs, and sponged on her and on her brother, the only other breadwinner in the house. Then one day her mother told him he'd have to stir up a bit, for Mary (Mrs. Evans) was going to have another, and if he didn't do something she'd have to go to the workhouse to be confined, and they'd be lucky if they didn't all have to go, for goodness knew what was to become of them without her wages!

So Bill made himself scarce again, and from that day to this they'd never seen top nor tail of him.

They got through somehow. One after another of the household goods had found its way to 'uncle's' [the pawnbroker's], and that they escaped the help of the hated 'parish' is a source of continual satisfaction.

Now both brothers were working, and with Mrs. Evans' wages averaging from ten shillings to twelve and sixpence a week, they were quite respectably well off — till that February day which had so much to add to their tale of experience.

Mrs. Evans, in order to earn her 12s 6d a week, worked in one of the dangerous processes of pottery manufacture. Many are the processes through which these articles of daily use have to pass between the conditions antecedent to the 'clay' stage, and the highly glazed and polished stage in which they reach the homes and institutions of the homeland and the lands beyond the seas. But Mrs. Evans got them when they left the dipper, who is usually a man. In the 'biscuit' stage they are brought to him, and with practised rapidity he dips them into a tub containing a mixture in which there is a percentage of lead. A girl takes them from him; then Mrs. Evans and her work-fellows get them and clean them with a sponge ready for the oven. All the workers in that 'dipping house' have more or less knowledge that they are risking health and perhaps life itself, while they handle the articles dipped into that deadly

149

tub; but the knowledge causes them little alarm, and they take their chances just as stoically as does the engine driver, the miner, or the expectant mother. This particular day was inspection day, and Mrs. Evans presented herself with others, to the certifying surgeon for another guarantee of fitness to encounter the daily risk. She dreaded this ordeal, for sometimes the doctor asked awkward questions, and she was afraid to death that he would find out that she often 'felt bad', and would be thinking that she would be better 'out of the lead'.

But that morning she 'passed' once more and assured herself with a sigh of relief that she was safe for another month.

She hurried home through the rain and the cold wind for her dinner of bacon and potatoes, and a cup of tea to make you feel 'puti' [lively] again. She dried her two and eleven halfpenny shoes and her thin cotton stockings whilst taking her dinner, and was just raising her cup to her mouth when – crash! went the cup and the tea all over her skirt. They were all startled, and her mother rated her for her carelessness and reminded her that she had done that same trick pretty often lately, and pots cost money! But Mrs. Evans did not let her mother see her face at this moment, and was glad that she (her mother) had no practical experience of wristdrop. So she bent down to pick up the pieces, and by the time they were carried out she was able to smile at her own stupidity and agree with her mother that she did not deserve more tea.

But on the way back to work, out of observation range, her face took on an air of gravity, and her eyes had a haunted look. Her thoughts took a shape which made every sensitive nerve quiver, and she shrank shuddering from a prospect which her fears opened out as ominously imminent.

Surely it could not be! Might she not then even be allowed to work for her children? No thought of the personal bodily suffering in store for her crossed her mind. But the children! And her poor mother! Would it have to be the hated workhouse for them all after all? After all their struggles and after having kept clear of the parish – except for poor father (ah, what a sting that is).

She donned overall and respirator, and worked steadily for an hour when – whatever was the ghastly pain which – ! Thought and speech fled before the monster which gripped her vitals, and she swooned. When she 'came to' she was in a cab with two fellow-workwomen, who were watching her with anxious, compassionate eyes.

Poor old mother! Her eyes had not yet wept tears enough, and there was another burden to lay on her frail shoulders. But the women were full of the milk of human kindness, and they helped Mrs. Evans on to the 'squab' [a rough kind of sofa bed]; and one ran for the doctor, and the other helped the old mother to rub the seat of the pain with turpentine.

The agony of lead colic defies description, and we will draw a veil over the sufferings of the next hour or two, till the 'doctor's stuff' began to take effect.

The neighbours came in to proffer sympathy and help to Mrs. Evans' mother after the workmates left. They were all sorry, but work was waiting at the 'pot bank', and every minute spent away from it meant less of the necessities of life at the weekend. They knew lead poisoning is usually a long business; but they did not remind Mrs. Evans or her mother of this. Instead, they bade them look on the bright side; and remember that there would be half wages as compensation. . . .

Mrs. Evans had to manage on half-wages over a year. But they did not have to call in the help of the 'parish'. To the end of her life she will suffer the effects of that year's illness. But she is deeply thankful to be able in spite of her disability to earn ten shillings a week at another branch of pottery manufacture.

Common Cause, 4 January 1912

All in the Day's Work: Mrs. Turpin

The clock strikes – *what* is it striking? Mrs. Turpin stirs uneasily, and again sinks back into slumber. But the last strokes penetrate the enveloping cloud of sleep, and recall her from a dream, wherein she is vainly seeking two of her children who had followed her into the train for a certainty, and yet, though the train had never stopped, and she had never taken her eyes off them, had mysteriously disappeared. Hark! the clock! Awake now and certain it had struck eleven times. Out of bed and scanning it frantically. It is not so bad as she feared. But it is *eight* o'clock. Eight, and to get through comfortably she ought never to be later than seven. How she will have to fly! How *could* she have slept so long? A glance at the sleeping baby in the orange box beside the bed. How cross he has been all night, bless him! It's his teeth, of course. How sick she feels, and for a moment sits on the bed, while all 'goes black'. Nothing new, however, and soon shaken off. Three minutes past eight. Her clothes are thrown on with lightning speed, and three schoolchildren have been wakened, the fire is lit and the kettle 'on'. Five minutes more suffices to 'wash the sleep out of her eyes' and 'straighten her hair'. By a quarter past, the bit of bacon for father and the boy who works is frizzling merrily in the Dutch oven before the fire; the children are downstairs, and she is buttoning on garments, and washing faces and combing hair, and putting out cups and saucers, making the tea, and turning the bacon. A glance at the fire. No, it is too 'blazy' to make toast. She ought to have got up sooner. Now the poor kids will have to have bread and treacle, and they are so fond of toast and dripping! Hark! there's the baby! How is it that, however soundly he may be sleeping when she leaves him, some instinct always tells him when she is gone?

Upstairs and down again. Down he goes on to the sofa,

where he protests loudly at mother's summary treatment until beguiled into forgetfulness by his nine-year-old sister. Now in come father and boy, who have to be back at work at nine, so, of course, cannot wait. She pours out the tea (if only she had got up sooner she would have had time to have a cup herself, and then she wouldn't feel so sick), gives the man the major portion of the bacon, and the boy the remainder. The children look on longingly, but without protest. They are too well drilled in the laws of the Medes and Persians, that those who work must always have the best. Their mother dips a piece of bread in the bacon-fat and gives a portion to each, and the remainder of breakfast is made up with bread and treacle. There is ten minutes' rapid feeding, mother replenishing cups and plates with the baby under her arm. In the intervals she keeps a sharp look-out for little caps and coats, and is relieved to find that they are within sight and will not need hunting for. Out go father and boy, followed by schoolchildren. She breathes a sigh of relief. Ten minutes to nine. She must be quick about her own breakfast. Of course the tea is all gone, and she sighs again at her wastefulness and neglect in over-sleeping, so that she lost first chance at the teapot.

But she *must* make a drop of fresh tea, for it's no use, she cannot 'make do' till dinner-time on a drop of slop. She must put a bit less tea in the pot at tea-time that's all, for she can't afford even a ha'porth extra. She toasts some bread, which she eats dry because the butter shows signs of giving out before Friday, and there's no getting any more. She feels quite fresh after the cup of tea, though she drinks it milkless, because she cannot screw more than eight pints a week out of her husband's wages, and a pint a day and a quart on Sunday (1s 2d per week) is so little among seven of them, and the father and boy are working and the children are growing. A quarter past nine. She must get the baby washed and begin to see about dinner. What a good job she got the washing done yesterday, even though she did have to finish after the children had gone to bed and her husband had gone to his meeting.

Half past nine. The baby is washed and dressed, and willing

to sit on the hearthrug and amuse himself with such marvellous curiosities as an empty bobbin, a newspaper, and a clothes-peg. Thank goodness it's June, and likely to dry outside, for the coals are getting low, and it takes such a lot of fire to dry all the clothes inside. A quarter to ten. As much of the weekly wash as the little backyard will hold is pegged out, and the rest is hanging on the clothes-horse in front of the fire.

Ten o'clock. The dirty pots are all in the little scullery, but there's no time to wash up now, nor is there any time to go upstairs. Miss Seaton, who came hindering yesterday, asked if she knew that milk contained all the necessary elements to sustain life; and hoped she gave her children a good milk pudding every day. Of course she said 'Yes, 'm'; it was easiest to get rid of her that way, especially when you wanted to be getting on with your work; but she (Mrs. Turpin) would like to know where the quart of milk per day (and a quart wouldn't make a pudding big enough to feed her five – leaving out herself and the baby) was to come from. Two shillings a week for milk puddings, when all she had to do upon, all told, was 28 shillings per week!

A quarter past ten. Mrs. Turpin, baby in arms, is at the butcher's purchasing half a pound of pork steak, a penn'orth of suet, and a penn'orth of bones. At the greengrocer's next door she gets five pounds of potatoes, a penn'orth of onions, and a penn'orth of pot-herbs [a big handful of scraps of vegetables of all kinds]. On Monday nights, in this country town of about 60,000 inhabitants, not a hundred miles from Manchester, the butchers are all closed, having agreed to take Monday for their weekly half-holiday, else she might have slipped out last night and got the dinner materials all ready, to save time this morning. Not that she could have done so after all, for didn't it take till nearly ten o'clock to finish the washing? And if she had left that how much better off would she have been? The bones, pot-herbs, some lentils, beans and peas, which have been soaking all night, are at last all boiling together on the fire. What a long time it takes to make broth! Everything to be cut up, and washed, and bothered with. But it is so cheap, and nothing fills their bellies so easily.

Eleven o'clock. Well, what next? Why, that child, bless him! He may well roar! He wants to go to sleep, of course. By a quarter past eleven he is asleep on the sofa. Now there's the washing up. And if it isn't raining! And the clothes not half dry!

Half-past eleven. The clothes are hastily fetched in. Those from the clothes-horse are deposited on the sofa-end, and others are put on the horse and placed round the fire. How's the dinner getting on? Time to be doing the potatoes and onions.

Twelve o'clock already? Well, the jorum [large bowl] of potatoes is 'on', though it's a tight fit to make two pans go on the fire at once. Now it's time to put the onions to fry.

By a quarter past twelve the onions and pork are frizzling in the Dutch oven before the fire. Will there be time to wash up? Well, there'll have to be, for there are not enough pots for another meal. Oh, lor! the boiler's nearly empty. She must have forgotten to fill it up last night, having the washing to finish.

Half-past twelve. The boiler is filled, and she is washing up, and turning the pork and onions, and stirring the broth, and 'trying' the potatoes. In come the children, hungry and noisy, and of course the baby wakes. But the nine-year-old takes charge of him, and the six-year-old sets the table, and by twenty minutes to one, when father and boy come in, the potatoes are 'poured', onions and pork 'smell good', and all are ready to do justice to them. The washing up is not finished, but there are enough pots to be going on with, so be thankful. All get a jorum of broth and a lump of bread. Then follow potatoes for all, and pork and onions for father and boy; and potatoes with a 'taste' of onions, and some of the broth for gravy, for the others. Mrs. Turpin's husband adjures her to get a bit of pork for herself, but she doesn't want any (if there's a bit left it will do for his tea) and the broth's very good.

Twenty minutes past one. Dinner is over, and the potatoes, broth, and nearly a loaf of bread have disappeared; but they're all full, bless 'em, and what a good job it is they're all well and hearty! The father and boy go off to work again, and the nine-year-old clears the table, and adds the dirty dishes to those already in the scullery. Now it is time for the children to be off. Another scrubbing of dirty faces, another hunt for lost caps. The baby yells to go with them. It's dull for him left at home with only a busy mother who hasn't time to look at him, bless him! Quite a quarter of an hour passes in persuading him to forget his woes, in the examination of a miscellaneous collection of articles brought out for his benefit. At last he becomes absorbed in a cardboard box which has a fascinating way of opening and shutting, and his mother is at liberty to place the clothes-horse round the fire once more, and to hang out the sheets a second time, since now it is June again. Drat that boiler! the water's not hot enough to begin the washing up. Well, she must put the kettle on, and do something else till it's ready. Look what a hearth there is! So she 'straightens up' the kitchen-living-room, a room about ten feet square, and puts away all the litter which a crowd of children and a careless man are always making. Miss Seaton says you should always make children tidy up after themselves. So easy to talk! If you were doing fifty things at once all day long you'd find it hard work to be going round after the children as well. Trouble enough to keep their bellies filled and their backs clothed without worrying your head off about their leaving a few things about. The straightening is followed by a vigorous sweeping of the red and blue tiled floor, interspersed by many excursions to the baby, to restore his lost treasures and to persuade him to further exploration amongst them. The little grate, with its oven on one side and the domestic boiler on the other, receives a rapid polish, the cinders are riddled and put at the back of the fire, the stone hearth wiped, and the ashes carried out. A shake of the hearthrug, a rub of the fire-irons, a 'scuffle round' the Windsor chairs and the painted dresser with a duster, and Mrs. Turpin sighs with satisfaction as she evolves order out of chaos, and the little room is 'fit to be seen' again.

Three o'clock already? What next? He wants another sleep,

bless him! His mother is glad to sit down to 'get him off to sleep'. She feels 'a bit tired', and actually dozes. Oh, how she *could* sleep! She looks at the clock with a start. Twenty past! How stupid of her to doze! She rises heavily, and lays the child on the sofa again. Now she'd better get the beds made, while he's asleep. So she goes into the little lobby which leads to the front door, and up the narrow stairs opposite it, first into the front bedroom, over the little front parlour – the latter of which is Mrs. Turpin's pride and her exasperation, being of no use to the family since it is impossible to afford two fires, and she can't live in the front room because the grate is not adapted for family domestic requirements, and besides, it's too much of a job to carry every meal into a front room – and yet every other woman in the long street has just such another parlour, so Mrs. Turpin supposes she must be just like the rest, and keeps it to look at, and to clean. So she thinks, vaguely, as she makes her own bed and the baby's, and then goes into the bedroom over the living-room, where her two girls sleep, and later into the tiny room over the scullery, just large enough to hold the bed where the two boys sleep. She had meant to do one of the three bedrooms to-day. Too late now. But she *must* get it in to-morrow, somehow. Must think of a dinner which won't be so much trouble as broth. A good big hot-pot perhaps. But that doesn't half take a time to prepare, too, though it's no trouble when once you've got it into the oven. And she had meant to have a suet pudding because it fills them so, and 'sticks' so long. And she mustn't have a big fire to boil, and one under the oven as well. Well, she'll have to bake the suet pudding. They like it baked better than boiled (only it doesn't go so far baked as boiled), and with some treacle on the pudding and a bit of bacon to the hot-pot (potatoes and onions sliced and baked) they'll have a good dinner, and if she can only get time to chop the suet to-night it will give her a good 'leg up'. Kettle and boiler now promise enough water to wash up. She tackles this as noiselessly as possible, in order to avoid waking her small tyrant, and it is nearly half-past four before the job is finished, because you can't get on when you have to keep attending to drying garments, and when it begins to rain again and you have to leave your washing up to fetch in the sheets. She wonders if there'll be time to fold the clothes before tea. She had meant not only to fold but to iron as well, because 'he' hates her clanking irons about and 'messing' with clothes after he comes home at night. He thought she ought to do that whilst he was at work, or else 'leave it till to-morrow'. No use to tell him that to-morrow has already got some of to-day's work piled on its shoulders, and that every day is too short to contain its due quota of work.

By the time the pots and pans are put away and the scullery 'riddled', it is twenty minutes to five, and the baby wakes and greets his brothers and sisters with acclamation. They are all hungry again, and wishing mother would be quick and set tea. Mother is thankful to find that the clothes are dry at last, and she can take away the clothes-horse, which is universally and cordially detested. The six-year-old again sets the table. What about toast-and-dripping for tea? 'Oh yes!' greets this pro-position in a joyous chorus. There's no doubt they eat more bread (and, of course, more dripping) when it is toasted, but they like it so; and her mother's heart is still sore that 'laziness' compelled them to turn out this morning without it. And it hurts so to be always considering the amount they eat. A whole pile of toast-and-dripping is made, the tea is made, and they gather round once more. Mother is careful to pour out the tea, because the nine-year-old is so lavish with the sugar-basin and milk-jug, and it's less trouble to do it than to insist on the exact amount going into each cup. How she wishes she could give them milk, or at least half milk and half water, instead of all water with a taste of tea just to colour it, and a taste of milk. The rounds of toast disappear like magic, mother watching half in fear, half in joy. Then out they go for half an hour's play on the open space just at the end of the street before it gets dark. The nine-year-old takes out the baby, strictly adjured never to let him sit on a cold step, to 'mind his back', and never to leave him for a minute. As Mrs. Turpin watches them go, she thinks of what the lady who came to see her when the baby was born said – she 'must remember always to take him out at least once a day'. Wouldn't she like the chance to take him, that's all!

A glance at the clock. Nearly half-past five! She puts on the kettle again, puts the bit of pork to warm, and begins to toast more bread. There won't be enough meat for two, and she'll not have to 'let on' that she notices the boy's injured glances towards the favoured father. He has a good appetite, and toast-and-dripping will have to do for him to-night. By the time the man and boy come in through the back door, and have washed their hands, all is ready for them. She is 'itching' to get at the clothes whilst the children are all out, but she knows her husband feels aggrieved if she 'can't even sit still while he has a meal'; so she starts mending the stockings, the while she listens with unaffected interest to what has happened to her workers during the day. Tea over, she clears the table and washes up once more.

By this time it is half-past six, and in come the children. Now follows a difficult hour for her, when her sympathies are torn in two, and she is hard-driven to keep the peace. For the man is tired with his weary work on the railway and not inclined to excuse racket and row. And the children are all confined to one small room and always seem to find tormenting one another the most fascinating occupation. All the while she is folding clothes, and mending stockings, and nursing the baby, alter-nately. She cannot help feeling glad when her husband announces that he 'has another meeting on to-night'; for that means that she may mangle and iron without irritating him; or, as she puts it, 'in peace'. At last he is gone and the irons are 'down' and she starts the mangling. She mangles all the plain things, such as sheets and towels, and her own aprons, etc. But she has a foolish liking for seeing her girls go to school in ironed pinafores, and her boys in starched collars, and that makes a lot of ironing. But never mind as long as she can get a chance to do it. By eight o'clock the mangling is done and the things are hung up to air on the clothes-horse, and now it is time to put the children to bed. She is feeling a bit cross by now, and they

159

hear some home truths, and get short shrift as she bundles them off. Half-past eight and they are all in bed except the elder boy, who is allowed till half-past nine – even the baby, who has 'gone off' with less trouble than usual. Time for the ironing, at last. She first starches the collars, rather a delicate process. Mrs. Masters, next door, has only one child, and sends her husband's collars to the laundry. She wouldn't be able to do it if she had five! An hour-and-a-half of steady ironing, only interrupted once by the teething baby. Done, at last! And the collars, and curtains, and pinafores, and sheets, are all hanging to air. Now, what next? The six-year-old's stockings to mend, for the hole shows every time she steps. And that boy has torn his breeches again! Here is the patch she put on last week, torn half off! Her husband comes in before she has finished, and teases her about being 'so fond of work'. But he good-naturedly gets a 'bit of supper' ready, and her heart glows with gratitude. Some bread and cheese and a cup of cocoa, and soon after eleven she is in bed once more.

Mrs. Turpin is tired.

She will be tired to-morrow morning when she rises, but she will gallantly face another day, much like to-day.

But it is said that she 'has no interest in public questions', and 'does not want a vote'.

Every day Mrs. Turpin solves a problem by reason of her experience of life and her heroic devotion to duty, which has hitherto baffled civilised Governments. She brings up her children on a sum which housekeepers on a large scale, with their advantages of buying in bulk, find totally inadequate to such results as she produces. The whole fabric of the State rests on the work she is doing, yet she is considered incapable or unworthy of expressing an opinion on affairs in which she is expert. So long as she is excluded, the Government will continue to 'muddle through somehow' in their domestic legislation.

The Englishwoman, July 1912

All in the Day's Work: Mrs. Bolt

A glorious summer morning. Five sonorous strokes from the Town Hall clock. The stone-flagged streets of a factory town in North-East Lancashire already show signs of life. From the electric tram depot one car after another comes forth to carry its human burdens to their daily toil. Here and there a man may be seen carrying a long pole, having a kind of mop made of thin wires at one end. Up and down the long street he goes, stopping here and there, in some streets at nearly every house, and applying his mop to the bedroom window-pane. A rattling hail-storm of sound results, calculated to wake the dead.

Mrs. Bolt lives in the middle of one of these long streets, and is fast asleep when the 'knocker-up' applies his instrument to her window-pane. Morning already! It's only a minute since she came to bed! But there is no time to lie; for there's a lot to do between now and six o'clock, when she is due at the factory doors.

'Fred,' says she, nudging with her elbow the sleeping man at her side, who had opened his eyes drowsily at the familiar noise on the window-pane, and then had turned over with a grunt. 'Fred, ger up! It's time to be off!' Another grunt from Fred.

Meanwhile she is dressing. She goes down the narrow, crooked stairs, leading into the back kitchen, which is about two yards wide and three yards long, in which is the set-pan [a boiler for washing clothes], the mangle, and the sink, which is of stone, like the flagged floor and the little back yard. On the slop-stone is a gas-ring, on which Mrs. Bolt places the little enamel kettle. She then washes her face in the back kitchen, but she does not take out her curling-pins. What's the good of bothering with your hair to go to the factory?

She then goes into the front-room, about four and a half yards square, which opens directly onto the street. It is Friday, the weekly 'siding-up' day; so she blackleads the bars of the grate, which is of the kitchen range type, a large oven for bread-baking on one side and a boiler on the other. Next she lays the fire, ready to light at tea-time. By the time she has done this, it is nearly half-past five, and after making a 'sup o' tay', she goes upstairs. Fred is summoned again from the land of slumber, and five minutes later follows her downstairs, yawning sleepily, as he, too, swills his face at the slop-stone.

A gill-pot of tea, 'sugared and milked', is ready for him by the time he has donned jacket, cap, and the woollen scarf which he wears winter and summer alike. They stand – there's no time to sit – drinking the tea, blowing it till it cools. Then she pins her factory shawl under her chin, and takes up two other shawls which lie ready on a chair. She hands one to her husband, as they both go upstairs and into the back bedroom, over the scullery. In the bed in this room lie their two children. The five-year-old lies with arms stretched out above his head, smiling as he dreams. The two-year-old has kicked off every bit of clothing; he opens his eyes as his mother picks him up and wraps him in the shawl, but is asleep again in a moment. The elder boy does not wake as his father wraps him in the other shawl and follows his mother downstairs. As they pass through the front room the man picks up a square tin containing the food for their breakfast, and two cans in which to make their breakfast tea; and Mrs. Bolt takes a bundle which contains the children's clothing. Her husband locks the door, and they hurry along the street, which now resounds with a clatter of clogs and is alive with old men and women, young men and maidens, boys and girls. Mr. and Mrs. Bolt meet many with similar burdens, on their way to the electric cars. On the opposite side of the main road is a street the exact replica of the one in which they live. Mrs. Earnshaw, who 'minds' their children, is up, and of course is expecting them, but there is no time to waste on words.

In this town the finishing stage of cotton manufacturing is done, so all the factories are 'weaving sheds', and nearly all the operatives, men and women alike, are cotton weavers; there is almost no other industry in the town. Mr. and Mrs. Bolt work at the same factory, and both are paid at the same rate. Both 'mind' four looms, and therefore are doing exactly the same work. The factory is five minutes' walk along the main road and down a side street, and they arrive just as the last whistle blows. The engine has already started, and as they enter the factory a deafening roar greets their ears.

Mrs. Bolt's looms are on one side of the factory and her husband's on the other. She threads her way through closely packed looms, by a passage-way wide enough for one person only, and soon her shuttles are adding their quota of sound, and the lengths of sheeting in her looms begin their day's growth under her watchful eye. The machine needs continuous feeding, and Mrs. Bolt's job is to replace, ever and always, the cops of cotton inside the shuttles. A cop lasts about three minutes, so Mrs. Bolt has not much idle time in keeping her four looms supplied.

Breakfast time, eight o'clock. The whistle blows. Each weaver releases the 'knocker-on' on each loom, the steam goes off, and a heavenly peace descends. Mrs. Bolt joins others who are going to the copper boiler, for boiling water for breakfast, for which each operative pays a penny a week. She fills her own and her husband's can, in which she has already placed the milk and sugar, and carries them back to her looms, where she finds her husband awaiting her. They sit on turned-up weft-cans, and eat their breakfast of bread and butter, between the slices of which are fried ham and eggs. Mr. Bolt announces that he has had a 'smash' [an entanglement in the threads of his warp] and that it has taken a full hour to 'get it reet'.

How hot it is! The roof is half glass, because a good light is essential to the production of flawless cloth; and it is white-washed to reduce the heat. But to-day's sun is fierce, and the temperature mounts higher and higher. The sleeves of Mrs. Bolt's cotton blouse are already rolled up. She unfastens the neck, and wishes she could take it off altogether. Beads of perspiration stand out on her forehead, and ever and anon run down the sides of her face, and between the momentary intervals of her cop-filling, she wipes it with her apron. It is impos-

163

sible, even to the noise-inured weavers, to hear themselves speak, but they have invented a kind of finger and mouth action, and Mrs. Bolt uses this language to convey to her neighbours her commentary on the heat.

The half-past twelve whistle blows at last. Mr. and Mrs. Bolt are at home by a quarter to one, being a little late to-day owing to Friday being pay-day, and their having to stop to get their wages before leaving the factory. The five-year-old meets them at the end of the street, and goes with them to dinner; but there is no time to bother with the baby, who dines with Mrs. Earnshaw. Nor is there time for a table cloth and an elaborate set-out for dinner. Mrs. Bolt wipes the oilcloth, which covers the square deal table in the middle of the room, with the dishcloth; and brings out bread, butter, knives, forks and spoons, and the milk which the milkman has left in a jug on the window-sill outside; and then goes to the 'eating-shop' at the end of the street, and brings sixpennyworth of hot potato pie, two twopenny custards, and a pennyworth of pickled cabbage. Some tea is made and poured into the gill-pots.

Whilst they are dining Mr. Bolt gives his wife his wages, except what he keeps for his own manly needs. If, as this week, his wages happen to be twenty-six shillings, he keeps six shillings and gives his wife a pound; if, as sometimes happens, his wages are only a pound, he keeps four shillings and gives her sixteen shillings. The only unalterable condition is that he must have a minimum of four shillings for his own pocket. Mrs. Bolt's wages this week are only a pound, because for four or five days she had in bad warps, and could not get on, owing to continual 'floats' and 'smashes'.

They leave the boy with Mrs. Earnshaw on the way back, and Mrs. Bolt has a look at her baby. The afternoon waxes hotter, till the temperature of the weaving shed is up to a hundred. Four hours without intermission Mrs. Bolt stands at her post, eyes and hands mechanically performing their never-varying tasks. At last the releasing whistle blows, and Mr. and Mrs. Bolt draw in the fresh air with relief as they trudge home. Mrs. Bolt calls for her boys on the way home, and by the time she gets there her husband has put the kettle on the gas-ring and is now resting and having a look at the evening paper. Mrs. Bolt puts a match to the fire. It's hot, but the children'll have to be bathed, and can't be bathed without hot water. Then she makes tea, and fetches the chips and fried fish from the little shop never far from the Lancashire factory home.

Tea over, she clears the table, and asks her husband to keep an eye on the children, while she, with a large carpet bag and a basket, sallies forth to the co-operative shop in the main street. She joins a shopful of women all bent like herself on buying enough butter, bacon, cheese, flour, eggs, tea, cocoa, soap, potatoes, and numerous other articles, to last a week, and finds she has 'made a hole in half a sovereign'.[1] Returning home with her load, she finds 't' Union man' waiting. Eightpence satisfies him – fourpence each for union benefits . . . Now here comes the rent-man, and hard on his heels the Death Insurance man. Mrs. Bolt declares her hand is never out of her pocket!

Her next job is to blacklead and polish the grate in the living-room, before it gets too hot with the fire. It is nearly half-past seven now, and Mr. Bolt, who up to now has been sitting on a chair in the open doorway, where it's cool, reading the cricket news, proceeds to wash himself, and to change into his 'second best' preparatory to spending the evening at the Working Men's Club and Institute.

At last the grate and fire-irons are shining enough to satisfy Mrs. Bolt's critical taste, and she is glad to leave such a 'hot shop' and to go upstairs to make the beds. Coming down, she debates with herself as to the advisability of bathing the children, or first swilling the flags [paving stones of kitchen or yard]. The children being both happily at play outside, she decides on the flags. She decides to do 'the front' whilst she is about it . . . finally, the doorstep. That finished, and Mrs. Bolt's front is as nice as everybody else's.

It is after eight o'clock. The panful of water has been ready some time, and the two-year-old is soon in and out of the zinc bath which occupies the hearth. He is sleepy, and 'drops off' before his brother's bath is finished. By a quarter to nine they are both in bed and asleep, and Mrs. Bolt is free to wash up the day's dirty pots, sweep the floor and scrub the oilcloth surround.

When she has finished the floor she goes to the little eating-shop for some potted meat for breakfast, as she is too tired to cook anything to-night. When she comes back, her husband has arrived, and they have a bite of the meat and bread for supper, Mrs. Bolt eating hers as she cuts up the food and packs their breakfast tins. She makes some cocoa, and sits down to drink it, falling asleep before she has finished it, and having to be roused by her husband. One more job! The clothes and shawls to place ready for morning, and then bed . . .

The Englishwoman, 1912

[1] Gold coins were still in use.

The Mother's Story

The loop-line train pursued its way from one end of the Five Towns and their environs to the other. It made a duty call at a northern outpost where the pit-shafts dotted the countryside, and into my compartment came three workaday women, looking a little blown and battered with their conflict with the north-east gale. As is the way of village dwellers, they were known to each other, and, as is the way with most of us, their thoughts were much coloured by daily environment.

'This is a strong wind, isn't it?' asked one of the other. 'An' I bet you'll feel it where you live, too.' (They lived in a colliery village, at the top of a hill.)

'Yes,' replied the one addressed. 'You can't shut our back door with your hands when there's a wind like this. You have to turn round and put your back against it and push with all your might. An' when it rains, the water pours under the door in a flood. Many a time when the children come down of a winter's morning they put their feet into it; and whenever it rains I always have to mop up bucketsful.'

The others looked their understanding of and commiseration with the situation.

'And what about the dirt and dust on a day like this?' demanded one of them. 'Can you keep clean? If you never have a brush and duster out of your hand, can you keep clean?'

Both the others made solemn assertions as to the impossibility of 'any woman alive' being able to cope with the havoc made by the wind on a day like this. The train had meanwhile transferred us a couple of miles further south, where the pit-shafts were now interspersed with pot-banks. We stopped at the most northern of the Five Towns, and the women left me. It was market day, and each had a basket or a bag.

The vision of their lives, of which they had given me a glimpse, remained. I knew that colliery village in which they

167

live as one knows vitally only one spot – that in which one's life took root. I know the houses where their daily battle with dirt is waged. The 'house-place', about four yards square, door opening on to the village street, a little kitchen beyond, with absurdly inadequate cooking apparatus; back-door opening, maybe, onto a tiny tiled yard, or, quite as likely, onto an open waste, exposed to the bleak countryside and the pit-brows. Imagine the wind sweeping through, leaving in its trail clouds of dirt and coal-shag, covering the beds, the table, the clothes, the cupboard shelves, the food! No, verily, a woman could not cope adequately with housing conditions such as these, though she were a ministering angel from heaven, and not a mere human woman of the earth.

The train stopped again, and there was my temporary destination. The cruel wind swept round every corner of every mean street, taking its tribute of pot-bank dust over every cottage doorway, and as I took my way from one part of the town to the other, I fell a-thinking again of the war of women with dirt, and realised afresh the impossibility of individual women in individual homes dealing with so huge and vital a problem as this. To settle this in which is woven the health and well-being of the race, women will have to act together, in association. This is pre-eminently their problem. Oh, for the power to deal with it! Turning a corner, I saw a woman approaching. Mutual recognition followed.

'Well, Mrs.—,' I said. 'How are you – and how's Polly?'

Mrs.— forgot to mention herself in her haste to tell me about Polly.

'Oh,' said she, 'she's got it over – three weeks ago – a boy.' Her face beamed with satisfaction, which, however, was soon overshadowed by another thought. 'She was bad – awful bad. But she's better now.'

'Well?' I asked, in answer to the shadow on her face. She knew, and I knew, that there was more behind. She came close to me and whispered something. Neither she nor I was surprised at the news – the doom pronounced by the doctor in attendance could have been foretold by ourselves. But she was the girl's mother, and mothers cannot reconcile themselves without a struggle to the destruction of the life which has drawn its life from them. I understood, and she knew it. But what is there to say when one comes straight up against the tragedy of a lacerated mother's heart?

'Well,' I said after a pause. 'Go and get your paper,' [Certificate of incapacity from certifying surgeon.] 'I'll be here when you come back.' She went, surreptitiously wiping her eye on the corner of her apron. Presently she returned, no longer shrinking under her load of woe, but with the light of battle in her eye. I looked enquiries.

'He asked if it was not time Polly was coming for her own paper!' said she indignantly. 'And I said, "She will as soon as she can walk again!" "It's a pity she got married," he said, and I said, "What else was there for her to do when she fell on compensation?" The 5s 4d a week won't keep her, and I'm a widow with four other children not working. How could I keep her? I miss her wages bad enough – even though she did only get 11 shillings a week. She *had* to get married to get kept, that's what she had to do!'

'Never mind!' I said. 'You weren't afraid of him, anyhow. You told him the truth!'

Smiles shone through her tears.

'Yes,' she said. 'What does he know about keeping a family on what you can get for washing?'

She left me, and as I went on my way thoughts of her and the girl filled my mind. I had known them nearly two years – ever since the girl contracted lead poisoning. I saw again the bonnie girl, who had not then lost all traces of the buoyancy and health of her childhood, of which her mother had told me. But even then the girl was developing a cough, and the doctors said there was lung trouble. The little cottage was always full of steam and soapy odours, for the mother's work had to go on all the week, in order to earn enough to keep the children. The steam made the girl cough, and the atmosphere was, of course, the worst possible for her. Then came a visit to a sanatorium. How much we hoped from that! The people at the chapel – for she is a good living girl – and others were all kind, and helped in different ways, and I heard of the 'young man' accompanying her on a portion of the journey.

She came back better. But the home conditions have been too much for her, and she has lapsed – that and the deadly poison which she took into her system whilst earning her 11 shillings a week. Then I heard of her marriage, and my last memory of them before this encounter was of the girl, now soon to be a mother, struggling with her cough in the steamy atmosphere, not made any more wholesome by the rain which was pouring down the walls, and making a little pool in one corner of the room; the ever cheerful mother at her washtubs, and the shy young man sitting in another corner. He had come to live here as a matter of course because her mother could not keep going without even the little help which the girl's compensation means; and he, loving the girl, wanted to help, and this was the obvious way to help best – or so it seemed to them.

How dare we women, whose lives are not cast where the shadows are so deep, judge the conduct of women whose whole lives call for a constant exercise of heroism? Rather should we resolve to treat the problem of downtrodden womanhood like the woman who shut her door against the north wind – we should turn round and put our backs against it. But this door – the door opening on to want and misery and injustice – cannot be shut by one woman's efforts. We must stand all together, and refuse to tolerate a world where women's lives are so cheap.

Common Cause, 11 April 1913

The Separation Order

It was in the month of March, 1913. In a certain village in the south-east of Lancashire, represented in Parliament by a member of the Government who is specially distinguished by his oriental ideas on the position of women, there is a political club of some standing where fortnightly debates are held during the winter months. It is usual in this valley to ignore the political position of British women – that having been conveniently regarded as not political. Owing to circumstances which are of no moment here, the winter just passed is an exception, and it was found impossible to ignore the 'woman's question'. On this evening, therefore, a crowded audience faced two debaters – one a woman who claimed equality for her sex; the other a young man, who denied her claim. Being of the legal profession, his views on women are naturally much coloured by his knowledge of the law. From his point of view the law always favours the woman, and he made much play with the statement that a woman is well protected by present laws, and instanced that of the law of maintenance – by which a husband is responsible for his wife's keep, no matter what she may do. . . .

It was another evening, a little later in the same month. Over the hills which shut in on one side the valley next above, is a manufacturing town of considerable size. Many of its women are mill-workers, and Mrs. Alice Bates belongs to this class. She and a neighbour, who works in the same mill, were deep in conversation as they wended their way homewards. Said Polly Brookes, the neighbour:

'Tha may put it off and keep putten it off as long as tha likes, Alice, and then tha'll hev to do it. Ger it done, and done wi'. What art a' waitin for?'

Mrs. Bates' steps lagged a little, and she heaved a tired sigh.

'Nay Polly, a dun know,' she said. 'A wouldn't cur abeaut

'im givin' me little or no wages if he'd nobbut be quiet. But
when he's allus kickin' up a row abeaut summat or other, and
acts as if he wur t'boss o' t'show, it does get on me craw. An'
then a say summat as a shouldn't do, and then th'fat's in
th'fire, an' theer we go on from year end to year end.' Her
voice trailed away dejectedly.

'An' he wur never no better, wur he?' asked Polly. 'A've
known thee nine 'ear, an' a never remember 'im no different.'

'Neaw,' answered Mrs. Bates. 'He wurn't long before he
begun. Before eaur Mary wur born 'e'd begun wi' his ways.
But a' could allus earn a good wage, an' he got used to havin' a
handful o' money o' his own. Then eaur Tom come; and it
took a lot o' money to pay for booth on 'em to be norsed, an' a'
'adn't so much to go on, and he got nastier. Then when eaur
John Willie come, a' wur beaun to give up my work, for a'
couldn' pay for 'em all to be norsed. An' his mother said a
good job mebbe, for neaw a' should have time to keep him a
proper hooam and he'd be better nor he had been. Bur he
weren't, not a bit. An' when 'a hedn't enough to keep gooin'
wi', a' got mad, an' caw'd a' aw sooart o' things. Ay, we hed an
awful time till th' childer wor big enough to be left, an' a'
could get back to my wark, an' hev a bit o' brass o' my own
again. Then, as childer begun to work he seemt as he didn't
think he should gimme nowt. Then th' childer geeat wed, and
a'm left wi' him agen. A' dooan't see as a' should keep 'im,
doesta?'

'A' should think not!' said Polly, indignantly. 'It's him as
should keep thee. Here tha are gettin' on to fifty, an' he's
never kept thee, nor never will, if tha doesn't mak 'im. Tha
mun make up thy mind and hev him up. That'll wakken him
up.'

'Nay, a' dooan't know as it will,' was the reply. 'He's been
had up twice before for bein' drunk an' feightin', an' a' coulda
had him up mony a time for neglectin' to keep th'
childer — ay, and for knockin' me abeaut, too.'

Polly looked round with a shocked expression.

'Nay,' she said. 'A' didn' knaw as he knocked thee abeaut.

A' thowt it was nobbut 'is nasty tongue and him givin' thee no wages. Tha shoulda hed him up long ago, tha silly thing. Tha'll stand owt, it seeams, just as if tha didn' waork for thy turn. The idea o' lettin' 'im leather thee when tha's keepin' 'im!'

'Nay,' interposed Mrs. Bates. 'He doesn't do it neaw – he dar'n't. It was when th' childer were little an' a'd nowt but his wages – as much on 'em as he choose to gi' me, that is. I used to get mad, an' then a' said owt as come into my heead, an' he couldn't stand it, tha knows. Men winnat stand naggin' when it's them as earns the brass. A'm noan grumblin' abeaut that.'

'Well, see as tha meks up thy mind to mek 'im keep thee,' said Polly, as she opened a cottage door at the bottom of the street in which they both lived, and entered.

Mrs. Bates walked up to the top of the street and unlocked and entered another door. There was a banked-up fire, kept in by a friendly neighbour, burning in the grate of the living-room. She cleared the dinner pots, and began to set out clean ones for tea. Before she had finished a man of about her own age entered, and after washing his hands, proceeded to occupy the armchair by the fire, waiting for his meal to be made ready.

'Tha can begin,' said Mrs. Bates presently, pouring him out a pint pot of tea, and placing before him some slices of bread and butter and potted meat.

He looked at the fare provided with a scowl.

'Is this aw there is when a chap's bin workin' 'ard aw day?' he grumbled. 'Why corned we hev summat tasty – a bit o' meit, or 'am an' eggs, or a bit o' fish, or summat woth eitin', astid o' this dry stuff?'

'Becos' there's no money for nowt better!' said Mrs. Bates angrily. 'It is mony a week sin' tha give me mooar nor seven shillings, an' it'll noan run to meit an' fish, let me tell thee!'

'Shut up!' he said politely. 'Tha never 'ad no mooar money when th' childer wur at hooam, an' tha allus seed as they 'ad plenty o' summat good. Trust thee for that. But I'm nowt a peaunt, [nothing a pound, i.e. of no account] nor never was.'

'The childer worked for what they got!' she answered pas-

173

THE WRITINGS OF ADA NIELD CHEW

sionately. 'Tha could 'ev it, if tha'd work for it. Wheer doesta think it's to come frae, when tha spends aw tha gets on summat else?'

'Thee shut up!' he commanded again. 'Tha's too much tongue by the hawf. It's thy business to provide me wi' summat decent to eit, an' then tha's done.'

'Well, we'll see if a've done!' she said, raising her voice angrily. 'It's thy business to keep me, an' tha's never done it yet; but by gord, a'll see as tha does! A'll let fooak know what sooart tha are! I'll summon thee, and see if tha cornd be med to gimme enough to keep me as well as thee, tha lazy heaund!'

He laughed derisively. By this time he had finished his tea, and proceeded to prepare for an evening out. The personal compliments which were mutually exchanged between them before he finally departed are not fit for repetition in a respectable journal.

After he had gone Mrs. Bates put her shawl round her head, and flew down the street to Polly Brookes, whom she discovered enjoying a tea of fish and chips, while she finished a tale replete with the doings of the nobility, especially represented by a certain Lady Geraldine.

'Come on!' commanded Mrs. Bates, a red spot glowing on each cheek, the light of a bitter resolve in her eye. 'Come on. A'm beaun to do it. A' cornd stand it no longer. A'll show him whether a'll be laughed at. He'll laugh o' t'other side of his face when he finds eaut. Come on, an' goo wi' me to th' police station. A'm beaun to do it.' . . .

A few days later Mrs. Bates and her husband, with Polly in attendance on the former, breathlessly awaited her turn in the police court. Mrs. Bates' married life was laid bare by her solicitor, and Mr. Bates did not shine during the recital. His solicitor made no attempt to deny that his client had not fulfilled his duty as a husband by keeping his wife, except during a short period when she could not earn owing to having three small children to look after. A demand was made for a separation order and an adequate maintenance allowance. The wages of the man were 24 shillings weekly; of his wife 21 shillings weekly. . . .

The magistrates conferred. 'Of course, he's a careless devil,' said one. 'The woman's had a hard life, and he's never helped her. She's getting on, too.'

'But she's getting a pound a week! What has she to complain of? She's able to keep herself.'

'We can't possibly give her an allowance out of his wage which would give her a larger income than he has!' . . .

'We have decided to grant the separation order,' said the chairman to the waiting court, 'with one shilling a week maintenance.'

Common Cause, 2 May 1913

A Daughter's Education

In one of Manchester's suburbs is a street (one of many, all planned exactly alike) of very respectable six-roomed houses. The front-rooms have smart little bay windows, and a pocket-size garden separates the house from the street. Mr. Barton, the proprietor of our particular house, is an eminently respectable man of the clerk class. His wages are 37s 6d a week – a very respectable salary indeed, and he has prospects of its rising as high as £2. In the year 1898 he had been married four years; and his home was a model of what a home should be. Mrs. Barton was proud of it. Some of the happiest hours of her life had been spent in saving up for, buying, and arranging her household goods, and she took great pride in having everything in apple pie order. She had had her work cut out to succeed in this, since the addition to the family had arrived three years ago; and of course there were always a few evidences of that beloved small presence lying about. But these dear small things only added to the homelikeness of the room, and were never an offence in Mrs. Barton's eyes.

To-day was Thursday – upstairs day. Monday was washing day; Tuesday was baking and general cooking day; and the mending needed looking after too. Wednesday the front-room's turn came; and on Thursday upstairs; and on Friday the living-room and scullery, so as to have Saturday as free as possible for a family outing. Every afternoon Mrs. Barton and her daughter took an airing in the park; and this afternoon she was waiting for the three-year-old to awake, in order to follow her usual custom. She looked down fondly on the little bundle on the sofa. How bonnie little Mollie was! The flush of healthy sleep was on the rounded cheek, the brown curls clung fascinatingly round the dear little head, one chubby fat hand and arm lay outside the cover. The mother's heart swelled with pride, and a recurring wonder overcame her – wonder how it

176

ever came to be that that all-perfect, all-beautiful child should be hers. This passed; other thoughts followed, and gradually her eyes became fixed, as though she saw some vision far ahead, and her mouth settled into determined lines. 'I'll do it,' she said aloud, just as little Mollie awoke with a cry of 'Mummy, mummy!'

That night after Mollie was abed, Mr. Barton sat in one armchair reading a magazine, while Mrs. Barton sat in another reading the daily paper. Presently she laid it down and said:

'Tom, I want to talk to you.'

He laid his magazine on his knee, drew out his tobacco pouch, lit a match and applied it; and when the smoke began to emerge satisfactorily, he looked at her with a lazy smile, and said: 'That's nothing fresh, is it? I bet I know what about, too. What marvels has that precious youngster performed to-day?'

Her face was very serious, however.

'Joking aside, Tom,' she said, 'Mollie's no ordinary child.' He smiled, but she took no notice. 'She's got a sound mind in a sound body, and she's had every care taken of her. But do you ever think ahead, Tom? She's a long way off being provided for –'

'You needn't remind me,' he said sharply. 'Look ahead, indeed! I'm haunted by the thought of what'll become of you and her if I peg out or if I lose my job. But I can't help it, and you might at least not mention it.'

She bit her lip and could not speak for a minute for the lump in her throat. Presently:

'I know, Tom. I am not mentioning it merely to remind you of what can't be helped, but of what can be helped. Suppose we can add a pound a week to our income. Think what a difference it would make!'

'Yes, it would,' he said satirically. 'But pounds aren't picked up in the gutter. The only pounds we can get are what I sweat for.'

'But you know quite well I could earn money, Tom!' she said. 'I was getting 28 shillings a week in Shipley's when I left to marry you. And the woman who took it after me is leaving. I was in buying some stuff to make Mollie a frock to-day, and heard it. I am sure I could have my job back, Tom. I'm sure Shipley hasn't made so much since I left. And think what a difference it would make!'

'Yes, it would,' he said sarcastically. 'What's to become of your home and of your husband and child, I should like to know? I suppose the fact of the matter is, you're about tired of us, eh?'

'Don't be silly, Tom. Does the home look as if I'm tired of it? Do you and Mollie get neglected? Act reasonably. I'm looking forward to when Mollie will want educating. I'm sure she's going to be clever, and I can't bear to think of her going into a shop when she's fourteen. But I can't save and keep respectable out of your wages. And I hate to think of you slaving away for Mollie and me all these years when I could be helping. And I'm jealous of you keeping Mollie all by yourself. I'm a desperately greedy mother. I want to help in keeping her.'

'Don't be silly,' he said shortly. 'Your job is to look after her at home.'

'She'd take no harm with your mother,' she persisted. 'Your mother's only three doors away, and she's always enticing Mollie there. She'd give the world to have her all day. And bye and bye the child will be going to school, and I should be left hours a day without her. And as to the housework, I can get it done easily at fourpence an hour. I'd earn a lot more than that at Shipley's.'

'Say no more about it,' he commanded. 'I shall not hear of it.'

He resumed his magazine, and Mrs. Barton hid her face behind the newspaper. There was a distinct coolness between them for some weeks, but time softens all wounds, including theirs. . . .

A year or two passed. Mollie began to attend a kindergarten. It was a little more expensive than Mr. Barton's income justified, but that was Mrs. Barton's business. Later, when the child was too big for the kindergarten, the parents held another conclave. The income would not run to a private school, and Mrs.

Barton could not bear the thought of her darling being exposed to the germs of measles and scarlet fever and whooping cough, not to speak of the annoyances of the importation of foreign bodies, in the way of parasites. The private school was all right – so was the other. It ended in the private school, however, and he made no comment on the decision. . . .

A year or two later he was staggered to see a young woman in the house at breakfast time, performing the duties usually undertaken by his wife. It was Saturday, and he could not ask questions in the presence of the stranger. At dinnertime she was gone, and he sat down with an air of expectancy, though he still forbore to make verbal enquiries. His wife answered his unspoken query, however, and said:

'I'm beginning at Shipley's on Monday morning. That young woman who was in this morning is going to do the housework every morning. Your mother will have Mollie in there out of school hours. I shall make 18 shillings a week clear.'

Mr. Barton was too stunned to answer, so he got a paper and read assiduously. He wore an air of injury for quite a year, and does so to this day if there is a hitch in the household machinery which causes him any inconvenience. . . .

Mrs. Barton is still at Shipley's. She makes much more profit for Mr. Shipley than her own wage amounts to, but she is keenly appreciative of that wage, which is steadily piling up in anticipation of the day when her precious daughter will need it.

That daughter is now eighteen and has not yet earned a penny. But she has won a scholarship at the University, and there is no prouder woman in England than Mrs. Barton, and she will pour out the money she has earned, like water if necessary, to keep her child at the University. Mr. Barton is by now comparatively reconciled to her work, and one of the pleasantest experiences of his day is to listen to her racy accounts of her daily encounters with the customers in Mr. Shipley's dressmaking establishment. And that clever daughter is no less the apple of his eye than of her mother's. . . .

Mrs. Barton and I met at a boarding-house in a North Wales seaside resort, where we were both taking a much-needed holiday. One night it was wet, and we ordered a fire and sat round it talking. With us were other boarders, amongst them a prosperous looking Manchester warehouseman with his wife and child. The conversation had been on women's work; and the prosperous gentleman told us with horror of a neighbour who lived in the next villa, whose wife had actually continued her professional work (teaching) after marriage. With much scorn he described the dreadful daily going to work of the wife as well as the husband, and ended with: 'No, it's not right. I don't 'old with it. A woman should make 'er 'ome 'er 'obby.'

Mrs. Barton and I looked at each other and smiled.

Common Cause, 13 June 1913

Assault and Battery

It was Saturday night. The streets away from the busy centre, where the market-place of a certain Lancashire town is situated, are usually very quiet at this time. On this Saturday night, however, one of these streets was alive with humanity coming out of the houses one after another, their number being augmented by strangers who passed the end of the street, and paused to find out what was 'to do'.

From one of the mean houses in this mean street sounds of shouting and of blows could be heard. A man's oaths mingled with a woman's shrill screams. One or two of the neighbours ventured in with a view to protest, but came forth almost immediately with frightened faces.

'Fetch t'bobby!' one of them (a woman) commanded, addressing nobody in particular. Several boys rushed off with alacrity to obey her behest.

'What's t'use?' asked another woman. 'It's nowt fresh. It's sickenin' livin' in the same street as that pair. Never a day passes as there isn't summat to do. A nice place for childer to be browt up in! Ah'm goin' to shift as soon as Ah can get a heause – only there's no heauses to be getten i' this teawn, an' yo' hev to live next door to any sort of riff-raff, becos yo' cornd find nowheer else to gooa. Listen!'

'Tha'rt nowt but a idle wastrel, Ah tell thee,' came from the inside of the house. 'Ah may wark mysel' i't' grave, an' t'harder Ah wark, t'mooar tha thinks there is for thee to spend! An if Ah dooan't wark an' think as Ah'll mek thee keep me, Ah've to be clemmin' [starving] hawf me time! Tha greit big idle good-for-nothin'!' There were sounds of a scuffle and of oaths.

'Hoo [she] goes too far,' said an elderly woman with a deeply-lined face. 'Hoo ought to know as no chap'll stand what hoo says. An' it's every day alike. Hoo's naggin' at him

181

mornin', noon an' neet. It'll not do. Yo hev to keep what you think on 'em to yersel. If hoo doesn't remember that, hoo'll hev to suffer for it one of these days.'

'Well,' said a younger woman passionately, 'Ah'd suffer then! If Ah had a brute like hoo's getten, Ah'd knock his neck eaut an' Ah'd swing for it before Ah'd tek it lyin' deawn. What's a chap get wed and get childer for if he's to act just as if he were a young felly wi' nobry to keep? An' he cornd keep his hands off her, neethur. It's not many weeks since hoo had a black eye as he give her when he come hooam drunk.'

Just at this moment a blood curdling shriek came from the interior of the house, and the crowd looked into one another's faces apprehensively. Almost at the same moment a policeman was seen approaching, accompanied by an ever-increasing crowd of curious people.

'Be sharp! Hurry up! He's killin' her!' were the cries which greeted him. He blew his whistle and entered the house, coming forth hurriedly a minute later to look anxiously for help, which was immediately forthcoming, in the shape of three or four constables. One occupied himself in keeping back the crowd. The others entered the house. A minute later a half fainting woman, with blood streaming down her face, was brought forth and hurried to the infirmary, followed by a sympathetic crowd, and a man was brought out between two policemen and hurried to the police station, followed by an execrating crowd. The sad-faced elderly woman and the passionate young one each took charge of one of the two frightened children, locking up what had been the home of a man and woman who had once seen an earthly heaven in the prospect of making a home together. . . .

Next week the man was brought before the magistrates, but had to be remanded because his wife was too ill to appear. One eye, the magistrates were informed, had been so badly damaged that it had been necessary to take it out. A week later she was well enough to appear, though visibly suffering. The magistrates duly made their investigations. The man was by no means a model husband and father. The plain facts of the case were that he expected everything to go on smoothly, and food, raiment and shelter to be manufactured out of everything except his wages. He was a gay fellow, and liked to be able to treat another fellow when he met him, and if his wife did have to work in the factory and had no money for luxuries such as he demanded for himself – what are women for? – especially wives! Instead of doing as so many other wives do, however, his wife never ceased nagging him about it! It was intolerable, and more than any man could stand with equanimity. It was not denied that he had frequently knocked her about; but (said his solicitor) there had always been 'great provocation'. Of course he had not meant to deprive her of the use of her eye; but on this occasion there had been even more provocation than usual, and her tongue had become past bearing, and he was so exasperated that he completely lost control of himself. . . .

The magistrates are men. Possibly a woman's tongue may have stung them some time, and they were animated by a fellow feeling for the rascal before them. 'There was great provocation,' said they: 'ten shillings and costs.'

Of so much value is a woman's body in a world where men 'protect' women.

Common Cause, 12 September 1913

A Woman's Work is Never Done

'If only we could live without eatin',' said Mrs. Best, 'how easy women's lives 'ud be! As it is, first thing as I open my eyes, it's breakfast; no sooner 'ave I washed up – sometimes before I can get to do it – it's dinner, all mornin' runnin' to the oven door if it's a baked dinner, and runnin' to pull pan lids off, or to draw 'em back, or to poke the fire up to make 'em boil, if it's a boiled dinner; an' then to think of a tasty bit for 'is tea; wash up tea things; and then a bite for 'is supper before we go to bed. An' all the while thinkin' what to 'ave for dinner termorrer. An' gettin' your work done in between, an' nervin' yerself to let the baby cry, because if you don't the pans will boil over, an' all the ashes will blow all over your clean clo'es as is dryin' on the line over the fireplace! I often tell me 'usbun' as if we'd no bellies women 'ud live longer!'

'Well, I don't bother wi' dinners every day, same as you,' answered Mrs. Temple, as she gently swayed her baby backwards and forwards in her arms. 'I believe in lookin' after a baby first. Me mother allis said, "Look after 'em for the first twelve months, an' then you can turn 'em loose." '

'Nay, you can't, neethur,' answered Mrs. Best. 'They're only just larnin' to walk then, an' you've to 'ave eyes all over yo'. When they're three months old, like mine, you can lay 'em down an let 'em roar while you peg your clo'es out. But when they're past twelve months, they'll either creep or they'll walk to wherever they want to go, an' yer 'eart's in yer mouth a 'undred times a day. They'll either be dabblin' in the dolly-tub, or they'll be pokin' yer boiler fire or they'll be gettin' the scissors, or diggin' i' th' coal bucket – nay, I've four, an' I know! But what do you get for dinners then, if you don't neethur boil nor bake?' with frank curiosity.

'Oh, whatever's 'andy. I don't trouble myself. If I can boil

184

'taters, I do it; but I go on the plan of lookin' after the baby first.'

'Well, you couldn't do that if you'd to live wi' Mr. Best,' commented the latter's wife. 'An' I'll doubt if you'll do it when your fourth comes.'

'Oh, Mr. Temple agrees with me,' answered Mrs. Temple. 'Neither of us thinks much of food.'

'Some women are born lucky,' said Mrs. Best with a sniff. 'Mr. Best is a blacksmith, an' when I grumble about 'im eatin' so much, 'e tells me I should eat an' all, if I'd to use me muscles an' sweat like 'e does. An' 'e doesn't take no excuse, such as th' baby's been that cross I didn't get time to do no vegetables. If 'e doesn't swear, 'e sulks, an' I can't bear to live wi' neither a lion nor a bear. So yer see I 'ave to manage to feed 'im, as well as look after t'babby.'

'Well, I didn't get one like that,' said Mrs. Temple. 'I don't think a' should a' got married if there 'adn't a' been somebody different to that.'

Mrs. Best's upper lip stiffened.

'What's wrong wi' 'im?' she demanded. ''E doesn't ever get drunk, an' 'e's good-tempered enough if you fill 'is belly. I don't know 'ow men does their work as lives on what they can catch. Wasn't your 'usband at 'ome 'avin Lloyd George,[1] a week or two back?' with suspicion.

'Yes, 'e was. 'E got a cold an' it got on 'is chest.'

''E may well get a cold,' said Mrs. Best, 'if 'e doesn't get nothin' into 'im to keep it out.'

'Well,' returned Mrs. Temple, with a suspicion of fright in her voice. 'I can't help it. This child will *not* let me get the work done. Last night I was washin' at bedtime. Every time I put 'er down she cried, an' every time I took 'er up she was as good as gold.'

'You 'ave to let 'em cry sometimes,' said Mrs. Best, 'or else learn to do things wi' 'em in your arms.'

'I've done both,' said Mrs. Temple desperately, as they sat down on one of the park seats, the latter with her baby in her arms, and Mrs. Best with hers in the pram beside her. 'But the neighbour on the other side 'as knocked at the door once or twice to know if I was killin' my baby, and sayin' as the noise was drivin' 'er 'usband to the public 'ouse, an' I must stop it off. 'Aven't you 'eard 'er?' (Mrs. Best lived on the other side of Mrs. Temple's house.)

'No, I can't say as I 'ave,' answered the latter. 'Not as I should notice it if I 'ad – only to feel glad as somebody else was 'avin' a taste same as me. But I'll bet as mine was makin' too much row for me to 'ear.'

'What makes 'em so tiresome, do you think?' asked Mrs. Temple seriously. 'She's well enough. She's gettin' fat. At a lecture I went to before she was born, it was said as a 'ealthy baby never cries.'

Mrs. Best laughed.

'It doesn't if you'll interest it,' she said. 'But if you 'ave to leave it starin' at nothing when it wants to be noticin' it'll let you know as it thinks different.'

'Some folks says let 'em cry, and *then* they'll learn to be good,' said Mrs. Temple. 'But I somehow can't do it. It tears me nerves to pieces. T'other day I got things in to make a dinner, an' she started to roar before I'd half got it ready, an' I was that flustered, I put sugar inter the 'taters, and salt inter the apple pie.'

'Aye, there's a lot of folks ready enough at teachin' yer 'ow to do things,' said Mrs. Best sarcastically, 'But if they'd to look after a teethin' child and do their 'ousework, an' get the meals ready as well, p'raps they'd know better what they was talkin' about.'

'One as told me to let 'em cry 'ad done it,' announced Mrs. Temple. 'She said as they roared a time or two, and then be'aved themselves ever after.'

'Yes;' said Mrs. Best, 'some women are born lucky, both as regards 'usbands and babbies, an' then 'ave a' aggrivatin' way o' settin' up as eggsamples to everybody else. When you've 'ad four babbies same as me, you know as there's at least four different sorts an' you've to adapt yourself to them – not them to you – an' every woman knows best what sort of a 'usband she's got, an' as it's 'er as 'as 'im to live with, I think as folks ought to see as 'e's 'er business, not theirs. You do as well as you can wi' your 'usband an' your babby, Mrs. Temple, an' never mind what them says as is so fond o' preachin'.'

They rose and wended their way homewards.

'What I allus says is,' finished Mrs. Best, 'as us women 'as too much on 'and. I could do me 'ousework an' be a lady if we'd no bellies to fill, and' if I'd no babbies to keep interested; an' if I'd no babbies an' no children, I could fill bellies an' get a bit o' peace in between; but look after childer an' do me washin' an bakin' an cleanin' an mendin' *and* fill bellies is donkey's work. I sometimes wonder whether us women *are* women – or donkeys!'

Common Cause, 24 April 1914

NOTES

1 Sick pay. National insurance and State pensions were brought in by Lloyd George in 1910.

As Others See Us

An Overheard Seaside Conversation:
Workers and the Upper Ten (Founded on Fact)

Mr. and Mrs. Brown are a hard working couple who live in a Lancashire industrial town.

Like most other hard working Lancashire folk, Mr. and Mrs. Brown can 'play' as thoroughly as they work, and are of the opinion that the annual 'Wakes' week is not a long enough playing time to compensate for the rest of the year at work. So when Wakes week comes they believe in making the most of it, and as the time draws nearer the desire to get right away from Lancashire and to see something the exact opposite of an industrial town becomes irresistible.

'We can have a weekend at Blackpool any time,' said Mr. Brown, when the discussion on where to go was in progress early in the present year. 'I don't want to be reminded of th'mill every time I hear anybody speak. Let's go to some place where they don't know owt about cotton mills, and see if we can forget 'em for a week!'

The final decision this year rested on the Devon coast, and thither Mr. and Mrs. Brown and their family, now all out of arms and 'getting up', duly repaired, when the annual Wakes week came round.

Mr. and Mrs. Sharp and family, neighbourhood friends, also decided on the West country, so it was a considerable and merry party which finally departed thereto.

Though they live in an ugly street in houses as like each other as two peas, and though the hours which are not spent in the brick box which is their Englishman's 'castle', are spent amidst deafening machinery, producing by minute and monotonous operations yards and yards of cotton cloth, these particular Lancashire operatives have a keen sense of beauty, and this

188

sense was gratified to the full by the ever-changing panorama of sea, sky, rocks and tree-clad hills, which broke upon their wondering eyes as they wandered about the beautiful bit of coast which they had chosen for their holiday. It seemed that they could not exhaust the surprises, as they climbed the hills and through the trees caught delicious glimpses, now of blue sky, then of glittering blue sea, and anon of a sister hill, with white houses peeping out here and there among the green trees.

One day they found a little corner beside a tiny beach enclosed between two high red rocks. The sun shone brilliantly overhead, and the soft clear air was as caressing as a zephyr. The big children had gone away on a private exploring expedition, and the little ones were soon absorbed with spade and bucket on the beach. The elders sat down beside the rocks, and basked. Many times will that lovely scene come back to them when they are on guard over the flying shuttles.

Conversation was superfluous. The men filled their pipes, and the women, just for once in their busy lives, sat absolutely idle. It was a secluded little spot, and only one or two other odd people were about.

Presently, though they could not see the speakers, voices fell on their ears, so startlingly near that they looked round involuntarily. It became plain that some other people were sitting just round the rock which hid them from view. Mrs. Brown and Mrs. Sharp were all attention now, for they had grasped from the very first words that were spoken, that the people round the corner belonged to 't'upper ten' or to 't'mesturs', and it was rather interesting to hear these people, whom usually one only saw occasionally from afar, in their motor-cars, or in their particular pews at chapel, at such close quarters as this.

'There!' said a man's voice in that languid drawling tone which is supposed to be a distinguishing mark of the Varsity, and therefore unattainable by plain working folk. 'There! This is all right, isn't it, Mater? Eh, Dolly? Here, Mater, let me wrap this coat under you. And where's your coat, Dolly? Ah, that's right. Oh, you're already fixed up, miss. There now, are we all comfortable? May I smoke, Mother dear? I know Dolly and Miss — don't mind, because they smoke themselves!'

'Of course you may smoke, darling,' said a woman's voice in fond tones. 'You know very well your old mother doesn't mind.'

'Righto,' was the cheerful reply, and there was a moment's pause while matches were struck and applied. Presently the neighbours round the corner smelt the perfume of a costly cigar.

'Isn't the place getting beastly full?' resumed the smoker, between his puffs. 'Really, you know, there'll soon be no place left for us except Central Africa or somewhere equally far off. Those beastly weekly trippers are invading every bit of our own coast, and even foreign coasts as well. Last year to escape them we – that is Mother and Dolly and I – went to France, but there they were. One lot had actually come from some rotten place in Lancashire for a day! You simply couldn't get away from them!'

'Oh, it's frightful!' said a young lady's voice. 'Did you notice those awful people who were crowding off to the sea front as we came out of our hotel just now? They're the sort of people who only have a bath once a year, and the men smoke thick twist, and the women wear such awful millinery! I can't bear to look at them. And as you say, there's no escaping them. Last year Dad and I went to Norway, but do you think there were no trippers? There were conducted trips or something I think, and they can rush round a whole country in a week for about five pounds. Father says that since it's been the fashion to have Labour men in Parliament, there's been no end to the pretensions of the working class. They are getting ideas out of all proportion to their station in life, as a consequence.'

'It's a good thing they can't afford to come to our hotels, isn't it?' asked the other young lady, who had been named Dolly by the young man. 'Whatever should we do if they could? I'm sure I can't eat my dinner beside people who don't bath every day. I'm so sensitive it would take away all my appetite.'

'I wonder why we can't arrange for them to go to certain places, and keep those places for them,' said the 'Mater' thoughtfully. 'There are plenty of places on the coast to which we don't care to go, and of which they could have a monopoly. And then such places as these, you know, would be free of them, and we shouldn't have the nightmare of having to be jostled by them wherever we go. You must arrange that when you go to Parliament, Jack dear.'

'Oh, it's too late for that sort of thing, Mother darling,' replied Jack dear. 'I *must* get into Parliament, of course, because it is just the thing to give a lawyer a leg up, but if I trot out that sort of proposal in these days I sha'n't stand a ghost of a chance. You forget that all those working-class beggars are voters now, and the only way to come it over them is to make out that you're strongly Labour, and think them as good men as yourself. And so it wouldn't look well to suggest that they mustn't come to the same seaside place as me – see, mumsey dear?'

'Of course you know best, darling,' mumsey dear replied. 'You mustn't do anything which will prejudice your career.'

'All the same, I do think something ought to be done to protect *us* a little,' said Miss —. 'We hear nothing else now-adays but the protection of this worker and that. But nobody thinks of protecting us. And some people speak as if the working classes were the only people who work! Don't we work, too, and at much more difficult jobs, than they – work which takes brains? It's the easiest thing in the world to work with the hands, but think of the kind of work we have to do! Here are you, Mr.—, have had to spend a quarter of a century in fitting yourself for your work – so difficult and intricate is the work of a barrister and legislator; and when it comes to the work of women, what working woman does as much as your dear mother? She has to run two or three large houses, and has the care of a retinue of servants, besides her family. I haven't patience really to hear all this silly talk about protection of

191

workers and so forth. We ought to make a stand against it.'

'Afraid it won't wash,' said Mr.—, between his puffs. 'The bloomin' working man knows too much nowadays. You can bluff him and hoodwink him, but you'd only give the show away if you talked like that to him. No! I'm going to find an industrial centre somewhere – for preference where they've strong Labour sympathies – and I'm going to play on that string for all it's worth. It's the only way nowadays.'

'You don't mean that you're going to be a Labour candidate, Jack darling?' said his mother with alarm.

'Oh dear no,' was the reply. 'Not at all necessary, even if they'd have me in the Labour Party, which is doubtful. Oh no. I only need to go at it in the right way, and then I can get their votes all right, and remain in my own party. Being one of *us* is an advantage. They like being represented by one of the governing class really. Only they're a bit restive, and you have to make 'em believe you understand 'em, you know. It can be worked, mumsey, don't be afraid.'

'Oh quite easily,' said Miss — in fine contempt. 'Father's member for — and the mill operatives absolutely adore him, and he doesn't pretend to have any sympathy with the Labour Party.'

'Oh yes,' said Jack with interest. 'I'd forgotten that he's member for —. It's a pity that he isn't here with us. He'd have the pleasure of meeting some of his constituents on the sea front. I was told at the station this morning, in explanation of the crowd, that it's —'s Wakes, and a large contingent of mill operatives from that salubrious resort are favouring us with their company.'

'Oh, *that* explains that awful crowd that we saw pushing their way to the front,' said Miss —.

'How do they manage it?' asked Dolly. 'I always thought the poor things had only just enough money to live on. And it's quite a long way from Lancashire to Devonshire, isn't it?'

'Oh my dear, how innocent you are!' broke in Miss —, before Jack dear had time to reply. 'Why, in the particular town that Father represents, they get nine pounds a week, and it's all spent up by Monday or Tuesday, and then they have to take their Sunday clothes to pawn! They buy strawberries when they're eighteen shillings a pound – when we daren't look at them – and when they come to the seaside they spend fifty pounds in a week!'

'No, really?' asked Jack's mother with a gasp. 'But they ought not to be allowed to do that – they shouldn't be allowed to earn as much as that – Oh, whatever's that?' she ended with a little shriek as from the cave beyond the rock came a quartette of two men and two women, the women with flushed cheeks and flashing eyes, and the men looking sheepishly uncomfortable, but with an angry glint in their eyes too.

Mrs. Brown opened fire.

'Ah've had abeaut enough of this,' said she. 'We've as much reet to breathe God's air when it's i' Devonshire, as we hev when we're i' Lankysheer, an' yo' didn' mek these rocks no more nor we did, an' we've bin listenin' to yer jawin' abeaut us, an' we've had abeaut enough, see?'

Jack's mother looked and listened with an air of horror which she might have worn if confronted by a wild beast at large. The others looked too much flabbergasted to express any other emotion, at present.

'But my dear woman,' began Jack, when he was interrupted by Mrs. Brown, and angrily commanded not to 'dear woman' her.

'Certainly not, if you object,' said Jack in a mellifluous tone. 'But my dear madam . . .'

'Well, if ever!' broke in Mrs. Sharp. 'Cornd yo' be civil, young man? Just remember as me and Mrs. Brown are neither yo'r dear woman nor yo'r dear madam, an' mind how yo speik to us, next time yo oppen yo'r meawth.'

'Oh!' gasped Jack's mother. 'Let us go, Jack darling. These are . . .'

'Oh, mater, shut up!' said Jack *sotto voce*, with much urgency. 'I'll manage 'em if you'll leave 'em to me!'

Mrs. Sharp's ears match her name, and before he could

193

resume, she said, 'Nay, yo'll not manage 'em, neither, young man. Yo've done enough talkin' and told enough lies abeaut decent folk for one afternoon, and so hev yo, Miss Cheeky,' she added, turning to Miss —. 'Don't yo come deawn to —, tellin' that fine tale abeaut nine peaunds a week, and pawnin' t' best clooas, and spendin' fifty peaund on a 'oliday. Ah'd like to know wheer we get eaur fifty peaund fro to spend if we're spent up an' hev to goo to t'pawn shop by Monday neet. And I'd like to know eaw mony on us gets nine peaund i' th' week, too! There's nobry on'y such like as yo as gets owt like that i' Lankysheer, nor nowheer else.'

A sudden thought struck her. She turned to her husband. 'Ah believe tha were fool enough to vote for owd — at th' last election, worn't ta?'

'Yi,' he answered savagely. 'But tha's no need to rub it in. Ah've larned a thing or two this afternoon.'

'Aye, so have I,' said Mr. Brown. 'Don't select — to come lookin' for your workin' men to mek fools on, young man. We'st hev to keep owd — till t'next election, but tha'll noan do i' his place, though tha does come tellin' us tha has "Labour sympathies", and owd — doesna pretend to have onny.'

Mrs. Sharp and Mrs. Brown called their children, and the party left, making audible remarks about 'some company not being fit to sit near to.'

The company looked at each other.

'Oh God!' said Jack, profanely. 'We can't sit on the sea front for them, and now we can't enjoy a solitary walk without their intrusion. These are the days of democracy, mother dear!'

Cotton Factory Times, 5 September 1913

Mrs. Stubbs on Women's Sphere

Mrs. Stubbs is the wife of a working farmer, some of whose fields are in Cheshire, some in North Staffordshire. I have known her all my life, and am never so happy as when listening to her discoursing on her views on things. She is a woman of views, and there are not many events or subjects on which she is not ready to express an opinion.

Mr. Stubbs too is by way of having views, and is as fond of airing them as his wife. He would not confess it to her for the world, but he never quite likes to make up his mind finally until he has heard what she thinks. She has a disconcerting way of expressing a view which her listener has never thought of before, and it is not safe to dogmatise too much until one knows whether she approves. In the village in which the Stubbs' farm is situated, Mrs. Stubbs' decisions on matters of doubt are regarded as final. In the bar of the village inn her sayings are quoted with respect, and even the vicar has been known to consult her in a matter of parish difficulty, and when you consider that Mrs. Stubbs is a 'good-living' strait-laced Wesleyan, you will realise that she is a power to be reckoned with.

We sat round the fire after tea in the comfortable farmhouse kitchen. One or two village folk had dropped in on some errand, and were lingering to have a chat. Mrs. Stubbs sat with a pair of boy's knickers on her lap, to which she was skilfully applying patches at each knee and at the seat. She is the mother of many sons, and is scarcely ever seen without some article of boy's clothing in her busy fingers. Mr. Stubbs was looking over the evening paper, after his busy day in the fields.

'Women's sphere!' he read out, contemplatively. 'They'n bin 'avin' another do in Parliament abeaut thease wimmin. A seigh one on 'em ses it isna as wimmin arna as good as men – on'y as they're different. Thur's a sphere as is

195

wimmin's and one as isna; and wimmin should be content wi' that as is thurs, and not want to usurp men's, like votin' for Parliament.'

'Who ses as votin' for Parliament is men's sphere?' asked Mrs. Stubbs.

'Why, everybody!' was the answer.

'Nay,' said Mrs. Stubbs. 'That canna be. If everybody said it was, there'd be noo dispute abeaut it. Somebody must be sayin' as it is and as it isna, or else we shouldn't be discussin' it. Let's know wheer we are. Who says as men's sphere is votin' and wimmin's isna?'

'Tha knows as well as I do,' answered Mr. Stubbs. 'Some on 'em says it is and some on 'em says it isna.'

'I know aw abeaut that,' said Mrs. Stubbs. 'But what I want to know and what tha 'asna towd me yet, is who it is as lays deawn the law as to what wimmin's sphere is, by keepin' 'em eaut o' votin'. Somebody's doin' it, or else they'd 'ave a vote, and wouldna 'ave to feight for one. Who is it, then as says votin' isna their sphere?'

Mr. Stubbs scratched his head.

'Tha makes me yed warch [ache], wench,' he said, 'wi thi "who says this" and "who says that". But it's allis like that wi' wimmin. You conna argue wi 'em. They wun goo ramblin' aw o'er the show, astid o' stickin' to point.'

He looked at the visitors for approval as he said this, carefully avoiding his wife's eye. She looked at him through her spectacles (for she could not see to patch on without them now) with a twinkle in her eye.

'Come on, come on, owd lad,' she said. 'Tha't not as bleent as aw that. Spit it eaut! Tha knows as well as I do that it's men as keeps wimmin eaut o' their proper sphere. It's men as says what wimmin's sphere is, and tries to mak 'em content in it. What I conna seigh is what business it is of men's. Why conna they be content wi' their own sphere wi'eaut wantin' to dictate to wimmin?'

'Nay, nay, Mrs. Stubbs,' said a neighbour, 'that fits the wimmin better than the men. Why conna they be content wi' their own sphere wi'eaut wantin' to dictate to men?'

'Well,' said Mrs. Stubbs, 'A reckon it's becos they're wantin' to 'ave a sey abeaut what their sphere is, and not leave it to men to sey. What dun men know abeaut what wimmin's sphere is? Wheer does men's sphere end and wimmin's begin? What is thur as tha does (to her husband) as A couldna do? Tha plews [ploughs], sows, reaps and teks the corn and cattle to market. Dost mean to sey as A couldna do it if A tried?'

Mr. Stubbs thought a moment. He came to the conclusion that his wife would probably make as good a farmer as he if she tried.

'Well,' he said, 'wheigh doesna tha do it, then? Tha doesna even milk the cow.'

'Becos A've summat else to do,' was the answer. 'A've to be dowin' things as tha conna do. Tha couldna put thease on ar Jack's britches. Tha couldna mek a peaund o' butter to save thi life. An' if tha looks after th'egg money an' the butter money, like tha 'as to do when A'm fast i' bed after a confinement, tha're sure to mak a mess on it, an' it taks me months to get things reight agen. An'as to nossin' th'babby – tha'rt a reggilar foo' at it, John Ennery, and tha knows it. Thur's some things as tha con do, and some as tha conna do, seigh?'

'That's just it,' said one of the visitors. 'That just illustrates wimmin's sphere, Mrs. Stubbs. Yo're aw reight i' your sphere, and Mestur Stubbs i' 'is, dunna you seigh?'

Mr. Stubbs kept silence. He knew from experience that Mrs. Stubbs had not done yet.

'Well,' she said, 'it seems a bit queer, doesna it, as Mestur Stubbs, wi'limitations, should monopolise votin' as 'is special sphere, and mae as con do my own work and his as well if A wanted, munner vote at aw? What is there abeaut farmin' as A dunna understand as well as 'im? He goes to th'rent day dinner, and proposes the landlord's health, while A stop awhom an' milk for 'im while ea's away, but it's mea as knows when th'rent day's comin' reaund; an' if A didna help 'im eaut wi' my butter money, ea'd bi i' a 'ole monny a time. If it comes to "sphere", Mestur Jinkins, thur's noow limit to my sphere, and there is to Mestur Stubbs'. Yet it's 'im as mun vote, and I'm none fit. Wimmin's sphere, indeed! If any o' my lads begin their "wimmin's sphere" at mae, they'n get a cleaut i' th'ear 'ole!'

'Well, you seigh,' said Mr. Jinkins, 'farmers arena everybody. It's true as most farmers' wives are well as good men as the farmers thersels. But there anna monny farmers in eaur country compared wi' other classes, an' them as rules things 'as to think o' what's good for the majority o' folks. Everybody knows as you, Mrs. Stubbs, (soothingly) are plenty clever enough to vote, bur other wimmin arna, you know. Men to their own sphere, wimmin to theirs, is my motto.'

'That's why you'n left Mrs. Jinkins lookin' after the shop while you come'n 'ere, A reckon,' replied Mrs. Stubbs. 'There's some things as wimmin dunna want to do, and wunna do if they'n any sey in it, like feightin' an' bloodshed an aw that that men are so fond on; bur there's one thing the stoopidest on 'em could do, Mestur Jinkins, and that's to put a cross on a ballot paper. If Mestur Stubbs 'as a nasty job before 'im as he's freightened to tackle, loike askin' somebody to pey up i' toime for th'rent dey, ea comes to mae wi' a face as wheit as a sheit, an' ea ses, "Canst spare toime to goo an' seigh owd Soo-an-Soo, an' ax 'im to pey up? A mun 'ave what ea owes or A conna find enough – even if tha lends mae a bit." An' if it's me weshin' dey, or me churnin' dey or A'm up to th' neck i' cleanin' deaun, A've to goo an' leave it . . .'

'But that's becos tha allis gets th'money,' interposed Mr. Stubbs. 'It's noo good o' mae gooin'. They wunna pey it to mae, an' they're freightened o' thee!'

We all laughed, including Mrs. Stubbs.

'Ay,' she said. 'A generally get it. Bur that's becos A'm i' earnest abeaut it, an' they know there's noo playin' wi' mae. A know what depends on gettin it, an' A mean to 'ave it.'

'Dost mean to sey as A'm not i' earnest abeaut it, too?' said Mr. Stubbs, with an offended glare. 'A've noo interest i' th'rent dey, A suppose?'

'Of course tha 'as,' she assured him. 'Bur tha's mae to

depend on, astna? Tha knows A shall get it, so tha leans on mae. Tha'd be a poor show without mae, owd lad, and tha's the sense to know it. The ballot box is shut to wimmin, and that's wheigh it shows such poor results. The fact o' the matter is, lads and wenches, that every mortal thing that's any bearing on wimmin's speciality – human loife – is wimmin's sphere, an' it's toime men stopped meddlin' wi' an' mono-polisin' what wimmin con understand better thin them.'

Common Cause, 6 May 1913

Mrs. Stubbs on Anti-Suffragists

The kitchen window of the Stubbs' farmhouse has a wide view, immediately of a good portion of the delicious rambling old garden, and of a corner of the farmyard and buildings; and further, of some of the Stubbs' fields, and beyond them, of the village on the hill. There is not a vestige of curtain to the window; Mrs. Stubbs needs every inch of the vantage ground it affords. However busy she may be, her lynx eyes never fail to see a small figure behind a gooseberry bush, and there is never time for youthful stomachs to be filled till they hurt before mother has discovered and banished the delinquents; and that special corner of the farmyard over which the kitchen window looks is not selected by the farmhands as a 'larking' or idling ground.

There is a path leading from the village over the fields over which the kitchen window looks, and as it is a path not only to the Stubbs' farm, but to another bit of the village and to the railway station on the other side of the farm, it is a fairly well frequented path, though timid people who are afraid of the Stubbs' geese, and of the cattle who sometimes have to cross the path on their way from field to building, and fastidious people who object to farmyard surroundings and odours usually take the high road a little lower down the hill. One day lately, Mrs. Stubbs had brought her churned butter out of the dairy onto the big white kitchen table, in order to weigh it up into pounds and half pounds, and to put the finishing touches. The dairy window has a poor outlook – merely on to a field – and the youngest boy was asleep on the settle, and needed an eye kept on him; and there were cakes in the oven which needed to be looked at occasionally.

Presently Mrs. Stubbs called out, ''Arriett! Hast welly [nearly] done? Bea sharp and mak' a road through. 'Ere's Mrs. Orthodox comin' across feighld, an' A know 'er's sure to be

NANTWICH
c. 1894

Previous page: Clarion Van, 1896 (Ada Chew standing to left at top of caravan steps).

RD OF GUARDIANS

ADA NIELD

Nantwich Board of Guardians, *c.* 1894 (Ada Nield second from right, front row).

Left:
Ada Nield Chew
and George Chew
with their daughter
Doris, *c.* 1903.

Facing page:
Ada Nield Chew
speaking at the
Crewe by-election,
1912.

Ada and George,
c. 1911.

Ada Nield Chew (standing on stool) at Suffragist meeting, 1912.

Left:
Ada and George in 1918.

Facing page:
Ada Nield Chew, 1920.

Ada Nield Chew, 1937.

Ada Nield Chew, 1938.

comin' 'ere. 'Er never goos past ar muck-midden without 'er's comin' 'ere. A wonder what 'er waants. 'Er ought to know it's noo use axin' mae to give 'er summat for school treats an' mothers' meetings an' things. 'Er knows A'm a Wesleyan, an' A give aw as A've got to give to th'chappil.'

By this time the Vicar's wife was at the door, being shown in by Harriett, the 'wench', whose head was tied up in a red handkerchief, and who had a bag tied round her body.

'Good afternoon, Mrs. Stubbs,' said Mrs. Orthodox politely, advancing into the freshly cleaned, sweet smelling kitchen.

'Good afternoon,' returned Mrs. Stubbs, with equal politeness, but without taking the hand which the Vicar's wife was hesitatingly holding out to her. 'A canna shake 'ands. Me 'ands are wet with the waater as A've to keep the butter in. Sit deawn an' mak' yersel awhoam,' pointing to the Stubbs' arm-chair in which the visitor seated herself.

After a little skirmishing in the way of talk about the children and the weather and the butter etc., the visitor disclosed the object of her visit, much to the satisfaction of Mrs. Stubbs' curiosity.

'We had a little meeting in my drawing room the other day, Mrs. Stubbs,' she said. 'It was just a little meeting of my friends, and I should have invited you to be present except that I know you have no time to spare in the afternoons.'

'Neaw,' was the reply. 'That A doan. An A'm none so fond o' foine drawin' rooms, neether, an' A'm not awhoam among such as loikes 'em. Soo it was aw the same, yo'seigh, as if yo' 'ad axed mae, and noobody's noo woss.'

'The outcome of the little meeting was,' went on Mrs. Orthodox, 'that a little branch of the Anti-Suffrage League was started, and though you couldn't come to the meeting, I am taking the first opportunity of asking you to join it, Mrs. Stubbs.'

'A branch o' what?' asked the latter, as she added another pound of butter – having put the imprint of a rose, which was the distinguishing mark guiding purchasers to the identity of the butter when added to that of other farmers' wives in the chief shop of the neighbouring market town – to the rapidly growing host of pounds and half pounds on a huge flat dish – 'What's it all abeaut?'

'Why, of course, you know about the dreadful danger that is threatening us – the growth of the movement for votes for Parliament amongst so many of our deplorably unsexed women, do you not, Mrs. Stubbs? Well, this League exists to express our horror of these creatures, and to say that we do not want votes, and that we will not have them. Now I am . . .'

'Oh!' interposed Mrs. Stubbs, in a tone which arrested her visitor's attention, and caused her to look anxiously at her. 'So that's it, is it? Yo' dunna want votes yersels, an' soo yo' dunna want noo other wimmin t'ave any. Wheigh, that's just 'eaw my little nippers act wi' one another. One on 'em'll want summat; an then t'other as never thowt abeaut it an' doesna want it, ea'll kick up a shindy abeaut t' other 'avin' it. But A dunna expect anythin' better o' little lads. They're on'y little savidges an' it teks me 'ears [years] to mak' 'em seigh 'ow nasty an' pig-'eaded it is on 'em t'act loike that. An' neaw yo' se'n as foine ladies loike yo' dunna know noo better neether! A shall begin to think my lads are little eengels, if grown-up wimmin wi' nothin' to dow canna act noo better.'

A look of annoyance crossed the visitor's face, but she tried carefully to keep the feeling out of her voice, as she said: 'You don't understand, Mrs. Stubbs. Women don't want votes; we resent the idea of having them thrust upon us, and the League is to protest against that.'

'Live an' learn!' said Mrs. Stubbs. 'A didna know as thur wor any wimmin as waanted to protest agen votin', bur as yo'n got a League thur mun be, A reckon. But yo' munna sey as wimmin dunna waant a vote, yo' know, becos that isna true. If wimmin didna waant a vote, yo' wouldna waant a League to try to stop 'em. A dunna seigh much, shut away i' this village, but it strikes mae as other wimmin as waant a vote mun be gettin' pretty strung to mek' yo' set up another show to feight 'em. Weigh conna yo' let 'em abeigh [alone]? Anna they enuf wi' them stoopid men i' th'Government, as anna sense enuf to weigh the signs o' thi' toimes, witheaut a toothre [two or three, a few] other wimmin as are too lazy to be bothered wi' a vote, an' dunna care eaw the men mess along witheaut 'em, settin' up for opposin' 'em? If thee'r tow idle to waant t'vote thersels, they mit let other wimmin as known better what they're woth abeigh.'

'No, no, Mrs. Stubbs, you don't understand,' said the visitor impatiently. 'We don't think women ought to vote – they're not fit. They'll bring disaster on the country . . .'

'It's noo use yer talkin' loike that,' said Mrs. Stubbs, as she finished the last pound of butter, wiped her hands and took her cakes out of the oven. 'A 'avna patience to listen to it. A darsay yo' 'ave a poor opinion of the gentry wimmin – A dunna think much on 'em mesel – but it's noo use talkin' to a woman loike mae baeaut wimmin not beain' fit for this or that. A know if A didna tek me share wi' Mestur Stubbs i' runnin' this farm, it 'ud be a poor do wi' it. An' if A'm fit t'elp 'im to run 'is farm, A'm fit to 'elp 'im to run 'is country. Yo' needna come 'ere cawin' wimmin names – A'm thankful me lads arna in. A wouldna loike 'em to listen to such rubbidge.'

'You persist in misunderstanding, Mrs. Stubbs,' said the visitor wearily, as she rose to go. 'It's not a question of the inferiority of women. But they've burdens enough without voting. You, for instance . . .'

'Th' votin' day's welly allis o' ar market day,' said Mrs. Stubbs. ' 'An' A've to dress up an take butter to market. It wouldna tek a minute t' stop th'oss at th'pollin' beawth an' nip in an' put me cross on th'paper, at's on'y once in four or five 'ear. A'm pretty thrung [busy], bur A'd squeeze it in some 'eaw.'

'Well, I didn't know you were a Suffragist, or I wouldn't have asked you to join us, of course,' said the visitor.

'A didna know it mesel,' was the reply. 'Bur A dow know enuf to know A amna an Anti-Suffragist, anyeaw. Good afternoon.'

Common Cause, 27 June 1913

Mrs. Stubbs on Militancy

A bright spring day was drawing to its close. The sun went down behind gathering clouds, and the westerly wind, which at noon-day had tempered the sun's rays, had now a keen edge and conveyed more than a hint of a coming midnight storm. It was nearing the 12th of May, and by that time Mr. Stubbs, like all good farmers, liked to have his year's potato crop under-ground, well planted and manured. To-day, every available person had been pressed into service, and even the small hands of the children had placed many potatoes at the requisite point of distribution in the even rows of ploughed earth, receiving a reward of a penny per row for their labours. Now the last seedling had been put in and covered, and the coming storm was viewed with complacency. Potato planting is back-aching work, however, and the settle beside the fire had an even more than ordinarily inviting look.

The milk had been duly despatched on its evening rounds, and Mrs. Stubbs' batch of golden loaves decorated the dresser, bearing testimony to the busy use of her hands during the day which some of us had spent in the fields. Those same hands were now clicking the knitting needles – putting new feet on Mr. Stubbs' stockings. In that big kitchen, even when the lamp is lit, it is too dim in the late evening to sew or to read, except near the lamp, and that is sacred to Mr. Stubbs, who looks upon the evening paper and the lamp as his special pre-rogative. To-night there was as yet only the fire-light, for Mr. Stubbs was out 'bedding' such of the livestock as was as yet housed indoors. Some of us were glad of an excuse to be idle; and Mrs. Stubbs can knit just as well in the dark as in the day-light, which is lucky, seeing that she says she could never get through her week's work if she wasted a minute of time.

A lifelong friend of Mrs. Stubbs and of my own, who once lived in the village, but who is now earning her living in a big city, was on holiday and had come in for a chat. She is a dear gentle creature to whom it would give pain to hurt a fly. That she is also a militant Suffragist is one of those queer anomalies to which time accustoms us. I long ago ceased arguing with her about militancy, and am content to enjoy and to count myself blessed in her friendship, but I rather anticipated hearing Mrs. Stubbs' views of militant tactics – which I knew would come before long.

It was the village cobbler, who called to bring home some shoes which he had had for mending, who started the theme.

'So tha't none i' prison, wench,' he said to my friend, with the familiarity of one who has known one in long clothes. 'Eaw's that? Owd Jinkins towd me as tha belunged to the winder-smashin' lot; and sin' then A've leawked every mornin' i' th'paper to seigh if tha'd done owt. It gives yer an interest in it, when someb'dy as yer know's gooin' to be copped.'

'Ay,' said Mrs. Stubbs. 'Eau is it, Mary wench, as tha'rt loose yet?'

'Because I'm a coward,' was the reply. 'I haven't courage enough to do what so many brave women are doing. Some day, perhaps.'

Mrs. Stubbs gave her a look of which the kindliness could be felt as well as seen. 'Nay, nay, Mary,' said she. 'Dunna be tragic. Sey tha's too much sense to get ta'en up. What good is it goin' to dow thee to goo to prison? What good does it ever do anybody t'goo to prison, for that matter? Tha rowins thi own 'ealth, an' tha owds wimmin up for a spectikkle – as kneauin' noo better thin men. Prisons an bin made bi men, an' loike most things as they'n tried to make beaut wimmin, they're noo good to nobody!'

'But don't you see,' said Mary, 'that's not it. We can't get attended to unless we damage property; and property's so sacred that doing that soon gets us into their man-made prisons. We are not responsible for their prisons, or for getting into them.'

'Neaw, that strikes mae as bein' soft,' said Mrs. Stubbs. 'To

205

sey you anna responsible for your own acts is to put yersels on a level wi' childer an' lunatics; an' to sey yo canna get attention beaut gooin' to prison is just as soft. Yo dunna get attended to if yo dun break winders . . .'

'But look what a furore we've created,' said Mary, eagerly. 'We're the talk of the country.'

'Ay, of course!' said Mrs. Stubbs, drily. 'If that's what yo caw'n gettin' attended to, yo've got what yo' waanted. Anybody as waants to get to prison con get theer if they tri'en. Thur's noo special distinction i' that. What are yo' meighterin' abeaut then if yo'n got what yo' waanted? A thought it was votes yo wan after.'

'You know it is,' was the reproachful reply. 'Whoever heard of our agitation until we began to go to prison.'

'Moost on us arna deaf an' bleent, and as tek'n any interest in what's gooin' on,' said Mrs. Stubbs. 'But it strikes mae as rather a 'opeless task yo'n taken on, if yo'n got to keep dowin' mooar an' mooar damidge just for keep fooaks talkin' abeaut it. What's the good on 'em talkin' abeaut settin' fire to 'eauses – that doesna bring votes no nearer. Men lik'n that sooart o' stuff, bless yer, an' dunna care eaw lung yo' keep'n it up. They'd any time sooner talk abeaut damidge an' destruction than abeaut dowin' summat sensible. Men an' lads an allis leave work to watch a feight. A'm surprised at wimmin playin' up to 'em like they are dowin', an' givin' 'em an excuse for dowin' what any wimmin ought to put deawn as much as we can. It's hard enuf for an ordinary woman to keep that soide of a man bottom-soide up i' ordinary everyday loife. Give 'em an excuse to feight an' to punish an' they'n keep on for ever, but that's aw yo'n get eaut on 'em.'

'But they did nothing before!' said Mary. 'We have at least made ourselves an annoyance to them.'

'Aye,' said Mrs. Stubbs, 'if aw yo' waant'n is to plague 'em, yo' con done that, o' coorse. Any woman as waants to raise the devil in a mon con dow it. Bur th' devil's noo good if yo' waant things mended. Ea's on'y good at destruction. If Mestur Stubbs is bent on dowin' summat as A know will do us noo good, A mak' up me mind theer an' then as it shanner be done. Bur A dunna begin bi werritin' un an' makin' 'is loife a misery to 'im. An' if eawr Joe, as is gettin' a big 'un neaw, an' thinks 'e knows mooar thin 'is feyther an' mother put together, talks abeaut doin' summat soft loike gooin' for a sojer or a sailor, A dunna start cawin' 'im a bad lad, an' makin' im 'ate the sight o' me; nor A dunna dow as 'is feyther is a bit too ready at – lickin' 'im into shape wi' the strap – thur's better ways thin them, lass!'

'But they're degrading ways!' was the passionate reply. 'We don't believe in wheedling. Women should be ashamed of getting what they want by coaxing.'

''Ere, 'ere!' said Mrs. Stubbs, as her husband came in, and took up his place in the armchair by the lamp. 'Noobody seighs mae wheedlin' an' coaxin', neether John 'Ennery nor the lads.'

'Neaw!' broke in Mr. Stubbs. 'Th' only toime tha wheedled an' coaxed was when tha was persuadin' mae t''ave thee. Bur tha's none done so much of it sin', by gow! Bur they're all loike that, arna they, Mestur Smith?' to the cobbler. The cobbler looked at Mrs. Stubbs with a laugh.

'Nay,' said she to him. 'Tha darsna say that's true. Ever'body as 'as lived lung enuf i' this village knows as John Ennery Stubbs was the soft un, when wea were courtin'. It was 'im as did the wheedlin' an' coaxin'! Bur tha'll never get what tha waant, wench,' to Mary, 'bu feightin' men wi' their own weapons. A dunna feight my lot, but they'n any of 'em confess in their sensible minutes as A know what's best for us as well as they dun, an' it's just as well to know what A think abeaut it before they dun anything fresh!'

'Aye,' said Mr. Smith. 'Wea aw know aa Mrs. Stubbs' husband an' lads are generally glad enuf to dow what 'er waants. Eauw does 'er manage it, Mestur Stubbs?'

Mr. Stubbs scratched his head.

'Nay, A dunna know,' he said, after a short pause. 'Bur if A goo me oown way it allis turns eawt wrong; an' if 'er says ''dow it'' it turns eawt reight. Soo A should be a foo' to tek no notice on 'er, shouldna A?'

207

'Ah,' Mary said, 'that's all right. But we have such awful tyrants to deal with.'

Mrs. Stubbs looked at her with an understanding kindliness, as she said gently, 'Nay, that's where tha makes a mistake, Mary. What's the good o' uz wimmin treatin' men as if they wan eaur enemies? They arna. They're eaur children, an' we're responsible for 'em. If my lads an noo respect for wimmin, it'll be becos A avna respected wimmin myself. Wea'n got to bring men to that frame o' mind when they'n be ashamed o' keepin' us eaut o' votin'. Bur your methods puts their minds off votin' awtogether, an' on'y stops 'em from seighing what's reight. 'Ere am A, tellin' my lads as feightin' is on'y fur savidges, an' as 'uman beins ought to know better than to feight; an' then wimmin must start the same game! You're behind the toimes, Mary wench; feightin's eaut o' date on'y fur young lads an' for men as dunna know no better.'

Common Cause, 20 August 1913

Letters to the Accrington Observer

1 Men, Women and the Vote, *26 August 1913*

It was a brilliant summer day early in the present month of the present year. At least, it was a brilliant day in Devonshire – I heard afterwards that in Lancashire it was close and overcast. But the air on a Devonshire hill, overlooking the English Channel, is not quite the same as that we breathe in the market-places of Lancashire industrial towns, and my companion – a schoolgirl daughter – and I climbed a grassy hill, where the thickly branching trees made a deliciously cool shade, a hill which overlooked the river Dart, and its quaint little castle jutting out into the water, till presently we emerged on to a wide down, covered with a thin layer of scorched brown grass. The river now merged into the open sea, which lay before us glittering and shimmering in the warm sunlight, reflecting like a sheet of glass the cloudless sky. Sheer below were the red rocks, round which the placid sea gently lapped, in playful, caressing mood. At the top of the hill the clear air entered one's blood like new wine, uplifting and exhilarating. 'Twas good to be there! And not by any means less good because we had both been working for some months at about the limit of our capacity. Only those who work know how to play. We lay down on the sunny hill top and just browsed and basked, feasting our eyes, resting our brains, and re-invigorating our bodies.

I think I was half asleep when the sound of voices reached me. I looked up lazily, and found that our hill-top had attracted other visitors.

'This is grand, is it not!' I heard, in an accent so unmistakably Lancashire that my attention was at once arrested.

'Yes,' was the reply, 'It is a bit of all right.' The accent now was obtrusively Cockney.

I stole a glance, and judged that two families, one from London way, and one from Blackburn way, were by way of fraternising together. The children wandered away to explore further, and being big children did not need running after, leaving two men, two wives, and myself behind.

'I suppose you don't see anything like this in Lancashire?' asked the Cockney man (they had evidently exchanged confidences in the ascent up the hill and were aware of the places of residence of each family).

'Well, no,' said the Lancashire man, with a comfortable laugh. 'We've a few places not so bad outside Blackburn but none like this! Nor you, I'll bet!'

'Oh, well,' said the Cockney, with rather a superior air. 'We're not as badly off as you in Lancashire, you know. The Thames is a pretty river, and Kew Gardens are a show, and we've some nice little places by the sea, too.'

'A sea like this?' I could not forbear to ask. 'A blue glitter like this? A coast-line like this? Red cliffs and green hills like this? Where?'

'Oh, well,' was the reply. 'Not exactly like this, but very pretty, all the same. And not like Lancashire! I once went to Manchester on a day trip, and I never saw so much ugliness on one day before.'

'True,' said the Blackburn man. 'But Manchester doesn't occupy all Lancashire, quite, you know. And then – you see, we're so busy making money in Lancashire we haven't time to think of beauty. We leave that for the Wakes, and then we don't mind how far we go to seek it – even to foreign lands.'

'Yes,' said the Cockney. 'I've sometimes thought of coming to Lancashire to see if I could make a bit. I heard the other day that working men make nine pounds a week there. I'd be content with half of it!'

'Yes,' said the Lancashire man, with a jolly laugh in which his wife and I joined, 'so would I, too.'

'So it isn't true!' persisted the other. 'But you're a spinner, aren't you!'

'No,' was the reply. 'It's all weaving at Blackburn. I'm a tackler, and that is reckoned a pretty good job. But I'd like to see four pounds ten a week for it, all the same!'

'So that other tale is true which I heard, from a Northampton man the other day, that the men get rotten wages because the women all work, is it? I'd like to get the hang of things, now I have a chance.'

We laughed again. The bewilderment of the South country-man about the men and women of the North is almost as great as if we belonged to another race and country.

'Well, what do you reckon rotten wages?' asked the Lancashire man in reply.

'I'm a shopman, and don't get very good wages, but I know men who are making thirty-five shillings a week,' replied the London man.

'Yes, and some less, I'll be bound,' said the other man. 'And so you will in Lancashire. There's no nine pounds being earned by one man, unless he's a boss of some sort, and there are usually a few hundred underlings to every boss. And even the agricultural labourers don't get such rotten wages as your labourers do, so I should think on the whole we might say that Lancashire men are better off, speaking generally, than your men are.'

'What in the name of heaven do the women work for, then?' asked the other man, in utter bewilderment.

Here the Lancashire man's wife broke in indignantly. 'Why to have a bit o' brass o' their own, of course. If me and my husband can earn three pounds between us that's better nor thirty shillings, isn't it?'

'I should think so!' answered the Cockney's wife. 'I wish I had three pounds a week coming in.'

'I don't know,' answered her husband. 'It wouldn't do for a man in my position to have a wife going out to work. I'm just counterman, and if my boss knew my wife worked I should get the sack, because people would think he didn't pay me

211

enough. And when you've said and done all, it isn't respectable for a married woman to work. She should make 'er 'ome 'er 'obby. What 'omes you must have in Lancashire!'

'Oh, have we!' asked the Lancashire wife, bristling. 'Well, anybody can come and look at my home any time and if they can find a better furnished one or a cleaner one I'll eat my hat!'

'But how can it be?' asked the Cockney. 'Do you work all night as well as day?'

'No, ah do'ant,' was the reply of the Lancashire wife, who lapsed into her native dialect in the heat of the discussion. 'Ah putts me weshin' eaut, an' ah pay sombry else to come an' cleean deawn. An' if ah had to wark aw day an' aw neet ah'd sooner do id an' hev a bit o' brass to do on, nor slave an' pinch on one wage. An' ah'd sooner bi th' hawf go to th' mill nor mope at hooam aw day.'

There was a thoughtful pause.

'But the children!' at last said the Cockney man. 'You can't rear healthy children.'

'Well, you've seen mine,' said the Lancashire woman. 'For anything I could see they're as well-grown as yours.'

'Ah, but what did Mr. Burns say the other day,' said the Cockney in a warning voice. 'The death rate in Lancashire towns amongst infants is simply awful.'

'Yes,' said the Blackburn man. 'He quoted Burnley, where there is always a high death rate because there are more back-to-back houses than there are in any other town in the country. But he forgot Nelson, only three miles from Burnley, where the houses are modern, and where the death rate is lower than in his favourite Battersea, which he quoted as being so much more favourable than Burnley, because Battersea mothers don't work in mills. But Nelson mothers work in mills, just as the Burnley mothers do. So you see that tale won't wash.'

'Aye,' said the Lancashire wife, bitterly, 'I'm gettin' sick o' these blessed politicians an' their tales abeaut wimmin! Wait till wimmin geds a vote! We'll mek 'em mind what they say, then, you see if we doo'ant. They think they can caw us for owt, neaw, but we'll shew 'em in a bit!'

'Hello!' said her husband. 'Votes for women on top of the Devonshire hills! I thought we'd left all that behind in Lancashire.'

'I thought I had, too, but it's in the air, and we can't escape it.'

Accrington Observer, 26 August 1913

2 Men, Women and the Vote, 2 September 1913

'Well, what do you think of this?' asked Alice, as the four of us emerged from the dense forest of trees which covered the hillside, on to the broad hilltop.

Immediately below were red rocks jutting out into the water. Across the water, to the left, was another green-clad hill, with here and there a white homestead peeping out amongst the trees. In the little river, also to the left, graceful craft, with gaily coloured sails, glided to and fro. To the right were two famous cliffs, one shaped exactly like a lizard, and in front was the English Channel, a broad, smiling, glittering sheet of glass, faithfully reflecting the blue of the cloudless sky.

'Oh, it beats the Rossendale hills!' was Dorothy's reply. Dorothy lives on the hills which smile on the Rossendale Valley.

We were not inclined to talk, however. The living picture before us was feast enough, in our opinion, and we sat down to enjoy it. But we were not to do this uninterruptedly, and presently a whole party of three men, three women, and several children appeared in view, and came and sat down close beside us. We could not avoid hearing the conversation which is now about to be recorded, nor was any attempt made to prevent one hearing it. The party had been in earnest conclave as they ascended the hill, and were now disposed to continue it.

'How horrid for you!' said one of the lady members of the party, 'to have a sister who acts like that! You don't mean that she speaks at outdoor meetings, though, do you? It will be properly arranged lectures in halls, etc., I suppose? Of course, that's bad enough for people in your position, who, everybody knows, are able to provide for all your women folks. I sympathise very much with you, dear.'

'But she does speak outdoors!' said one of the men, savagely. 'Nothing's too outrageous for her taste. An old orange box at a street corner, a dirty coal wagon at the crossroads, an empty stall in the market place — nothing's too disagreeable.'

'How frightful!' exclaimed the lady who had spoken previously. 'But she doesn't do it in the neighbourhood of home — don't tell me you have to endure that, dear?'

'But we do!' was the angry reply. 'Do you think a woman who'll bawl on a box at a street corner will stick at anything? I never know when I shall drop across her. She makes a regular fool of me. Stands at the street corners where I have to pass, and where everybody know me, and sells beastly rotten suffrage papers — begs people to buy — just like a common street-hawker. Another time she's not selling, but has her arms full of silly leaflets, and rams them into the hands of every Tom, Dick and Harry who passes!'

'And, oh, my dear!' spoke one of the ladies, 'she hasn't the least respect for her clothes! She stands knee deep in the gutters, and, of course, she can't put up an umbrella with all that awful stuff in her arms, so the rain pours down on her hats and frocks. How can anybody be nicely dressed who messes about like that? I have put my feelings in my pocket many a time and have stopped the motor and begged her to get in and come home, but she never will, and, of course, people grin so much when they see us together under those circumstances that I have given up noticing her at all when she's doing it. It's the only way.'

'Oh, what a trial for you both!' said the lady who had spoken before. 'How horribly selfish of her!'

'Oh well, I don't know about that,' said a man who had not said anything before. 'She can't really enjoy doing those sort of things, you know. I'll never believe as long as I live that a woman like your sister likes doing the sort of thing you describe. I can imagine that everything she does in that way is a continual ordeal. So it's anything but selfish. Mistaken, if you will, but let's give her her due, and admit that she's brave.'

'But couldn't she go somewhere else and do it, if she must do it!' grumbled her brother. 'Why must she be under my nose, making me a laughing stock to the neighbourhood?'

'Yes,' said the previous lady speaker; a fat person with half a dozen bangles on her arms and a dozen rings on her fingers, so that one couldn't help thinking of the nursery rhyme, 'rings on her fingers and bells on her toes.' 'You can't but admit, Harry dear, that to do these things in the town where her brother is an important citizen certainly is selfish and thoughtless, to say the least of it.'

'Harry dear's' face took on an obstinate look. 'No,' said he. 'I can't even admit that, unless you also want me to say that her brother ought to be her first consideration.'

'Well, of course he ought!' the fat lady indignantly replied. 'I'm surprised at you, Harry, dearest, questioning that at all, with the example you have had before you all your life. Did I not always put your dear father's interests before my own, right up to the day of his death, and have I lived for anything since except my darling boy? Can you imagine my doing such things in W—, where you and I and all our family are so well known? I ask, can you imagine your mother disgracing you by shouting on a box at a street corner, or standing in gutters acting as a street-hawker?'

I was too much absorbed in listening to notice much else, but I could not help noticing, at this point, 'dear Harry' biting his lips to keep from smiling, whilst the other two men puffed hastily at their pipes. My companions and I, sitting on the grass near by, discreetly turned our heads, though my schoolgirl daughter very nearly gave the show away. Fortunately her convulsive giggle was drowned by Harry's reply.

'No, mother darling,' he said. 'I can't quite see you in either of those positions. But you see, dear, it's quite a long time since you were very young – you can't disguise your age too much, you know, with me about – and times have changed.'

'They have indeed!' agreed his mother. 'Girls used to be too nice to do that when I was young. Perhaps the dear girl will marry, by-and-by, and then she'll forget all that nonsense. Though I'm afraid she's spoiling her chances. She really can't expect men to come to gutters and street corners in search of wives.'

'Oh, it's all right, mother,' answered Harry. 'This particular girl's provided for. I may as well out with it now as any time. I'm going to marry her.'

There was a longish pause. We four now listened breathlessly.

'No, really, old chap!' congratulated the girl's brother, who recovered first, holding out his hand. We gathered from his cordial manner that Harry is an eligible whom a sister did well to marry.

'I'm so glad, Harry, dear!' said the brother's wife, also shaking hands. One read relief and genuine satisfaction in her tones.

By this time Harry's mother was able to speak. 'My darling boy!' she exclaimed. 'What news to spring on us so suddenly!'

'Well,' explained Harry, 'it was only settled last week. You were all going to be told on Saturday, when she arrives here. But you were so concerned about her future prospects, that I could not forbear to reassure you, mother.'

'Well, she's a dear girl, after all,' said his mother, 'and of course this dreadful business about the suffrage was merely a phase. She'll settle down now, and will make an excellent wife, I'm sure.'

From the calculating expression which her face assumed I judged that she was trying to remember how much money the girl's father had bequeathed to her, and that it was a satisfactory amount.

'Oh, don't be too sure,' said the third man, who now spoke for the first time. 'Didn't you know what a rabid Suffragist my wife is! She's secretary of our local society, and the meetings are held in our drawing-room, and she's always got some crank or other staying with us. And I even came across her at a meeting in the market-place the other day, with a bundle of papers under her arm and a red, white and green sash tied round her!'

'No!' gasped Harry's mother, looking incredulously at one of the ladies who sat beside her. 'And what did you do; did you bolt?'

'Oh, no,' was the reply. 'I took her for better or worse, you know. I'm bound to stick by her whatever she does, so I collared some of her bloomin' leaflets, and began to give 'em out.'

'Oh!' gasped Harry's mother again. 'But I'm sure dear Cicely won't want to do it after she's comfortably married, will she, Harry dear?' looking at him anxiously:

'She'll have to do just as she likes,' said Harry. 'She wouldn't promise to marry me unless I'd promise to treat her as a "full-grown, self-respecting human being." And she added that of course marriage was a side line for women, just as it is for men, and that she didn't mean to be swallowed up in me just because she'd married me. And she shan't be, either, bless her!'

'But she'll be shouting on *our* orange boxes, and standing in *our* gutters!' gasped his mother.

'Never mind,' said the girl's brother, with a smile. 'It's an ill wind that blows nobody any good. She won't be able to patronise *ours* so much!'

Accrington Observer, 2 September 1913

3   Men, Women and the Vote, *9 September 1913*

It was a hot day in the last week of last month in the present year. In the cotton mills of Lancashire the air was close and stifling, but in a certain Cheshire village it was more than bearable. On a pleasant lawn, 'under a spreading chestnut tree', round a tea-table, sat four women. The deep wicker chairs invited ease, the tea in the delicate Worcester china invited refreshment, and the cakes with the whipped cream on top were a dream. (I quote the verdict of one who tasted them.) There had been a wedding earlier in the day, at the house to which the lawn belongs, where the sister of the bride lives, and these four tea drinkers were all that remained of the party which had gathered round the wedding-breakfast table. The happy pair had long ago departed for a distant coast, and at the point the conversation had now reached their destination was the topic.

'How lovely it will be there just now,' said Alicia. 'Lucky Jennie!'

'Thrice lucky Jennie!' said Margaret, whose sister Jennie is, and who was the present hostess. 'I'm going there for my honeymoon, too.' The others laughed.

'Don't try to pose as a young thing, my dear,' advised Dorothy. 'We saw that tall daughter of yours in her brides-maid's gown to-day. It's time you were putting on grand-motherly airs, and leaving honeymoons to those who've never had any.'

'Ah, that's where you make a mistake,' answered Margaret. 'You young things have no capacity for appreciating honey-moons properly. It's only after you've braved the rocks and the storms together that you can appreciate the placid seas of an idle honeymoon, just as those who work are the only people who really know what a holiday means.'

'That's why you and Dorothy went off for a holiday without your husbands, I suppose,' said Alicia, drily.

Margaret smiled. A shadow crossed Dorothy's face.

'I can't help thinking, you know,' went on Alicia, 'that in spite of her being such a loss to the school, Jennie's right in giving up her teaching and devoting herself to home-making, now she's married. It's a woman's mission in life, when all's said and done.'

'Meaning,' said Dorothy, very quietly, 'that I haven't a

218

home because I leave it every day to take my share in managing my husband's business.'

'No,' was the hasty reply, 'I didn't quite mean that, dear. But is home just what it might be to your husband, with your being out of it so much?'

'Why not?' asked Dorothy. 'I'm usually in it when he is, and often when he isn't, because I haven't a Club to go to, as he has. And even if I don't happen to be there when he is, what of it? He appreciates me all the better when I am there, that's all.'

'But surely,' pursued Alicia, 'there's a feminine touch which a woman's presence in the home imparts, which makes all the difference.'

'What is it, Alicia?' asked Margaret, earnestly, 'I've been trying to find out precisely what that feminine touch is, for years, but it's the most elusive will o' the wisp I ever pursued. Is it the having of everything in apple-pie order? Is it the kind of carpet one has on the floor, the sort of fire-irons which decorate the hearthstone; is it the food – or what is it?'

'Oh, I should think it's the way a woman does things, you know,' said Alicia, wisely. 'A man doesn't know how to lay a table, for instance. He forgets the flowers, or he doesn't notice that the cloth is dirty. I have even heard of a man spreading a newspaper on the table, and eating an enormous meal off it. It doesn't make the least difference to his appetite, as it would a woman's. Everybody knows the difference when there's a woman in the home. That's the very essence of home-making, my dear, and which is part of a woman's make-up, and which makes her different from a man. A woman does things in a feminine way, and a man does things in a masculine way, and there you have the whole thing in a nutshell.'

'Oh, no, we haven't,' objected Margaret. 'It's not nearly so simple as that. If a woman's way and a feminine touch were all that is needed to make a home, any woman's way and any feminine touch would do. A man wouldn't need a wife to have a home, yet most men (and women) when they speak of a home, have in their minds the trio for whom home chiefly

219

exists – husband, wife, and child. As you know, though I never touch housework, even to the laying of a table, I am a busy woman, earning my living with my fountain pen. Yet my home is kept in perfect order – in better order when I am out of it than when I am in it. Recently I left it for several weeks, and when I got back all was as it should be, and my husband had punctually served and well cooked meals, a table neatly laid, and the missing buttons restored to his garments. So that, the "feminine touch" and the "woman's way" not being lacking, he should have been perfectly happy in my absence. My "perfect treasure" of a home-keeper was able to keep much better order with only his delinquencies to cope with, than when there are mine and the children's as well. Yet that home was merely a shelter till I got back, and the minute I was in it again it was home again. So you see, Alicia, dear, it's not the "feminine touch" – it's something else.'

'But you've admitted my point!' said Alicia. 'It's the wife who makes home for the man. Therefore home's the place for the wife.'

'Oh, rot, Alicia!' said Dorothy, impatiently. 'Don't be so absurd. Do homes exist only for men? Don't women need homes as well? And what makes home for a woman? The "feminine touch"? And only her own particular touch? Must a woman scour her own doorstep, and wash her own saucepans, in order to have a home? As a matter of fact, what is usually termed "home-making" has no connection with the actual thing. You know that my husband and I can never take a holiday together, because our business cannot be left without the supervision of one of its managers. I've had my holiday, and next week he is to go away for his. I shall be going home every night to a lonely hearth, as he did whilst I was away (only I've no Club to call at and to stay at till bed-time, as he had). Do you think the house will feel like home to me with him away, even with the children there? It's not the glueing of the wife to the hearthstone which makes home, my dear. As Margaret says, it's something else.'

220

'I shouldn't know what to do with myself,' said Ethel, who is science mistress at a girls' high school. 'How boring to have nothing to do all day long!'

'Oh, I like that!' was Alicia's derisive reply. 'And the times I've heard you discourse on the iniquity of the average working woman's day!'

'Oh,' said Margaret. 'At last we're coming to it. We've all to be cooks and washerwomen and general house-scavengers in order to fulfil the role of home-maker. At least, we must if we're married. If we're single we may have a charming little home such as yours is, and may take a useful part in the world's work as well, like you and Ethel. You both maintain nice homes, on the work you do. And that same work blesses the world as well as yourselves. You know perfectly well, Alicia, that you are the best kindergarten teacher that ever was born, just as Ethel's the best science teacher. And Dorothy revels in acting as watch-dog over her husband's business interests, and he would be the first to acknowledge that he is making a much bigger income with her help than he could make without it. As for me, do you suggest that I ought to fret myself into scrubbing pots and pans, which I detest, when I can use a pen with much better effect, both in the way of kudos, and of giving pleasure to people who like reading my stuff? Yet according to your logic, Dorothy and I, because we have both husbands and children whom we adore, and who reciprocate our affection, ought to give up the work we can do best and become house-scavengers and cooks! Why mayn't we do what we like? People always do best that which they enjoy doing.'

'But,' objected Alicia, 'who's to do the house-scavenging? I don't like the idea of shirking.'

'But the irony of it is that one doesn't shirk, according to your logic, unless one is married,' said Dorothy. 'It's perfectly right for you, who teach babies so delightfully and profitably, to employ somebody who can't do that to cook your meals and wash your dishes. But it is all wrong for Margaret, because she's married, to employ somebody, though she writes so charmingly, or for myself, who hate housework, to delegate that to somebody more capable, and to do what I can do better – look after a business.'

'Of course, now you put it that way, I see it, especially in your own two cases,' said Alicia. 'But aren't you two exceptions? On the whole shouldn't women be home-makers first? Though I'm an ardent Suffragist, I sometimes fear where the movement's going to lead us. We mustn't injure the home, you know.'

'Oh, Alicia,' said Margaret, 'don't be a sentimental ass! Haven't we just shown you that we *are* home-makers, by virtue of the love which sanctifies our home relationships? And love does not depend on the personal use of pots and pans and scrubbing brushes.'

'But somebody's got to like those things, or what's to become of us all?' asked Alicia, with a troubled face.

Margaret laughed. 'You needn't worry, dear,' she said. 'For a long time to come there'll be plenty of women like my treasure indoors, who often says to me, when she sees me grubbing over my pen, buried in mss. paper, and with ink all over my fingers and the front of my blouse, "Aye, I'd sooner do my work than yours!" By the time all women have learnt to hate our present primitive methods of domestic management too much to adopt them as a life work, those same methods will have followed natural lines of advance, and will be so organised and specialised that they will fit the needs of the women of the day to which they belong. It will be our grand-daughters who will have to deal with that problem – or possibly our daughters. But certainly not we – so why worry?'

Accrington Observer, 9 September 1913

4   *Men, Women and the Vote, 14 October 1913*

Mr. and Mrs. Jones live in a villa on the outskirts of Accrington. One evening during the present month they sat on either side of the drawing-room fire, Mr. Jones with the evening paper in his hands, and his wife with long lengths of red, white and green muslin on her knee. She was sewing these lengths together.

Mr. Jones had been too deeply absorbed in his paper to notice what she was doing, but presently, when he had turned the paper inside out several times, he laid it on his knee, and glanced at his wife. His pipe had been smoked out, and he proceeded to refill it with lazy leisureliness. His eye fell on the gaily coloured heap of material on his wife's knee.

'What in the world are you doing, my dear?' he asked. 'Making a frock for Elsie, or what? Surely it's late in the year to be making up flimsy stuff like that. And what crude colours! It's much more artistic to get subdued colours – such as that thing you're wearing now. That soft shade of warm brown is just the thing for autumn. But those colours you are so industriously working on are enough to give one a headache. You can't surely be going to mix them? They're bad enough separately, but a mixture is only fit for a circus.'

'Oh, it's not to wear, dear,' answered his wife. 'At least, this muslin isn't to wear. The lengths of ribbon (she held up three rolls of red, white and green ribbon) are to be made into sashes, to be worn. The lengths of muslin are to drape rooms, and to make into tricky little flags.'

Mr. Jones paused in the act of lighting his pipe.

'Tricky little flags!' he repeated. 'In heaven's name, what for? Surely you're not having the children's party before Christmas? They'll want another then, just the same.'

'Oh, no,' replied Mrs. Jones, with an under-note of tremor in her voice. 'They're not for the children, dear. These are our suffrage colours, and the flags are to decorate our platforms – indoor and outdoor.'

'Oh!' said Mr. Jones. There was silence whilst he puffed at his pipe. Then, with rather a searching glance at his wife, he said, 'What are you doing with suffrage flags and drapery?'

'Why, Paul, dear, you knew quite well that I joined the non-militant movement when a branch was formed in Accrington,' she protested.

223

'I had forgotten,' he replied. 'One doesn't hear much about the non-militant lot, and I had clean forgotten they have a branch here.'

'Yes, that's just it,' she eagerly broke in. 'You just now announced to me, when you were reading your paper, that Annie Kenny has again been arrested, and the papers see that you don't forget the militant movement. But we may organise, educate, and agitate by all the recognised constitutional methods, and you forget we exist! Really, Paul, I never heard a much better argument for the necessity of militancy.'

'Rot!' was Mr. Jones's conjugally polite rejoinder. 'We don't think about suffrage when we read about the militants. We only think what disgraceful creatures they are. But where are we to have the felicity of seeing all this brilliant array of flags and bunting! Is it a special jubilee of the Accrington non-militants which is coming off?'

His wife swallowed a lump in her throat before she replied, patiently and good-temperedly, 'No, dear. But we're going to try to let you and other Accringtonians know that what we are out for is woman's suffrage. We're going to try to convince you that there is a strong body of local opinion in favour of votes for women.'

'By decking yourselves out in rainbow colours and parading the streets with flags?' he asked.

She swallowed another lump. 'No,' was her answer. 'But by a campaign of outdoor and indoor meetings, a door-to-door canvass, and a great distribution of literature all over the constituency. You are always telling us to convert the people to the justice of our demands and then we shall get it. So we're following your advice.'

'All over the country?' he asked. 'Good Lord, what a job you've taken on!'

'All over the country more or less,' she replied. 'But more in those constituencies where you men return an opponent to Parliament and less where you return a supporter.'

'Oh, I see,' said Mr. Jones. 'So that's why Accrington's going to get a special dose, is it? Poor Mr. Baker!'

'Poor women of Accrington rather,' replied his wife, with some spirit. 'For the life of me, I can't understand how you Liberal men, who profess to believe in democracy, can support a Liberal who doesn't believe in it. If you had no vote, and I had, I wouldn't vote for a woman (because, of course, it would be a House composed of women and a Government composed of women, if all women had votes and no men) who didn't think men ought to have votes as well.'

'Oh, you don't understand, my dear child,' was the reply. 'It is not likely you would. Of course, as you know, I do believe in women's suffrage, and on that matter I disagree with Mr. Baker; but then he's so splendid on other things that I can't let a trifle like that influence my vote.'

'That's what I don't understand,' said Mrs. Jones. 'You speak of the Liberal Party as the party of progress, the democratic party, the working man's party. Yet you can coolly support your party in denying working women the elemental right of governing themselves.'

'Well, well,' said Mr. Jones, testily, as he re-lit his pipe, which he had allowed to go out in the heat of the argument, 'it isn't likely you can understand, and I don't believe in arguing with a woman. They always wander away from the point. But do explain what is going to happen in our specially favoured town.'

'Well, dear,' said his wife, 'if you won't argue with me, I do hope you'll come and argue with the people who are coming down here specially during the week beginning October 20th. There are lots of men as well as women coming, so that, if you don't care to argue with the women, you may meet foe-men of your own sex who may be worthy of your steel. There are to be ''suffrage shops'', decorated with these brilliant colours, the Town Hall and the market-place are to hum with suffrage discussions, and I believe the theatre has been taken.'

'And what part are you playing?' asked Mr. Jones. 'I do hope you're not learning to speak, and that I shall drop across you at street corners as I pass. I didn't quite bargain for that dear.'

'Oh, no,' she answered, with a cheerful laugh. 'You needn't worry, darling. I won't do anything to disgrace you. As to speaking at a street corner or anywhere else – couldn't do it to save my life! But you won't mind my wearing a sash, and giving out leaflets, I hope, Paul? And may I have one of the MAs or BScs who are flooding the town to stay with us during the week?'

'H'm!' said Mr. Jones, 'Man – or woman?'

'Oh, I think a woman, dear, unless you'd rather have a man?'

'No, let it be a woman,' he said. 'I shan't be supposed to entertain a woman much, and I don't want to have to sit up all night talking suffrage to a man. Lord, what fools they must be to go about preaching women's suffrage!'

'I'm sorry you think so,' said Mrs. Jones, gently, and the conversation ended.

Accrington Observer, 14 October 1913

Articles

The Economic Position of the Married Woman

It is not at all an unusual view that the difference between the wages of men and women in the industrial world is attributable to the fact that a man has always a present or potential wife and family to keep, whilst the same argument does not hold good in the case of a woman. The whole position of women as workers is such a muddled one, owing to their economic functions, their way of getting a living, being mixed up with their sex functions – wifehood and motherhood – that it is little wonder that there is confusion in our ideas when considering it. The contention that men are paid on the assumption that they have a wife and family to keep is plausible, and satisfies people who are unable to do any thinking on their own account, and who are therefore disposed to be content with any kind of superficial explanation of what puzzles them; but it will not bear examination. If this is a definite, general principle, with a governing effect on wages, it will apply so generally and forcibly that convincing data will be forthcoming in support of it, as is the case in the effect of trade unionism on wages. What are the data in support of the theory we are considering? Opinions are not facts and are generally inconclusive. Meanwhile there are one or two facts which need a satisfactory explanation before conclusions are safe.

The other day, in the course of my work, I met a woman whose husband is a labourer. A full week's wage brings him in eighteen shillings, but three months' wet weather has meant twelve weeks of a much lower wage than that. The wife has a child under three years of age; during the past year she has suffered two miscarriages, and is again expecting another child.

She is not fit to work, but would do so if she could, because they are, of course, not living but starving on her husband's wage. So in this case (one of thousands) the husband is not paid on the assumption that he has a wife and family to keep, unless it is suggested that less than eighteen shillings a week is enough to keep a family upon. And if men are paid on the assumption before mentioned, why do so many men get more than this? It is not suggested that they have more than one wife to keep, presumably; and if not, why this difference in their wages?

I daily employ a woman in domestic work to whom I pay fourpence an hour. This is the usual rate in Lancashire, and, be it noticed, it is practically the same as that paid to the husband of the woman mentioned above, though in the one case the man has a wife and family to keep, and in the other the woman is supposed (incorrectly) to have nobody to keep. It is admitted at once that this is not the usual rate for domestic workers everywhere, but Lancashire contains more skilled women workers than any other part of the country;[1] they act as a lever in pulling up their sisters' wages in nearly every occupation.

But what, then, becomes of the argument that men are paid better than women because they have a wife and family to keep? Miss Rathbone[2] says that 'juvenile and female labour have an influence' (which is not denied, by the way). But women do not compete in railway work, and wages are notoriously low on railways. Nor do women compete with men as labourers. Yet labouring is the worst paid of men's occupations. On the other hand, cotton spinning and engineering are among the best paid of men's occupations; in neither of these do women compete. So that, without denying the inevitable dragging down effect of any ill-paid work, which women's mostly is, it is clear that this point is laboured out of all proportion to its importance, and that there are other factors governing wages which are much more powerful. Even the worst paid men in the cotton trade will compare favourably with labourers in the matter of wages, probably; yet nowhere are there more women working for wages. Does the evidence not point out, rather, that it is competence and skill, which are a greater force in governing wages, and that it is largely because women are so unskilled that they are paid less wages? Surely it would be wiser for women to recognise that unless they are prepared to demand and to fit themselves for any branch of work which is necessary in the community's service, they will for ever occupy a subordinate and dependent position?

Common Cause, 25 January 1912

NOTES

1 Presumably a reference to the wages paid to women workers in the cotton industry, then Lancashire's largest employer of labour, both male and female.

2 Eleanor Rathbone, campaigner for family allowances and later MP.

The Problem of the Married Working Woman

It is desirable that married women should be economically independent, and free to develop their humanity on lines best suited to that object. The bondage of the married working woman is twofold: the dependence of her young children, and the primitive stage in which domestic industry still remains. In other words, her babies and her domestic jobs are the chains which bind her; and it is these chains which must be broken before talk of human development for her ever becomes more than talk.

There is not the least need to hold up holy hands in horror at this plain statement of fact. It does not mean that the mother is going to desert her child, or that homes and babies are going to be neglected – quite the contrary. Only those who have no knowledge or conception of the magnitude of a nature force such as mother-passion, could possibly read such a meaning into it.

Human progress is not merely a matter of individual opportunity. It is our power to combine which marks our human development. This is seen in all the human world which is controlled by men. Men now combine to achieve marvels in the way of progress outside the home; fathers (though they may not individually have any children) combine to educate the children of all fathers (except of course the small class whose income puts them out of the necessity of being regarded as problems). It is only in the sphere of home and what are termed the 'domesticities' that progress and combination stop dead. It is only in the world of women that the laws governing progress are not allowed to govern. No wonder that woman in her world falls short of what is expected of her! For we develop by that which we do, and if we are compelled to live and work in a world which is at variance with all the laws of progress, how can we ourselves make progress?

Therefore since combination is the law of progress, and woman, married or unmarried, must be free to bestow on the world her human gifts, she must of necessity be free from that which shackles her.

She does not wish to be free of her babies, and could not if she did, but she could collectively make provision for the care of her own and other babies much better than she can do by remaining an untrained domestic worker, and a mother who keeps the baby quiet in the intervals of scrappy cooking, scrubbing, washing and mending. No woman is individually good enough, however fiercely maternal her passion, to have the unaided care, day and night, of a baby; and when this is scrambled into the day's domestic work of an average working man's household, it means that the little human plant is being injured irrevocably. Child lovers of knowledge and education are making clearer to us every day that understanding and care are as necessary for the infant as for the child of school age.

One suggestion therefore, which follows naturally on the views outlined above, is that there should be nurseries for all babies; places made specifically for them, and in charge of these there should be trained mothers. It is not at all necessary that they should be individual mothers though many naturally would be; one of the most loving, capable and successful baby trainers I know is not herself a mother. The point to be careful about would be that those women and only those would be entrusted with this work – a State service of high rank – who are not happy apart from babies; and whose absorbing delight it is to study patiently and tend faithfully the tender humanity under their care.

This would open a new and glorious field of work to women, in which their special sort of human genius would have scope for development. It should not mean a new profession for middle-class women *only*. Mothers would naturally predominate in this work; and by far the larger number of mothers belong to the working class. Given an opportunity they could develop power for baby culture quite as easily as women who are better-off financially. I know personally some splendid world mothers of this type, whose genius has been cramped and comparatively wasted on the care of the few babies with whom intelligent women of the working class have to be contented.

The cost? The cost of a Dreadnought[1] or an added tax on all incomes over £1000 a year. Separation of mothers from babies? There would not be any – more than is good for mother and baby. Middle-class mothers do not keep their babies in their arms night and day; but they would be offended if one suggested that they are worse mothers than working-class women. Many Lancashire women leave their babies ten hours a day (much too long); but only politicians of the Burns[2]-type imagine them to be lacking in maternal love on that account.

The babies disposed of – and much the better for it, since they would be in trained not ignorant care – there remains that old man of the sea – the general cook and bottle washing business. The married working woman who has no babies is a slave to her pots and pans.

Well, slaves should break their chains, and they who want women to be free should help in the chain-breaking, not try to rivet the links closer by advocating domestic teaching in *all* schools for *all* girls, fostering the idea in the mind of girls that simply because of their sex, they must inevitably be ready some day to cook a man's dinner and tidy up his hearth. Women should insist that girls should be trained for whatever they show a liking for, as boys are, and that if they have no liking for scrubbing and cleaning (or home-making, as it is erroneously called) they should no more be expected to do it than a boy would.

Quite a sufficient number would for a long time (habits of centuries are not got rid of in a day) like domestic work sufficiently, or would show no particular capacity for other work to keep the domestic wheels oiled. But if we insisted on training girls to be *human* instead of merely feminine, and brought them up with the idea that it is disgraceful not to serve humanity, and that to be dependent for the necessities of life upon either an individual or society without giving back in return is immoral and dishonest, girls would naturally rebel against the narrow world circumscribed by household drudgery. Rebellion, refusal to do and to submit, are the first steps to progress; and if we consciously discourage the domestic ideal in our girls, domestic work will of necessity have to step out of the painfully primitive stage into line with progress generally. The time is passing when either a class or a sex must necessarily be sacrificed to the privileges demanded by another class or sex, and women must either help in the passing or remain a drag on progress.

Domestic work on organised lines, which I have not space to elaborate, would open up another paid field for women.

Meanwhile the line of progress, as far as it is clear to the present writer, is for married women to insist on demanding the right to paid work, and to refuse to perform domestic jobs simply because they are wives. In Lancashire the prejudice against married women's work does not exist; but the women are largely slaves to their domestic work, for the simple reason that family well-being, in the way of good food and raiment, and a 'bit o' brass i' t'bank' are placed first. But the remedy does not lie in compelling the women to stay at home, for they would lose far more than they would gain. In human development they are far ahead of individual working women anywhere else, and that is much more valuable to the race than the doing of domestic jobs by women who are at home all day. Should the income of the men and women cotton operatives be increased – and there is no reason why it should not if the income of the cotton masters were reduced – and it became the fashion for domestic work to be performed by paid and daily helpers, and the babies were cared for during the hours the mothers were at work by trained mothers in special baby homes (quite near by) the Lancashire woman would lead the van in the intelligent progress of her sex and class.

Clearly if women are to take part in all the world's work, reserving to themselves perhaps, that which deals specifically with child life and home-building and decoration, and with the feeding and clothing and housing of the people, in return for that done better in other fields by men, – clearly all work must be open to them. They must train in efficiency and must shoulder responsibilities – and so grow in humanity.

The path to much that women want and must have is blocked by the need of legislation. Which brings us again round the circle to the need of the vote. It is as well to be as clear as possible as to the path of reform we wish to take. I suggest to reformers that to relieve working-class women of the dependence of small children and to organise domestic work into a paid profession is the path to human progress, and that to endow individual mothers and to compel husbands to be employers, and to pay their wives, is the retrograde path to further sex and class degradation.

Common Cause, 6 March 1914

NOTES

[1] Huge and expensive battleship of that time.

[2] John Burns MP, was active over many years in organisations to lower the infant mortality rate, but on various occasions announced that the chief cause of infant deaths was bad motherhood, in which he included mothers who went out to work. See also above: p 54 note 2, and pp 212–13.

Let the women be alive

To the Editor of *The Freewoman*

Madam, – One recognises and delights in your magazine as a really 'free' platform, whereon are expressed real living thoughts, where there is no need to keep back half one's mind for the very good reason that in saying what one really thinks one is but beating the air, since its unpopularity or its clashing with some interest will safely ensure its never seeing the light.

Since a friend brought to my notice Mrs. Charlotte Perkins Gilman's *Forerunner* – an all too brief monthly refreshment – never have I so much appreciated, so hungrily and thirstily eaten and drunk of any mental food as that provided by *The Freewoman*. And that not by any means because I am always in agreement with your own or your writers' opinions, but because your work all bears the impress of vivid, fearless thought, and that whatever the opinions expressed, is meat and drink to the sincere student who is out to learn the truth, however unpalatable the truth may be. One feels your process of growth as you write; and one feels oneself growing as one reads! And growth is no less the joy than the law of life. I am one with you in feeling that the Suffrage papers and the Suffrage societies insist too much on the be-all and end-all of the mere vote. But, after all, what else can one reasonably expect or hope for? Each and all are governed and *paid for* by women who belong to a small and privileged class; and she who pays the piper may surely call the tune? Most of these women are quite sincere in their desire to use the vote, when obtained, to abolish sweating and misery, inequalities and injustices amongst their poorer 'sisters'; but they have only the vaguest ideas as to how their having a vote is to enable them to do this. Most of them would be horrified at the idea of using their vote, or of helping in any other way, to bring about the evolutionary revolution which will result in every woman, as well as every man, having to work (really work – at something useful to the community) for the bread they eat. Proposals for, and work directed towards this end, come under the heading of 'Economics' or 'Socialism' – or something – with which they, as Suffragists, have no concern! The woman who frankly acknowledges that 'equality' means equality in bread-earning (apart altogether from marriage), in responsibility-sharing, who recognises that the woman who lives on 'rent,' or 'interest,' or 'shares,' or unearned income of any kind is a parasite, just as a man is who lives without working: who recognises that a woman who lives on a man's earnings, even though 'respectably,' married, is as much a prostitute as her outcast sister of the streets – such a woman is repudiated as 'going too far,' and as being a hindrance to progress (in getting a vote). In this movement, as in every other, without a single exception, only what pays is acceptable, and it is thought to pay better to disguise what those of us who know what we are out for, and who are honest with ourselves, want to do with the vote when we get it.

But there is one slight discrepancy in your reasoning on which it would be interesting to have further information. The WSPU, you say, does not want the vote for another ten years. Yet it is the only society to-day which repudiates the idea of votes being won on any terms save those of equality with men. Other societies are willing to take any small crumb, and even a promise of a crumb in the visionary future is quite enough to satisfy some of them (witness the Women's Liberal Federation, who meekly submit to indignity and betrayal time and time again, from the party they work for – nothing is too much for them to stand). Yet you argue that all the societies are alike in not recognising the larger issues of their 'woman' and not 'votes' movement. Surely if they (the WSPU) are willing to stand out for what to them seems best worth having – equality – even though they put off the attainment of a smaller share, they at least show their sincerity, and possibly larger vision, than those who would be content with votes for women householders at the same time as votes are granted to all men (many of those who pay to keep the Suffrage societies going do not want more than the householder vote; but can those who pay to keep the WSPU going really be in ignorance of what they are paying for?)

As you say, it may be for 'limelight' effect only. But, then, you also say that limelight is absolutely essential, and urge the other societies to make use of it! I ought, perhaps, to say that I am myself, at present, a law-abiding Suffragist, and a member of the largest Suffrage society – the NUWSS.

And – may I say it? – you appear to have a childlike faith in the immediate possibility of organising women workers into trade unions and indicate that herein lies the salvation of womanhood – just as if you had stumbled on something quite new and undiscovered! I have personally had a large dose of practical experience, which makes your advice (to me) as amusing as it is stale. I was, years ago, the first member of a trade union formed amongst a certain number of sweated girl workers (thereby hangs a tale calculated to teach an effective lesson to any woman on the possibility of trade unionism for women), and for more than a dozen years have been engaged in the task of organising women workers, and my experience is that until you have awakened a social conscience in a woman, there is not the least hope of getting her to sacrifice threepence or fourpence of her weekly wages for some vague (to her) benefit, which she (personally) may never receive. I do not state this as a fact, but my distinct impression is that wherever the educating, awakening influence of Suffrage workers has been at work, there one finds it much easier to induce women to see the necessity for industrial organisation, than where there is darkest ignorance about 'votes for women,' and everything else. The practical impossibility of organising an unskilled, badly paid, intending-to-become-a-parasite-on-marriage worker is a truly formidable obstacle. But it is by no means the only or the hardest one. Last month I spent a week in Yorkshire, personally interviewing women workers who earn anything from ten shillings to twenty shillings weekly

– aristocrats amongst women workers – urging upon them the necessity for joining their trade union (already existing – for men and one or two women – and promising substantial benefits). With few exceptions, they were adamant to all argument. 'We are all right – nobody else matters,' was their immovable attitude. Nor could the spectacle of women in another town six miles away, who are getting several shillings per week more in wages for the same work, move them into action. Nor was it the fact, which is, in my opinion, the greatest obstacle to trade unionism amongst women – the abandoning of wage-earning on marriage – a factor in this case, for the married women are nearly all wage-earners in that particular town. No. The fact is that unless you can get a woman to see the utter degradation of her industrial and political position as a dependant and belonging of man, there is as little hope of industrial organisation for her as for political power. If there is, lying dormant, one spark of latent desire for freedom, for growth, you have some ground to work on, some hope of results. And one of the best means, I rather think, of appealing to this dormant quality is to rouse a sense of resentment against obvious inequality, as in the voteless condition of women compared with man. It may be this, merely, at first. But first steps must be taken, and if this is an effective way, and leads to growth and power, it is the right way. What is needed, then, it seems to me, is education, as much by the Suffragist as by the trade unionist, and not by one more than the other. But my experience – a fairly extensive one – is that if you want any help with any kind of real educational work amongst women, you must go to the Suffragist for it. If she wants a vote, she is at least alive. And it is heart-breaking, as well as useless work, trying to raise the dead. Many women, especially of the working class, grow up to adult age without ever having lived. It will be a long business, and will need a new generation, bred and reared by freewomen, to leaven the lump of inanity. 'Tis a long hoe to row!

13 April 1912
The Freewoman, 18 April 1912

The Economic Freedom of Women

The pressure of social and economic development is forcing this very debatable question on the attention of all serious students of social problems. The reiteration of pious beliefs; the heated denial of bondage which demand for freedom implies; the pathetic appeals to women to go back thankfully and contentedly to the conditions of a hundred years ago; the solemn warnings of preachers and teachers of what they fear will result from the actions of free women, make a confusion of tongues and confliction of opinions in which it is difficult sometimes for a plain woman to realise exactly where she stands. It is with a view to attempt some definite realisation, not necessarily as a final and fixed conviction, but as an essential prelude thereto, that this study is undertaken. As a preliminary, it is necessary clearly to acknowledge and fix in our minds one fact — being a fact, provable by official statistics, it would be waste of time to dwell on it — that social and economic pressure, felt by women as well as by men, is a factor in this problem which may not be ignored.

To clear the ground, it may be necessary, even at the risk of tedious redundancy, to state exactly what we mean by the economic position of the individual. To sustain life, we have three primal needs — food, clothing, and shelter. Luxuries and comforts of many other kinds have been made necessaries to most of us by modern life; but the first three are the basis without which we cannot live at all. A moment's thought will remind anybody that these needs could not be supplied, even for ourselves alone, individually. Left to ourselves, at the stage of specialisation reached to-day, each one of us would perish miserably in an attempt to feed, clothe, and house ourselves.

It is common knowledge that our food comes from many lands, and the combined labour of thousands of people is necessary before it stands on the table ready for us to eat; the same is true of our clothes; and the work of many skilled work-men goes to the building of our homes before they are ready to shelter us. The conditions of life to-day, more than ever in our history, are complicated and interdependent, making it impossible to deal with them as a whole, without considering the people as a whole. We are approaching a time when it will be impossible to ignore the larger half of the people – the female half – when in process of that readjustment of social and economic conditions which is not only being forced on us by evolutionary progress, but which is the earnest hope and desire of the social reformer.

The task of taking the women into account is to some refor-mers so appallingly difficult that they are inclined to shelve this aspect of the question, and to postpone its settlement. Mean-while, there is an ever-growing unrest amongst the two sections of society who feel the pressure of changing conditions most – the section whose labour produces the necessaries of life for all, and the women of the country. The unrest grows, and is becoming so menacing that there is growing conviction amongst the more serious and thoughtful type of social refor-mer that it will have to be tackled. If that be so, then it had surely better be tackled seriously, and women should fit them-selves to approach the settlement in a helpful and informed spirit. They should know definitely what they want, and why they want it. If they want economic freedom because they are convinced, and can show, that it is necessary in the interests of the race, they have a ground for their demand of which the ultimate realisation is sure.

In considering the economic freedom of men, it is never necessary to drag in our notions of their conjugal and parental duty. We can, and do, frankly consider them as producers, as civil and social servants, as human· beings with a necessity to earn a living on the one hand, and an opportunity to serve society on the other. But in a study of the economic position of women, no such easy task awaits us. We have, on the contrary, to consider women, not as human beings, with a need to live and a power to serve, but as a wife of a particular man, as a

240

mother of particular children. We have even, according to the view generally accepted, to consider her as a potential wife and mother of no particular man and children. Nor is this all. We have even to pry into her domestic arrangements, and pass judgement from our view of her relation to the house she lives in. A woman's relation to her husband, her children, and her 'home duties' have for many long ages been mixed up with her economic relation to society, and this is the reason why so many people are unable to make up their minds as to what they mean by the economic freedom of women. It needs quite a gymnastic feat of the imagination, quite a revolutionary shock to the mind, to attempt to consider women apart from their actual or possible husbands and children, and apart from their 'domestic duties'; and to see them in the light of economic factors in society. 'Women and children,' in the light of dependants on men, have for so long been classed together that many people go through life without realising that women ever grow up. The 'duties of home' are so inseparable (quite naturally so, since they are all the duties most women acknowledge) from any consideration of women that the phrase has become a shibboleth which serves in place of thought to those who find thinking an impossible or a disagreeable process. But, to get even a glimpse of what economic freedom for women really means, it is quite necessary that we should try to perform this feat of the mind and imagination; for it is an indispensable condition that we should realise that women are adult human beings, of the *genus homo*, quite as much as the males of their species. As such, they, of course, have primal needs. They eat. They wear clothes. They live in houses – much more than do men. What do they do to supply the many needs of the community, of which their own are by no means the smaller part? Men, except the unemployed, at the top and bottom of the social structure, all take part more or less in the many services which the continuance of civilised society demands daily. They it is who bring the food from many lands; who fashion most of the fabrics which clothe us; who perform every office (till it reaches the drudgery of the cleaning) in raising the homes in which we live; who get the coal from the earth's bowels; who 'man' the railways and the ships; who fill the posts of Government; and who generally keep the world moving. Men, therefore, are economically free. That there are degrees of freedom, governed by factors which are not of moment here, may be conceded at once. But everybody who earns enough to live upon gives back to the whole something in return for what the whole gives to him. It may be necessary, *en passant*, to remark that though it is true to say that the man or woman who works not at all, or who tumbles over each other in 'flunkey' service for individual people (as must be the case where nineteen servants are kept to supply the personal requirements of one woman), but who are 'economically free' in the usually accepted sense of the word, are not so in the sense in which the present writer understands or discusses economic freedom. Such people are free, in the first case, because they are not obliged to give anything back for what is given to them; and in the second place because they give to one person service which others give to society; but both are dependent on the producers none the less, since no amount of money could buy if want of money did not result in goods produced.

Economic freedom, then, in a large generalisation, means the equal freedom of women with men in opportunity and obligation to earn their living – to cease living as parasites, either on individual men or on society – to give back their share in return for what is given to them. As before stated, in considering any phase of economics as related to men, we have a straightforward issue, and need not pry into the man's relations with his wife, children, or home. But in the case of women we have no option. So for purposes of convenience it may be well to separate the sheep from the goats – the married and the unmarried. To take the last first. It is becoming more and more impossible every day for fathers and brothers, even of the middle classes, to maintain an army of daughters and sisters at home, and it has never been possible for the 'working man' to do so. But in the past the girls of the working classes were content to be domestic servants, and to-day they are not so content, and never will be content again till domestic service follows development in other spheres, and is organised on lines which will make it acceptable to women who have a growing thirst for human freedom. It is easy to convince the bitterest opponent of economic freedom for women that girls and unmarried women must work at something, because nobody can afford to keep them. But few people take their necessity to work as a serious reason why they should be trained to work efficiently; and that since they must be workers they are an economic factor which cannot be ignored without danger to other workers. There can be little doubt that the greatest obstacle to economic freedom for women is the deeply rooted notion, in the minds of many of themselves, and in the minds of almost all men, that they are merely playing at work for a time until they undertake the 'duties of wife and mother' – in which case they are expected to give up their duty to society, and to plant themselves as a life-burden on a male-producer. The writer has had many years' experience of trade union work amongst women workers, and is sadly convinced thereby that the greatest obstacle to the trade organisation of women is this intention to become a parasite on marriage. The only women of the industrial classes who organise so splendidly and completely as to be able to command what may be regarded as a living wage, are the cotton operatives of Lancashire; and it is a remarkable fact, with a distinct bearing on the problem under discussion, that more married women work in this trade than in any other. Most men consider the conditions of their work, and the wage received, in the light of a life-job. So does the Lancashire cotton weaver, and both act accordingly, with similar results. But it must be recognised that though the trade organisation of women is as capable of improving their economic condition as it is in the case of men, especially when backed by the political power of the vote; yet, if the women cotton weavers of Lancashire were not experts at their trade, and as highly skilled, and, therefore, as valuable as producers as are the men, they might not be able to command, as they do, a monopoly of the trade, and would certainly not be able to command, as they do, exactly the same rate of pay. And herein is a deduction to be made. If women are going to demand, or, what is much more like, are going to be forced to take their share in providing for the world's economic needs, and to relieve men of the burden of their maintenance, it will be absolutely necessary for them to become experts, and to demand the training which fits for efficient service. And this is as necessary in the interests of men workers as of women. Men realise, as proved by their trade organisations, their systems of apprenticeship, that the untrained man who may pick up a smattering of knowledge of their trade, sufficient to enable him to perform minor parts of it, is a menace to their own stability and prosperity as workers. But they are slow to recognise that what is true of a man in this connection is equally true of a woman. Instead, they are inclined to say, 'Keep her out! Drive her back to her home!' Their very natural fear of being ousted from their place in the scheme of things obliterates the view that a moment's reasoning would show them – namely, that since women must work to live, the best plan for both men and women would be to treat that fact seriously, and to help, and to insist on the women making use of every possible means to increase their value as workers. Most doors by which woman could, if she were willing, obtain the skill necessary to command a living wage, are closed to her, because there are no ways whatever (open to her) of getting into them. There are others out of which she cannot be kept, as the tailoring trade, for instance, and particularly in those trades associated with the distributive processes, which do not require long periods of apprenticeship. In the case of the tailoring trade, men for many years bitterly resented the entrance of the women, and rigorously refused to admit them to their trade union; and even now it is only the worst paid jobs which are allowed to come in the way of the women. A tailor serves a long apprenticeship, and his trade union has fixed prices below which he may not work. Now observe where the danger comes in, in allowing the women to enter the trade without skill or organisation. The writer was at one time intimately acquainted with the inner working of a factory run by a contractor for the manufacture of Government clothing, and can vouch for the truth of the details here given in illustration of this argument. Four hundred and fifty people were employed in this factory, of whom four hundred were women. They were largely the daughters of railway workers earning less than thirty shillings a week, so it can scarcely be argued that 'their place was at home.' It was understood that the Government stipulated that the sleeves of policemen's tunics should be sewn in by tailors. The sleeves were sewn in by tailors – on one afternoon only during the four months the order lasted – on the afternoon when the Government inspector came round. At all other periods during the four months the sleeves were sewn in by women. It is presumable that the work of the men and the women was indistinguishable. But the pay was distinguishable, since in the case of the women it was fivepence per pair, and in the case of the men it was one shilling-fivepence. Now, who gains by conditions such as these? The women did not, since they worked longer hours than the men (taking their work home at night), and still were not, and are not, able to earn enough to keep themselves in return for all their toil. And the men actually lose, as the inference is that if they insisted on equal training and equal pay for women they would share the work, since there would surely be no inducement to employ women in preference to men if their work were no cheaper. The community, of course, are heavy losers by such conditions, as, the less money earned by the people, men and women alike, the less they have to spend, and the less demand for goods produced. This apart altogether from the national danger of wasting natural wealth – the health of the wealth producers – which insufficient wages and consequent poor conditions of life place in constant jeopardy. Some people argue that to demand equal pay for women would be to make their conditions harder. Why should it? If that were true, the conditions amongst Lancashire cotton operatives would be amongst the worst in the country. That the exact opposite is

the fact is surely conclusive proof that the way to better conditions would be for men and women alike to recognise that
unskilled, unorganised workers are a menace to, and a drag on
the skilled and organised. To declare, as some people think it
sufficient to do, that women have no business entering men's
trades, is but to beat the air. Women must live, and in order to
live must work, and, of course, have to follow whatever chan-
nels afford the best opportunity of getting a living. Men and
women cannot separate their interests in the world of work any
more than in the sphere of home; and surely the speedier way
to progress would be to utilise the wisdom and work of both in
obtaining relief from pressure of modern conditions. There are
no doubt many occupations now monopolised by men of
which they will always have a monopoly. But there are many
others in which women could fit themselves for competency as
easily as do men, and in these men and women alike must put
aside unnecessary sex prejudices, and recognise that they must
rise or fall together. And there are many other trades and occupations, waiting to be organised and developed, so soon as
women are alive to their responsibilities, and men are sufficiently alive to help instead of to hinder, in which women
could be of special use and value. There are, for instance, baby
and child culture, so little recognised or practised, as infant
mortality returns testify; there are the organisation and
development of the present primitive condition of domestic
work (which will be absolutely necessary in order to enable
women to attain to economic freedom); there is the efficient
feeding of the people, now so absurdly badly done, and many
other lines of work waiting and crying out for the organised,
intelligent effort of the women who are at present either
wholly dependent on men, or who are crowding the few
avenues of employment which are open to them. But the indispensable preliminary to this is a frank recognition that women
are now out of their homes permanently, and that for good or
ill they are obliged to take part in industrial work; and that
unless they are for ever to remain a subordinate, dependent
sex, and a permanent drag on the advance of civilisation, all

doors must be opened to them, all the training to fit themselves for efficient workers, far from being withheld, must be actually forced on them, and rigorously demanded of them. This brings us to the married woman, for, in order to deal seriously with women as wealth producers, and as the equals of men in the world of work, it is an essential that girls shall be brought up to regard their work as a serious part of life, and to approach it in this spirit. The further consideration of this aspect of our study, the place of the married woman in industry, will be reserved for another article.

The Freewoman, 11 July 1912

Mother-Interest and Child-Training

There is, quite naturally, much confusion of thought as to what is the part of maternal duty in that long and careful tending of the young human plant which is necessary before we can produce the fully developed adult human being. The confusion arises from the fact that the maternal part is mixed up in some of our minds inextricably with what are regarded as equally sacred duties – duties to houses and clothes, to pots and pans, and to food. We can never think clearly about this matter till we accustom our minds to regard women as individual human beings; and the difficulties, pointed out by a correspondent in a former article, will not appear so formidable if we can succeed in detaching women from our preconceived ideas of what their 'duties' are. The first statement quoted by the correspondent was made when the point under discussion was the proposal frequently advocated by reformers, that the mother should have a legal right to half her husband's wages (should his economic position be so low that there is no available margin to draw upon), and to a legal allowance (should his income be big enough), in return for her performance of the duties of wife and mother. I pointed out that if this were done, a mother would still be economically bound, because in most cases the amount would make no appreciable difference to existing arrangements, and in almost every case would not be enough to provide wholly for the maintenance of the children. And, since a woman is indeed bound to her children in a totally different and more vital way than she can ever be bound to her husband, it is clear that so long as he only provides for the children he owns the mother, too, and the tie by which he has her bound can only be broken by her ability to provide for her children without his aid. A woman will suffer any degradation of mind or body rather than see her children starve – she is made that way. That is why, when women

248

recognise their glorious duty to the race, and set out to perform it, there will be an end to the starvation of the bodies and minds of children. And not till women see that it is within *their* province, not only to bear and nurse, but to provide for the young, will this duty to the race be properly done; the latter task gladly shared, but not monopolised – because all monopolies tend to abuse – by the men to whom mothers of this type would allow the privilege of fatherhood.

The difficulties are many, no doubt. Some are due to artificial barriers, which women (and men) must break down. Most difficulties are caused by our age-long habit of looking upon what is, and what has been, as altogether desirable. We have, for instance, an exaggerated view of the inevitableness of the utter dependence of a mother on somebody or something – her husband, or the State. If anybody is so bold as to suggest that the human mother is not necessarily any more incapacitated by the absolutely natural and healthful condition of motherhood than are other female animals, the meaning is taken to be that of repudiation of maternity. And this in spite of repeated history of all ages, and of present-day evidence, that human mothers not only can, but do, perform Herculean tasks the while they rear their young. So terribly afraid are we that women will not be mothers at all unless we bind them in some way, either to husband or State, that we raise frightened heads at every mention of a possibility of making them really free – free to be mothers or not, as they shall choose, and as they only can choose when willing and able to provide for their own children. Taking these difficulties into account, it is perhaps not wonderful that the second statement to which exception was taken, that 'wifehood and motherhood must be divorced from the tyranny of primitive domestic conditions, so that women as well as men may be enabled to earn their living, apart altogether from marital and parental relations,' is interpreted to mean that mothers shall have no joy in motherhood, but that they shall arbitrarily tear themselves away from their newly-born babes, at once and for always.

It is not very curious that men should have this truly ghastly fear that it is possible to weaken the maternal tie; but it is inconceivable that a woman can honestly fear it. How little such people can know of what they fear! Have they really not imagination enough to realise that what they fear is the supposed possibility of 'weakening' the mightiest force in the universe, the great lifestream from which all power flows? This fear will merely afford a smile to any woman who has ever yearned to hold, or has ever held, that ever-new, ever-marvellous gift of ages in her arms – her own newly-born babe. Any woman who has lived through years watching the daily growth of her child, who has followed it with her yearning mother-care, surrounding it always, whether a yard or a thousand miles divide her from its physical contact, with her protecting love – she knows, freewoman or bond, that no mere presumptuous man-made or woman-made law on earth can lessen by one jot that blessed bond between her and her child – a bond which is to become her glory in the full, free future, but which is the instrument of her degradation and shame, and, through her, of the degradation and shame of the human race, in the blindly groping, prejudice-bound present.

Why is it necessary to keep wifehood and motherhood bound to primitive domestic conditions? Let us try to face facts squarely. We want – some of us – women to be economically independent of their husbands. But we, and they, want to be wives and mothers. To the larger number of women, the only way to the latter is by dependence on man and by undertaking certain washing, scrubbing, and cooking duties. The fact that a woman may have a positive loathing for domestic cobbling is not taken into account at all – it does not matter, apparently. If the State endows her when she becomes a mother, it is, presumably, paying her to look after her baby, because the baby belongs to the State. And, of course, she cannot be allowed to go to the factory and to pay somebody else to look after her baby, because, naturally, if the State employs her to do certain work it will want that work done in a particular way! What is the good of being a master if you cannot command obedience? So there is a proposal to pay the mother to tend her child. But she has another employer also – her husband – for whom she has to undertake a number of 'domestic duties.' If she neglects these in order to attend to her State duties, may this other employer not have a right to complain? And who shall determine how much of one and how much of the other duty is the right proportion?

It is, presumably, only proposed to endow poor mothers – mothers whose husbands earn less than £160 per year. To make the endowment sufficient to relieve a woman of economic dependence on her husband, it would be necessary that the sum should be substantial enough to keep her and all her children who are not old enough to keep themselves. Is the State really going to do as much as this for its poor women, in order to enable them to tend their babies? If not, it is sheer nonsense to talk of a small weekly dole, given to prevent poor mothers from earning their own living, relieving them of economic dependence on their husbands. Such an interference with their already restricted liberty would but bind the shackles of dependence on them closer, and would tend still further to the perpetuation of a producing race with slave instincts. You cannot breed a free people from slave mothers, and husband-kept or State-kept women can never know the meaning of liberty.

We are so used to 'keeping' women – to herding them together as a dependent whole – that there is another point which seldom occurs to us. They are individuals, and differ individually. Many women are quite fit to be mothers, both mentally and physically, who are totally unfit to tend young babies, either their own or anybody else's. A very special kind of woman is needed for this most important office. During years of much peregrination, I have met numbers of women who for various reasons have no child of their own, but who are none the less mother-women. The special talents of these women, by our stupid social and economic arrangements, are lost to the community. I have one woman in mind. Her own three children are now completely grown-up; but her arms are always aching for babies, and babies love to be in those arms. She is a veritable sunbeam – a cheerful, laughter-loving mother-woman. Her infinite capacity for mothering is wasted on three children, though that number is quite sufficient for one woman to bear in these days. She should be employed, either by parents or else by the State, in the same way in which the State employs women to teach children of older years, to mother the babies of the women who, though passionately loving and beloved mothers, are capable of satisfactorily performing other work, and are quite unfit (not physically, but temperamentally) to tend young children. Why should talents – differing in women equally as in men – be wasted? Why should we always make such a virtue of putting square pegs in round holes?

And why do we always specially want to do this to the poor? In the circles above the producers – or the 'insured persons' – mothers do not necessarily tend their own particular babies. They hire other women to do it. But it is not suggested that they thereby lose all interest in their children. And if it is the infantile death rates which alarm us, it may be pointed out that personal mother-tending is not the only factor in that problem, because the death rates are lowest amongst those classes where there is least of this.

A well-to-do woman may leave her children in the care of others for years, and nobody suggests that we shall pass a law to endow her, so that we shall be able to enforce our views of her maternal duties on her acceptance. Again, it is the liberty of the poor which we propose to restrict, and the fact that some of us propose to endow working mothers – with a view to binding them still closer to the domestic cobbling business – without even consulting their own wishes, is not the least item in the charge against us.

But there are many earnest people to whom endowment of motherhood seems the only way out of a deplorable state of starving maternity and childhood. But is it, really? Why not demand the same facilities for poor mothers and their children as those enjoyed by women whose husbands are better off? If it

ARTICLES

is not wrong for a well-to-do woman to spend a few hours away from her child daily, it cannot be wrong for the poor woman. If it is beneficial for well-to-do children to have specially selected women, and specially selected rooms, gardens, and every other facility for healthy growth, it could not be bad for the children of the poor. Instead, therefore, of giving an individual mother a few shillings a week – not enough to enable her to hire a nurse, or even to live where the air is pure, one supposes! – why not make beautiful baby gardens, quite near to the homes of the parents, and gather in all the hungry mother-women into this truly blessed State service, and let individual mothers, like individual fathers, follow whatever bent they are fitted for. Fathers, by the way do not love their children less – but possibly more – because they leave them for a number of hours daily. Then why should mother-love be conceived to be of so much weaker quality? Or, if we object to State cared-for children before they are five (we do not object to State-educated children), why should not father and mother combine to keep the baby gardens and to pay the 'mothers'?

A baby loves and thrives on a sunny mother, and the company of other babies is as dear to its baby soul as is the company of other children as it grows older. My baby would have been as carefully looked after by my friend as by myself, and any baby would grow better in such an atmosphere than shut up in a little house with a nervous, irritable mother, who is oppressed ever with a sense of crowding, stifling, absurd little duties, which absorb the whole-hearted attention which should be given to the child. Babies are well or ill looked after by individual mothers, as circumstances allow. But in the former case it is often done at a quite needless cost of nervous energy, and in the latter it is doubtful whether endowment of individual mothers would mend matters. The impelling natural pressure on a mother to tend her child is so great that if she does not there is some cause which endowment will not cure.

But what about the 'domestic duties'? Well, what about them? Is there some changeless, immutable law, binding on

253

women who marry, to thereafter spend their days in keeping little houses clean and in cooking little dinners? No woman who has anything more interesting to do, and who can afford to pay somebody else to do it, does her own family washing. No woman scrubs her own doorstep if she can find a job more to her taste. Why should it be so horrible for poor women to contemplate somebody else doing these jobs for them than it is for well-to-do women to have them done? 'What! Is the labourer's wife to keep a servant?' say the wives of our shocked rulers. 'Where, then, will *our* servants come from?' Again we are up against the ancient bugbear – primitive domestic conditions. But why keep them primitive? At one time the poor had no sanitary conveniences. But even the poorest townsman now has his scavenger servants, taking away some of the disagreeables of civilised existence. Why must the poor man's wife always be regarded as his only household scavenger? At one time she also spun and wove his clothing. He still gets clothed, though she has ceased to do this. No doubt his home would not cease to be a home because other people besides his wife kept it clean. Middle-class women have strangers invading the home to do the domestic scavenging, and middle-class homes are as fixed a national institution as are the homes of the poor. Anyway, if it is necessary to organise domestic cleaning on lines which will give the working man's wife an opportunity to work out her own economic freedom, who shall say it has no right to be done? Why do our ideas of reform nearly always take the form of restricting the liberty of women? Why should the State lay it down, for instance, that if a woman chooses to be a mother, and neither she nor her husband have income sufficient to save her from State interference, that she must give up whatever work she may be efficiently performing, and devote herself in future to housework? Is she to have an endless succession of children, in order to keep up the endowment (since babies have an awkward habit of leaving babyhood behind)? or, when her children are grown, is she to try to pick up the threads of her former work – if she can? For she must face the fact that though she may be strong and capable as of

Say hello if you want to collect

PRIVATE!

Trespassers will be prosecuted

yore, yet the opportunity to begin where she left off may be lacking. Is this strong, capable woman to be pensioned off in early middle life, or, existing only as a child-bearer, is she to be cast on the scrap-heap when her individual baby-tending is of necessity over?

Women *cannot* live individual lives and develop on individual lines whilst nearly all are forced to follow one occupation, and are dependent for a livelihood either on men or on State endowment.

It should be unnecessary to say that it might be desirable for women's industrial or professional work to be performed by substitutes some little time before and after the birth of a child. But an interruption of a year, at most, once or twice in a lifetime ought not to tax our powers of arrangement, either industrial, professional, or economic. Many people take holidays of that length, and if their salaries are sufficiently large there is no need to call in charity, to keep them, meanwhile.

There is nothing to fear, either to the home or to the child, from the freedom of the mother! No arms will ever be so sweet to a baby as those wherein the mother-heart is found; and a mother's precious office will never be superseded, even amongst the crowding delights of a childhood tended by all the picked brains and hands in the country (which should all be used in the glad service of *every* mother's child). But a mother who has at last struggled to her feet, who has shaken off the shackles which bound her; who stands free before the world, capable of providing for her own and her child's needs, and therefore dependent on none; who has grasped the meaning of human motherhood – which is no less than the mothering of the human race; a mother who grows daily with her child's growth – ah! *what* a mother the children of the future shall know!

The Freewoman, 22 August 1912

If you would like to know more about Virago books, write to us at Ely House, 37 Dover Street, London W1X 4HS for a full catalogue.

Please send a stamped addressed envelope

Book Tokens

Give them the pleasure of choosing

Book Tokens can be bought and exchanged at most bookshops.